4.2.01

W9-DFX-375

My Silk Purse and Yours

My Silk Purse and Yours

The Publishing Scene and American Literary Art

George Garrett

University of Missouri Press
Columbia and London

For acknowledgment of previously published material, see p. 305

Library of Congress Cataloging-in-Publication Data

Garrett, George P., 1929–
    My silk purse and yours : the publishing scene and American
literary art / George Garrett.
        p.   cm.
    Includes index.
    ISBN 0–8262–0866–5 (alk. paper)
    1. American literature—20th century—History and criticism.
    2. Authors and publishers—United States.   3. Literature
publishing—United States.   I. Title.
PS225.G37   1992
810.9'005—dc20
                                                    92–17695
                                                    CIP

∞™ This paper meets the requirements of the
American National Standard for Permanence of Paper
for Printed Library Materials, Z39.48, 1984.

Designer: Rhonda Miller
Typesetter: Connell-Zeko Type & Graphics
Printer and Binder: Thomson-Shore, Inc.
Typeface: Palatino and American Classic

For my children—William, George, and Alice. And for my grand-children—Jennifer and Ruth.

Let there be no child
who comes into the world without some hope,
some joy in him. And we shall have begun . . .
—Virgil's fourth Eclogue, "Pollio,"
translated by David R. Slavitt

He is himself a creator, and has lived in creation all his life, and so he understands and continually reminds himself that in a world of everlasting creation there is no justice. The original artist who *counts* on understanding and reward is a fool.

—Joyce Cary, "Preface" to the Carfax edition of *The Horse's Mouth*

Contents

Other Books by George Garrett

Fiction

King of the Mountain
The Finished Man
In the Briar Patch
Which Ones Are the Enemy?
Cold Ground Was My Bed Last Night
Do, Lord, Remember Me
A Wreath for Garibaldi
Death of the Fox
The Magic Striptease
The Succession
Poison Pen
An Evening Performance
Entered from the Sun
Whistling in the Dark

Poetry

The Reverend Ghost
The Sleeping Gypsy
Abraham's Knife
For a Bitter Season
Welcome to the Medicine Show
Luck's Shining Child
The Collected Poems of George Garrett

Plays

Sir Slob and the Princess
Enchanted Ground

Biography

James Jones

Criticism

Understanding Mary Lee Settle
The Sorrows of Fat City

I.

Essays

The manner of the Arcadian shepherds was, when they met together to pass their time, either in such music as their rural education could afford them, or in exercise of their body and trying of masteries.

—Sir Philip Sidney, "The First Eclogues"

Traces of the Elizabethans

I wrote this piece by invitation for the "Sophisticated Traveler" section of the *New York Times*. This version is a little bit longer than the version they published in 1991.

Once upon a time, my driver tells me, he drove Bing Crosby and Bob Hope all over England and Scotland looking for interesting golf courses to play. Hope and Crosby were wonderfully funny, he says. The driver, a cheerful Scotsman, allows that he knows a lot about Americans and their odd interests and habits, but he has never yet met one like me. He has never before driven anyone who wanted to go very slowly along very old routes and roads, looking at landscape, with books and notebooks, maps and guides scattered all over the car, trying to keep count of streams and old stone bridges, searching for ruins and monuments, farmhouses and guildhalls, a parish church here, an inn or market cross there, and sometimes a sudden view of what the Elizabethans called "a great house," one of those palatial mansions we now call "stately homes."

Waltham . . . Ware . . . Royston . . . Huntingdon . . . Stilton . . . Stamford . . . Grantham . . .

We are going along an ancient route (it was a Roman road), a two-lane blacktop running the 378 miles between London and Edinburgh—the Great North Road. We are following its leisurely course through gently rolling countryside with wide fields of grain and hay, cows and sheep in pasture, fruit trees in rows, and slow narrow rivers and streams twisting away toward the sea.

I jot down notes: *Wonderful apple trees between Tuxford and Bawtry. Dark earthy windmills and wide views beyond Huntingdon. Pear trees between Doncaster and Wentbridge . . .*

The shape and look of the land—forest and meadow, fen and moor—change every few miles, as does the weather, now bright, now an armada of clouds, now mizzling rain. But the essential landscape has changed only slightly over centuries. Sir Robert Carey, a dashing cousin of Elizabeth I, who covered this same

3

route at a full gallop, changing horses every dozen miles, going faster than we, to carry the news of the death of Elizabeth I to her successor, James VI of Scotland, would find much of it still familiar. And the driver takes it all for granted, part of his normal environment. I am an outsider who has come to this world from books I have read and for the sake of some books I am writing, seeking what I have so far only imagined, searching for traces of the Elizabethans. Because my time is short this time, I have hired both car and driver, a luxury worth every pound and penny if your time is strictly limited and you need to be looking rather than trying to remember to drive on the wrong side of the road.

The driver soon catches on to my alien habit and, hawk-eyed, slows down to point toward the distance. "Look there!" he cries. "There stands another of your old ruined castles."

I have already, on several trips, logged many happy hours in and around London and made the obligatory pilgrimage to Stratford.

Much that belonged to medieval and Elizabethan London went up in the smoke of the Great Fire of London in 1666 and in the bombs and flames of the Blitz in World War II. Yet more than enough survives to keep an interested traveler busy standing on the very spots where they stood, walking on the old stones and the ground they walked on; and it is often an enchanted ground. Many great names of Elizabethan times, proud, enigmatic, often looking vaguely dangerous, are to be found in full-dress portraits (the courtiers usually wearing brilliant and bejeweled clothing more costly than our world's most luxurious automobiles) in the National Gallery and a whole range and variety of public museums. There are also the breathtaking contemporary miniatures of limners like Isaac Oliver and Nicholas Hillyard and Simon Benick; and there are the remarkable sculpted (and sometimes painted and gilded) tomb effigies, not only those of kings and queens, including Tudors and Stuarts (Elizabeth's, in white marble, is by her celebrated contemporary Maximillian Colt) in Westminster Abbey, but also those of citizens of various sorts in surviving parish churches. A noteworthy example is St. Helen's Bishopsgate, which for a time was Shakespeare's parish in London. There are shards, tantalizing odds and ends to be found at the Museum of London, especially the collection of jewelry—the "Cheapside Hoard." The sprawling and amazing Victoria and Albert Museum has a marvelous collection of the age's flotsam and jetsam in Room 52, the Renaissance Room: miniatures, furniture, bits and pieces of clothing, a whole paneled room, the Great Bed of Ware, musical instruments including a virginal Elizabeth herself played on. And there are special things preserved in places close by London. Greenwich's National Maritime Museum displays a justly celebrated example of period embroidery—the "Bradford Table Carpet." The whole area is a thicket of museums, some grand and famous, some small and less obvious. Among the latter is The Bear Gardens Museum, Bankside, a theatrical museum in an old warehouse on the site of an Elizabethan playhouse, the Hope, and close to the place where Shakespeare's Globe once stood.

More alive than the museums, however, and the things, however precious or humble, preserved there, are the places where, in fact and in flesh, the Elizabethans played out their fabulous lives. In the proper light (or darkness) at these places you can push imagination to its outer limits and almost see the ghosts there. Middle Temple Hall (1572), an Elizabethan dining hall for lawyers and law students, then and now, is beautifully unchanged and has at its west end the dais where Shakespeare's *Twelfth Night* had its first performance on February 2, 1602. Beneath the extraordinary hammerbeam roof of the ancient Hall of Westminster, you can stand where Elizabeth enjoyed her coronation banquet and where some great men, like the young Earls of Essex and Southampton, were tried and convicted of high treason.

Frugal out of dire necessity, Elizabeth I built no new palaces or public buildings, choosing instead to hold her court in the palaces of her extravagant father and grandfather. Here, more a matter of image than reality, but nevertheless, like many other great myths, a powerful memory, "Merry England" bloomed and thrived. In London, itself, like a small perfect jewel, St. James Palace is still in use by the Queen Mother and other royals and officeholders; and out along the Thames, easily accessible, other palaces remain. Part of the gatehouse marks the spot of Richmond Palace, a favorite of Elizabeth, where she died in 1603. At ancient Windsor Castle, now as then, the court gathers for the Garter Ceremonies on

St. George's Day, April 23. Given by Cardinal Wolsey to Henry VIII, Hampton Court, a wonder of complex Tudor brickwork, is where Elizabeth almost died of smallpox in 1562. Its rooms and chambers, including a royal tennis court, are full of fascinating things.

But of all the places known well to Elizabeth, none seems so much alive with ghostly presences as the Royal Palace and Fortress of London, or, as it was and is more familiarly known, the Tower of London. Crowds or not—and it is sometimes very crowded with tourists from all over the world, themselves a sight to behold—it is not to be missed by anyone looking for signs of the Elizabethan world. Not merely because Elizabeth, as a princess, was held prisoner there, entering from the river by Traitors' Gate and, it seemed, more likely to die there than to live to be a queen; and not merely because her mother, Anne Boleyn, was beheaded there in the quietly beautiful space of Tower Green, a place where many another, including the Queen's favorite, the Earl of Essex, died hoping for a last minute reprieve from her; because, even now, it is more than a museum. Every tower and stairway, house, cell and dungeon has its earned name and long history, but there are more lively links to Elizabeth and her age. For one thing, there are the Yeomen Warders of the Tower, the "Beefeaters," who wear, as they have ever since the time of Elizabeth, *her* particular uniform—black, high-crowned, brimmed hat; at the neck the starched white ruff so fashionable in the late years of her reign; scarlet tunics tricked out with black and gold; soft black shoes with rosettes. These are not actors in funny costumes, but honored veteran soldiers in their official uniforms. Together with an escort, the Chief Warder of the Yeomen locks the gates of the tower every night at ten just as he always has since her time. According to this centuries-old scenario, he and his escort are challenged by a sentry nearby the tower named the Bloody Tower:
Sentry
Halt! Who goes there?
Chief Warder
The keys.
Sentry
Whose keys?

Chief Warder
Queen Elizabeth's keys. God bless Queen Elizabeth.
Sentry
Amen!

This event is called the Ceremony of the Keys.

Another place rich with royal myth and resonance lies just outside London near the Great North Road—the Old Palace of Hatfield. All that remains is the Great Hall and the oak-shaded park, standing near to and just below the huge Jacobean magnificence of Sir Robert Cecil's Hatfield House. Cecil served both Elizabeth and James, and in the Long Gallery of that mansion are preserved and displayed (among many other items) gloves, hat, and stockings of Elizabeth, and a roll of parchment which purports to trace her genealogy all the way back to Adam and Eve. But it is the Hall and the park of Old Palace which serve as living memorials to the day, November 17, 1558, the age that bears her name began, that day when the great lords came in all their finery to walk through fallen leaves and find her and greet and hail her as their Queen. She was sitting in the shade of an oak with her ladies-in-waiting, reading from her Greek New Testament. When they knelt before her, she quoted from the Psalms (in Latin): "This is the Lord's doing and is marvelous in our eyes." Perhaps even more marvelous was her success, for she inherited a troubled, nearly bankrupt kingdom, always threatened from within and from all sides. Yet she ruled for forty-five years from that moment at Hatfield. Her presence is felt there, and all that is missing now is the crowd of great lords and gentlemen, those cutthroats clad in silk and satin, in damask, brocade, taffeta and velvet, fine lawn and cambric. But the Elizabethan flower gardens of Old Palace, newly created by the present Countess of Salisbury, in their riot of blooming color, can serve to give a sense of those colorful creatures and the shades of the rainbow they affected with apt Elizabethan names like Peachflower, Maiden's Blush, Popinjay Green, Flame, Ash, Drake's Color, Dead Spaniard, Devil-in-the-Hedge, Marigold, Gooseturd Green, etc.

Then as now, the English loved gardens and gardening, flower gardens for beauty, scent and perfumes, herb gardens for healing and pleasure, knot gardens (like the great one at Hampton Court) for decorative fun and games. No wonder, then, that the most celebrated and archetypal Elizabethan, William Shakespeare, planted a fine garden when he used his profits as a playwright and actor to buy the biggest house in his hometown of Stratford-on-Avon—New Place. New Place is gone, but its well-tended garden remains, including all the flowers he mentioned in his plays and poems and an ancient mulberry tree said to be taken from a sprig of the tree he planted. True or false, there is no question that much of Stratford is perfectly exemplary of the life of the age: the Church of the Holy Trinity where Shakespeare was christened and is buried; the half-timbered birthplace on Henley Street; the guildhall and the King's New School he attended; Anne Hathaway's Cottage, etc.; all are well equipped with the furniture, the tools and implements of that time. It is true that pressing crowds of tourists make Stratford sometimes seem most like a kind of theme park, but it is firmly authentic and worth all the effort.

We are still moving north: *Topcliffe to Northallerton to Darlington to Durham.* I am still making notes: *Dark slow water of the Swale at Topcliffe . . . Sheep for sale at Northallerton Market . . .*

If Queen Elizabeth did very little building herself, she inspired and encouraged others to build grandly. Her long reign became a season of great houses, many of them still standing and accessible to visitors. Alike only in their palatial dimensions (they had to be fit for the Queen, for she often visited them during her summer progress), these houses make a bold statement. Bravely indefensible, made for show and for pleasure, they deny danger and assert peace and plenty. With their expensive materials and even more expensive glass, with a wealth of carving and gilding and implausibly intricate paneling and plasterwork, with elaborate decoration inside and outside, they assert a plentitude their builders may, in fact, never have quite enjoyed. So much of what was factually true of the age has vanished, as if Prospero in *The Tempest* had waved a wand to end the revels. But these illusions remain as solid as the timber and stone and bricks they are made of, as shimmering as the glass the Elizabethans loved.

Everybody has favorites: Ightham Mote in Kent (saved because Cromwell's soldiery got lost and burned the wrong house); magnificent Penshurst, seat for the celebrated family of Sir Philip Sydney and poetically praised in its finest hours by Ben Jonson; Sherbourne Castle in Dorset, because it was built by and lived in for a time by Sir Walter Raleigh; the half-timbered Tudor fantasy of Little Moreton Hall (Cheshire); Compton Wynates, elegantly composed of brick and stone and a forest of chimneys in Shakespeare's country—Warwickshire; Longleat in Wiltshire, though altered in later centuries, its classical entrance front completed in Elizabethan times.

Two deserve special mention because, one early and one late, one conservative and the other all built anew, they define the limits of the period; also because they are easily accessible to interested travelers and because the people who built them are fascinating and influential Elizabethans. Both houses, of course, are graced by elegant gardens and surrounded by acres of park.

Burghley House, near the ancient town of Stamford (one of whose inns, Le George, in my opinion serves the best Bloody Mary in England), was the seat of William Cecil, Lord Burghley. Cecil served the Queen, first as Secretary, then as Lord Treasurer, for forty years. When he was dying, the Queen sat on his bed and spooned him broth. His tomb and effigy are in St. Martin's Church in Stamford. Built to include the remains of a twelfth-century monastery, Burghley House was finished in 1589. The high-vaulted kitchen, with huge utensils and a fireplace large enough to roast an ox, served the monastery. Much altered inside (a direct descendant, the Sixth Marquess of Exeter still lives there), the exterior is purely of the period: three dignified and well-windowed stories topped by a forest of turrets and towers and an obelisk. From any angle the house looks different, a celebration of abundant and seeming disorder, an odd wedding of classical and gothic elements. The paradoxical union of wildness and propriety reflect the character of the Queen as much as her most faithful statesman.

Coming out of the final years of the reign, Hardwick Hall suggests another frame of mind, something like Hollywood show-and-tell. It stands proudly and beautifully on a hillside, its great glass windows blazing with any touch of sunlight, a startling vision from the M-1 highway.

Elizabeth Shrewsbury, called Bess of Hardwick, began life in genteel poverty and ended it as the richest woman in England not counting the Queen. She outlived four husbands, each richer than the last, and managed her own business with a Midas touch. Friend to the Queen (and to Mary, Queen of Scots as well), she had built several great houses before, at seventy, working with master mason Robert Smythson, she created Hardwick Hall. It has magnificent rooms—especially the Great High Chamber and the Long Gallery displaying a multitude of beautiful things and flashing her coat of arms and initials everywhere. The three-story facade, with so many windows they inspired a nursery rhyme—"Hardwick Hall / More glass than wall"—is capped by six towers, each with her initials, *E. S.,* huge in fretted stone, like shouts against the sky. It is appropriate that among the animals kept in the park these days is a herd of Texas longhorns.

Morpeth to Alnwick to Belford to Berwick . . . Wide skies and hills ahead . . . downhill to cross the Coquet at Alnwick . . . Moors to west . . . Bamburgh Castle visible below Belford . . .

As for my driver and me, we make it to Edinburgh and then take another way back, going through the quiet border country, his home country, where reivers once rustled the cattle of the Elizabethan English. By now he is a full participant in this new American game. It is he who first spots the towering brick ruins of Norham Castle guarding the English side of a ford on the River Tweed; he, too, who insists we seek out the stark and lonesome stone pele tower of Smailholm, loved by Sir Walter Scott and set in the middle of a farmer's field near Kelso. Together we run up the steep narrow stairs, twisting counterclockwise against invading swordsmen, to peer through a high arrow slit and look south toward the England of Elizabeth which, ironically, upon the death of its great Queen, gained Scotland and its king without so much as firing a shot.

Child among Ancestors
The Elizabethan Influence

And this is my eternal plea
To him that made Heaven, Earth, and Sea,
Seeing that I must die so soon
And want a head to dine next noon,
Just at the stroke when my veins start, and spread,
Set on my soul an everlasting head.
Then am I ready like a palmer fit
To tread those blest paths which before I writ.
> —Sir Walter Raleigh, "The Passionate Man's Pilgrimage"

Even though I am aware that there are a considerable number of living and working American writers who write as
if the Elizabethans (and many other among their ancestors) had
never existed, and even though I know all too well that for large
numbers of students these days (even, maybe especially, students
of creative writing) the past drops off into a primitive and simultaneous darkness somewhere in the life and times of Robert Lowell,
the past becoming a constant season of chaos and old night indifferently containing the unread works of Chaucer, Spenser, Milton,
Dryden, and Hart Crane . . . a few people seem to have managed
to escape the perfect democracy of oblivion by one accident or
another; for instance, Louise Bogan by being a woman and working for the *New Yorker,* or Virginia Woolf for being English upper-
middle class and for marrying Leonard who was not. . . . Anyway, in spite of all these depressing things (and others too sad
even to mention), I find it impossible to imagine life and art, in
this country and our own language, without the profound and
continuing influence of the Elizabethans.
It is difficult to imagine myself as someone uninfluenced by
them and uninspired by their example. Yet to make any sense at
all, to untangle the snarl of personal influence, it is necessary to
go back to a condition of ignorance and partial innocence and to

11

try to trace how that influence came to be and in what sequence and with what changes it developed.

It begins appropriately with their literature, particularly the plays of Shakespeare and the poems of the Tudor and Jacobean period. Begins therefore in college. Which gives me time and occasion to say that I like to think that, even if I had never managed to write and finish anything, purely and simply as a reader, then, I would still have been much influenced by their works and words. Beyond that kind of guessing, though, I was greatly and eagerly influenced. In part by modernity. My college days were the salad days of the criticism of T. S. Eliot and of the Fugitives. They did not profess to be great admirers of the Elizabethan poets in general, but they were active propagandists for the Metaphysicals. And what was good enough for them was (as they kept on telling me) more than good enough for the likes of me. It was later, though not very much later, that I learned by a lot of reading and a little thinking that the differences between the Metaphysicals and the mainline/mainstream Elizabethans were more a matter of emphasis than anything else and that the quarrel was basically intramural, a minor problem to be negotiated between people who shared most of the same conventions and expectations, most of the same artistic interests, and pretty much the same wide range and habits of language. A family feud.

About the same time I dropped off the back of the bandwagon of the New Criticism. Much as I admired the practice of it and some gifted performers. It didn't take me long in those happy sophomoric days to figure out they didn't really *know enough* to be saying what they were saying.

What were some of things which, with a lot of help, I stumbled across, the things which were to last me from then until now and were to influence most of the writing of all kinds which I would attempt? At first these things were almost purely literary. I knew next to nothing about the *life* behind and in and of the literature and, to add complexity to my native ignorance, I did not know yet that I did not know. In the literature I was pleased to learn that gifted and inspired artists made good and often fresh use of a whole deck of conventions. That is, I was pleased to discover there could be a real and useful connection between reading and writing. Next I greatly admired their ceaseless interest in and ability to articulate characterization. Pre-Freudian, pre-Jungian, sometimes working with equally improbable and much simpler theories, they could go as deep into human beings as anyone before or since them—this included, by the way, the self-reflexive characterization of speakers and narrators.

Above all, though, I believe that then as now I was wholly overwhelmed by the range, openness, and vitality of their language, all the layers of it, from the most coarse and vulgar to the most highfalutin, the often indecorous joining of the vernacular with the rhetorical, all welded together somehow without any visible cracks or seams. Simultaneous with this richly various language, probably part and parcel of it, was the bringing together of an equal variety of images, of tones and moods, of subjects.

I did not know it at the time, but I was beginning to learn something about the true sophistication of culture.

It was only much later that I would begin to perceive the truth that the Renaissance was not really the beginning of anything, not a stage along the way leading up to, of course, us, but rather the wonderful tag end of something old and fully formed.

In any case, these notions, together with a deepening experience of reading (catching up, really, in this illiterate era), looking for and finding some of the same characteristics even in the most unlikely places and periods, these things have consciously and unconsciously influenced all my work in every form I have been able to work in ever since in both poetry and prose. Including this paper. Including, yes, the screenplay for *Frankenstein Meets the Space Monster.* Which I wouldn't have even entertained, let alone worked on, if I had not been much influenced by Renaissance writers and, before that, if I had not been much challenged and influenced by a whole string of courses, undergraduate and graduate, taught by D. W. Robertson, Jr.

Next (and briefly) there are the very special problems encountered in the making of two published historical novels and one more in the works.

The relevant problem—there were many others—was seeking and finding and developing a kind of language which would do to represent and to evoke the tropes and tones of voice from the sixteenth and early seventeenth century. Not to parody the languages of those times. Nor to imitate. But rather to create, if possible, a modern equivalent.

This involved a great deal of reading, of course. Especially Elizabethan prose, Elizabethan satires, and Elizabethan translations. Translations, with all their inherent flaws, can often give us a very strong sense of the second language.

Early on I made a choice not to base my own style, or styles, on any specific example, except here and there from Raleigh's *History of the World.* The way to do this was to be as vaguely familiar with as many texts and kinds of texts as possible without being directly beholden to any. With the Raleigh the problem was simpler if not easier. Mostly it was handled by a conflict and contrast between two primary styles, old and new. A single passage from *Death of the Fox* dealing precisely and overtly with that contrast will give you the idea:

> My son, it is the prerogative of the old to inflict upon the young a tedious celebration of the past, spent seasons, festivals, and holidays of lost time. And as the world goes, it falls the duty of the young to hear them out or to seem to; and remains the privilege of the old to practice that prerogative, though the exercise serve only to prove the folly thereof. For the old hold no patent, license, or monopoly on wisdom, which, being mysterious and, all reasonable men will agree, invaluable, is beyond the possession of one man or another, one station or one age. For youth, though bound to ignorance out of inexperience, is not likewise condemned to be foolish. For if the purpose of the old be to transmit such wisdom as they deem they have come into, together with a history of themselves and their experience, judiciously framed and arranged in quiet afterthought, and thereby to preserve for the young the best of what has been, and so to defend them from the repetition of many errors and follies of the past, then their intent is surely foolish. It is doomed and fated to fail. The young will either listen, nodding assent and masking an honest indifference, thus learning chiefly the fine art of duplicity at a tender age, or they will listen truly, but without full understanding; as newly arrived in a foreign country, one listens out of courtesy, with much frowning concentration, to a strange tongue, the grammar of which is less than half mastered. Or, should a young man be fortunate enough to be free from need to listen to elders or heed the clucking of old ganders, whose chief claim to excellence is to have lived long

enough to be unfit for anything except a stewing pot, he will stop his ears or walk away in insolence, leaving an old man to mutter at his own shadow by the fire.

Nonetheless, with knowledge of the vanity of my purpose and some foreknowledge of its likely failure, I would seek . . .

I would seek . . . what?

A clumsy exercise in an antiquated style, lacking the time for revision and polish; so that even if I were not to be credited for any substance whatsoever, I might win grudging approval for virtuosity.

Time will bleed away, an inward wound, until I truly bleed.

If time were blood and the executioner struck off my head now, there would be nothing left in me for a crowd to see. A drained and cured carcass only. For I have been gutted and cleaned and hung up by time like a pig in the cellar. They say—do they not?—that I have the pig's eye. Just so . . . I can find no fault now with that. What is gossip may sometimes be poetry.

"Old men are twice children," the proverb says. Perhaps he will bear with me for the sake of my second childhood.

The Succession had to be more diffuse, wide-ranging. More layers of language had to be suggested, because there were so many characters acting over such an expanse of time.

Here I moved further away from literary reading—to letters, to Robert Carey's great autobiography, to jest books and the like. Some of the jokes in *The Succession* come directly out of jest books. Others I made up in the process of writing. Which my wife and most patient critic reckons was the moment I was at last more or less at home in the times. When you can finally make a plausible joke or two in the language of ghosts, you are at least getting there.

The most important thing I learned from studying and imagining the lives of these our ancestors (here reduced to brutal simplicity) was something close to T. S. Eliot's notion of the "dissociation of sensibility." Close, but no cigar. Over and over again I encountered a sustained duplicity, a characteristic involving feeling and perception as much as any ideas, a capacity to entertain, simultaneously, paradoxical, indeed contradictory feelings and perceptions. That capacity stands like an ocean between us.

I have only one more point to make here: that for the making of these two novels I was much more concerned with the life of the times than the literature. But soon enough it was perfectly apparent that the only good gate leading to their lives and times was made out of words. So much else that they created and loved and lived by and for is long gone. The words—which, with a very few exceptions they cannot possibly have taken as seriously as the wealth of vanished clothes and jewels, the lost and forgotten great houses and tombs and monuments . . . Shakespeare was dead right: "Not marble, nor the gilded monuments of princes shall outlive this powerful rime." Their words are not only their greatest gift to us, but they are also the only true map we have to lead us to their world and safely back to our own.

The Star System
A Jeremiad

This was written for a special issue of the *Michigan Quarterly Review,* edited by Nicholas Delbanco and dedicated to the subject of American fiction. It is to the tactful Delbanco that I owe the defining subtitle. I had thought of it, at the time, as a cheerful and even funny piece, though some of the fun was—in the writing, and I hoped in the reading—to be found in the spoken, vernacular *style* of the piece, set as it was in a serious academic quarterly. I see now that Delbanco was right. There is a bit of very old-fashioned raging and raving here. Think of it as being like the two-by-four the farmer uses to get the mule's attention.

I would much rather not be writing about this. Because if I do and if I tell the truth, as I perceive and feel it, I am bound to offend many and probably annoy all the rest. But I will do it. For reasons which may become clear as we go along. Maybe so.

Let me say, here and now, that I am going to abide by the general ground rules and will be dealing, more or less strictly, with the limited world of American fiction. But please bear in mind that I see fiction as a living part of a living literature; and that includes all of us and all the going forms of contemporary writing— poetry, drama, nonfiction, essays, even criticism, journalism old and new, what have you; and, as well, must include all of the known and going forms of narrative including (yes) film, TV, radio, and, by all means, the "interactive" computer narratives which are coming along these days. It is a serious flaw of the American literary mind-set which allows us (all too often) to pretend that all of these things are not closely related, are not always interwoven in a single, if not quite seamless whole. Or maybe it is not mind-set. Maybe it is (as I think in my more cynical mode) a deliberate pretense on the part of self-serving parties and practitioners to keep, dog fashion, the limits of their little territory somehow defined and exclusive. I blame part of it on the Iowa Workshop, which insisted on the separation of the poets and the fiction writers. For its own purposes. Not everybody has followed that design, and it certainly is not the only way to go; but it has been hugely influential and advantageous, too, to those who followed faithfully. Time, most of history, certainly *all* literary history up through Dryden and, I would argue, on through the Augustan Age in England, is on my side. There were always hierarchies of forms, allowing for an interchange, an *intercourse* between critical thinking and popular practice and fashion. But, truly, we find ourselves well into the eighteenth century before some chaps begin to separate poetry and prose or to separate poetry from other forms of discourse merely by the fact that it may be in verse. In terms that Aristotle and John Dryden, and most likely Fielding and Swift and Pope, would have understood and acknowledged as *given*, Faulkner, Joyce, Woolf, Mann, and Proust were poets in every way and every bit as much as, say, Eliot, Pound, Yeats, Williams, Moore, Stevens, Frost, etc. Indeed the former had a certain critical edge because their poetry comes in the shape and form of fully realized fable rather than in evocative fragments. Moreover, and I do believe Aristotle and Dryden and all the others in between and some pretty good ones later, too, would have to allow for the fact, other even more widely influential fabulists, let us say Fellini, Kurosawa, and Bergman, are by definition poets of the highest order. What I am saying—and no fooling—is that when it comes to poetry, you can have your Plumly and I'll take Proust, thank you. You take Mark Strand (poetry and prose) and I'll take Thomas Mann, if you please. Dave Smith is to be measured not against the examples of James Dickey or even the magnificently versatile Robert Penn Warren, but, rather, against Faulkner at his finest.

I am only kidding to the extent that (as you see) I don't really believe at all in the favorite American literary parlor game of literary *ranking*. I am just arguing that all our literature is part of a wholeness which (for whatever reasons) we sometimes choose to forget. I confess that I once used the same argument, allowing all our literary creators to claim the name of poets, in a discussion with Donald Justice. Whose answer was that of the active generation surely James Merrill could under the best classical standards take his place alongside the great Masters. Maybe so . . .

Am I being too cranky and pedantic? Well, after all, I finally got my Ph.D. last year, after thirty years; and, in the time that may be left to me, maybe I ought to be allowed to make up for lost time and sound as academic as I please. But not for long.

You need to know a little bit more about me to evaluate my point of view. I am a witness here, but I am not a disinterested one. There are a few facts which may be pertinent. I started reading and writing before I could actually do either. That is, I was regularly *read to*, by my father and my mother and by others in the family, before I was well out of the crib. For richer and for poorer, we lived in a house with (as it turned out, when my father died and we sold the house and counted them) many thousands of books. Everybody read and everybody wrote, too. Before we *learned how to write*, we dictated our stories and poems and plays to those who did. And there were always some writers in the family, some pretty good ones on both sides. (So? There was also a dancer, a musician, a P.G.A. golfer, soldiers and sailors. A little of everything.) By habit and example we learned to be, I hope, *open* to almost everything without being entirely undiscriminating. There was room, among the many mansions of the heaven of literature, for Shakespeare and Kipling and Dickens and Stevenson, for Hemingway and Sinclair Lewis, for *The Harvard Classics* and the Hardy Boys, for *Don Quixote* and *Don Sturdy and the Temple of Gold*. I read all the time, then, and I still do. And after I became a teacher and then later a certified (by finally being published) writer, I did not put away childish things, but just added to them. I have for thirty-some years judged countless contests and grant applications and prizes. And I have edited poetry and fiction, too, for various magazines and presses. And I have reviewed books all the time, individually and in clusters for chronicle reviews and in mountainous caches, over the last few years, for the annual "Year in Fiction" essay for the *Dictionary of Literary Biography Yearbook* where in ten or twelve thousand words I try to do my best to report on a calendar year's worth of American fiction. At this time I am still doing at least some of all of it. And I think it would be perfectly safe to say that I read more fiction, at all stages of its development, than anybody else in this country. And in terms of published books, I may be wrong, but you cannot convince me that I do not read more novels and story collections than the entire professional staffs of the *New York Times* (Sunday and daily) and the *Washington Post* (ditto) put together. Add on, say, *Vanity Fair, New York,* and the *Village Voice.* And I am not a bona fide speed reader, either. Not such an outrageous claim. You will surely have noticed that they all review pretty much the same books. And close readers will also have noted the irrefutable internal evidence that they read each other's stuff, reviews, pretty closely, too. And *really* close readers will notice how phrases on book jackets, inevitably and slightly translated, reappear in their reviews. Now. You can argue *selectivity* all you want to. I'll give you some points on that one, but will argue back that a true and honest selectivity would not produce such *uniformity* of agreement in various places as to which books are worthy of attention and which are not. I would also argue that, for these professional book arbiters, by the time they have taken care of their friends and enemies and have paid off professional obligations of one kind and another to publishers, selection has been greatly simplified. Of course I can't claim, and I don't, to *know* as much as they do, collectively or individually. And I remain helplessly dependent on them for *information,* if not for judgment or wisdom. Anyway, by all rights, I ought to have a sense of what is going on. And I simply do not. And that is the one and only thing I am absolutely sure of.

You want to know something? I will bet you good money that I read more short stories in any given year, in magazines and book collections, as well as in manuscript, than Shannon Ravenel or William Abrahams. But they have the answers every year (though I read *them,* too, and notice that they are not overburdened with memory of their earlier certainties and that their answers tend to change as the years go on and by). I am sorry I don't have many answers. I envy their scope, authority, and confidence. They have strategic points of view. I am down in the trenches. A literary grunt with a limited view of shell bursts, flares, and rusty barbwire. And I claim to be a writer, too. Oh, if I only had good sense, I would try to be a lot more like Faulkner in this matter. I saw him once, at a polite distance in Princeton. While I stood there, a hot-shot New York editor came up and gave him a new novel that he thought Faulkner would really enjoy. And Mr. Faulkner (somewhat to my surprise) thanked him kindly for the book, but added that he probably would never get around to reading it. "These days," he said, stuffing his pipe, "I only have time for the Old Verities."

God, I wish I had spent as much time on the Old Verities as on the many ways and means of contemporary American fiction, fine and dandy as it is! Of course, as I gather from his family and friends, Faulkner was, as ever, half kidding. He read everything he could get hold of. All the time. An old friend of his told me once: "He would read matchbox covers and cereal boxes if there was nothing else." In that sense a kindred spirit. . . .

Something more before we get down to what the middle-aged survivors of the 1960s used to call the nitty-gritty. (I wonder if guys like Daniel Ellsberg and his celebrated psychiatrist still use expressions like that.) Not only do I not have a good sense of the Big Picture, but also, try as I will, I *miss things*. Lots of things. It has become, over the years, a kind of a desperate game, trying *not* to let anything escape my attention, slip through the cracks, as they keep on saying. Well, truth is that I don't even come close. And unlike the *Times* and *Post* people, in the anarchy of my effort, I sometimes even forget the work of my friends. Example: to my everlasting shame, I read and greatly valued (I even wrote a blurb for the book jacket) and then just plain *forgot*! for the "Year in Fiction," one of the better novels of 1985, *Scorpio Rising*, by R. G. Vliet. Russ Vliet was a poet and fiction writer I much admired. I just forgot. . . .

Point one, then. There is so much being done that it is easy to overlook a lot of it; and, in truth, a whole lot of very good fiction is overlooked each and every year.

It is my best and considered judgment that American fiction is, overall, a reflection of American life and society; that our fiction is large, very large both in sheer numbers, *quantity* of production, and in its wild variety of forms. Like our great country, it's seething with diversity, wild with plurality. There are dozens and dozens of good—and I mean very good—writers, a crowd, a multitude of them. Even within the limited parameters of my aesthetic tastes. Or yours. Look, I may think minimalism, as a *program*, sucks. I may think of smartass metafiction as a social disease. But I am continually surprised and delighted and (all right) instructed by superb writers who do nothing else but be minimal and smart-ass. The basic rule of thumb is that the more open and supple you allow yourself to be, the more of them (good writers) there are to be found out there. And you know what? I think this situation is purely and simply wonderful. If you like to read fiction, if you really enjoy it, it is a great time to be alive. Now, of course, it may be somewhat inconvenient for those folks who make their livings by generalizing all about the contemporary literary scene and its trends; I mean professional critics and reviewers and their academic accomplices, the specialists in contemporary literature (of one kind or another) who, together with (yes!) the writers they bet on and praise, have a vested interest, the most obvious kind of self-interest, in maintaining their own arbitrary status quo, their artificially created Establishment. Artificial? Pray remember we are talking about "serious" fiction, mostly. Serious fiction has no establishment based on *sales*. Unless you want to quibble about hundreds (in a nation of millions). And do not forget the publishers, large and small, who must use the distortions of the Establishment to simplify their difficult tasks and to (pardon the expression) maximize their slim profits or, anyway, (again, please) minimize their losses.

I am here saying (yes) that in our time the Establishment, in its loosely collusive and more or less related forms, is not honestly representative of what is really going on in American fiction, day in and day out. I am also trying to imply that to the extent that they know better, those who help to maintain, preserve, protect, and defend the Establishment are dishonest people. And those in the Establishment who *don't* know better are too ignorant and stupid to be believed.

Take your pick, members-in-good-standing of the Literary Establishment, in my book you are either liars or dupes. No, I'm only hurrahing you. What I'm *really* saying is that you, O judges and salesmen and hypocrite readers and writers!, are really just like all the rest of us. Caught up in the System.

There are really no officers in the army of Contemporary Lit. We are all grunts.

Point two, then. The Star System, which works for journalists, professors, critics and reviewers, publishers, foundations, and, don't forget, the Stars too, has no real basis whatsoever in fact or in truth. The Star System is about as applicable to our real life and times as, say, Courtly Love in the Age of AIDS or the Feudal System in the Era of Affirmative Action.

The Literary Star System *may* (I will allow for the possibility) be a necessary and relatively efficient way to deal with the literature of the past, especially of the remote past. But the closer we get to the present, the greater the distortion of both facts and truth, and the greater the extent of the injustice.

Stars—and you know who you are, O Voices of Your Generation, Spokespersons for Decades, and so, alas, do we—I am not saying you aren't any good. Am not even saying you are not all you are cracked up to be. I am saying—and you will be hard-pressed to prove otherwise: you will have to read at least as much as I do and know a little bit more; and you don't; and you won't—you are not head and shoulders better than many, many, many living and working American writers. And you know it. No matter how many times you read your happy press clippings, you can't get rid of your doubts. Poets are the worst about this. Some of my poet friends and colleagues get, *really!*, instant facial tics and migraine headaches if I merely mention the names of poets whom they haven't heard of. A powerful weapon. Fun, too. Reader, do you remember James Dickey, in various places, insisting that we are the only intelligent life in the universe? It would be unbearable to him, and us too for different reasons, to discover another James Dickey out there somewhere banging out anapests and three-stress lines.

Names? You want names, of course. Examples from the world of American fiction. Well, you won't get them from me. They know who they are. And you know who they are. Any recently published anthology (anthologies are the Rogues' Galleries of our time) will tell you. This issue of this magazine will give you all the names you need. And one thing about the Stars that I have noticed. No matter how they got to be Stars, by hook or crook, they don't *stay* where they are by being anything else than *ruthless,* ruthlessly self-serving, invincibly ignorant of anything going on outside the castle walls. Merciless folk. Note how they want and get full credit for every little half-ass act of generosity they perform. They want not only to be deeply admired, but also well remembered. And like the legendary elephant, they never forget.

I may be (and proud of it, too) an advocate and mediator for the literary peasants, but I have also been among the Stars, here and there—completely by accident of course—on panels and committees and so forth and so on. And I can report to you that (in my best judgment) most Literary Stars are shamelessly mean-spirited and vindictive and utterly self-serving. And, as far as I can tell, with only a shred, call it a fig leaf, of moral rectitude. You will surmise that I really don't *like* them very much. True enough, but irrelevant. I love my family and friends. I have a large family and a lot of friends. Socializing with Literary Stars has never been my idea of an upscale experience. Tell you the truth, I can't figure out how they can stand each other's dreary company. Only excuse I can see for it is that, like some corrupt Renaissance court, they can't afford to let each other out of sight for a moment. Let that, the company of each other, be their reward.

Do you think I am being pretty silly, foolish? Well, here is the text for this sermon. You did notice that my rhetoric here is the rhetoric of preaching. Which is as good as any other, as long as everybody understands it. My text comes from St. Paul's first epistle to the proud and worldly wise congregation in Corinth. "Where is the wise? Where is the disputer of this world? Hath not God made foolish the wisdom of this world?" (I Corinthians 1:20).

If you can't stand preaching, we can always be political. Why not?

I speak here on their behalf, the working majority. They are, here and now, my constituency. The truth is that, just like the society at large, our literature is much more democratic than any of the existing Star Systems will allow. You know what? In terms of quality, I can in a matter of minutes put together an anthology of American story writers, writers you have never heard of, that will be in every way and by any standard as good as the finest collection of Stars you can assemble.

A few years ago, as an exercise, I used to get each of my creative writing students to take a single year in the 1920s or 1930s or early 1940s and read straight through the *New York Times*, Sunday and daily, and the *Herald Tribune*, for book reviews and for literary news. Then to come and to report to us as to how, say, 1929, *saw itself.* Next step was to compare and contrast that vision with the later judgment of the literary histories.

This exercise taught a lot of different things. One good one was humility. O Stars, cultivate a little humility and you will be stronger and better for the experience! Of course, it indicated that even in this self-conscious and manipulative century, characteristics which may be as commonplace as (and not unrelated to) our merciless savagery, tacit and active, with each other at all levels, even here, in the good old twentieth century, there have been huge discrepancies between reality and status quo.

I remember once, in the late 1950s, trying this selfsame argument out, in terms of poetry, with Stanley Kunitz. (It was in a restaurant in Middletown, Connecticut, Stanley, in case you have forgotten. Refresh your memory.) And you shrugged off my arguments, Stanley, with an example. "If Robert Frost came along now," you said, "we would surely recognize him." Brash and sassy and full of bile and irony, I said: "Yes, sir, I reckon you would recognize Robert Frost. We have certainly come that far." Second time around, do you get what I was saying? Somebody else at the table, I think it was my old friend Dick Wilbur, allowed as how *in this age* no talent could go undiscovered and unrewarded for long. He seemed mildly wistful that this was so. Never again would there be exciting and happy posthumous discoveries. Somebody else (who? I wish I could remember) jumped in and went too far, too, claiming that even poverty had finally disappeared. Soon there would be nobody left to feel sorry for. We laughed. What else? This was, after all, the late and high 1950s. Everybody was still reading John Kenneth Galbraith. *Assured of certain certainties,* as Eliot wrote once. . . .

What am I getting at here? I am saying that there are no *real* Stars in American fiction these days. Stars are few and we are many. And from experience, the experience of reading, not writing, not as one among the many, permits me to assert that, by and large, the many are very good. It is wonderfully exciting and rewarding to be a reader of American fiction in this day and age. We have so many exciting and rewarding writers. Young ones and old ones.

This, the active and visible presence of the elders in our literary culture, may be, ironically, the *newest* distinction of our time. May be, after all, its finest and most distinguishing characteristic. Writers of every race, creed, color, country of national origin, sexual preference, etc. American, myself, for as long as any white folks have been here. American, then, to my genetic code and the marrow of my bones. I can be pardoned for wishing that our wondrous plurality extended beyond political and social life to include our literature, itself, as an honest and accurately reflective part of the vital national debates going on. But to have worthwhile debates you have to have more than one side, more than one self-serving point of view, and maybe even a little passion, also. Our Stars, and the Establishment of which they are ornaments, have too much to lose to be real and serious participants in our political and social life beyond the most reflexive, simpleminded, and stereotypical levels. Truth is, they have even less to contribute than the Rock Stars so many of them yearn to become.

What's to be done about all this, if anything? Maybe nothing. Too many people, including many of the new and younger writers, read much too little. They don't even have time for the Old Verities. They just barely have time for the Stars. So, in the end, the Star System may finally come in the future to be as real as it is false now as a model and description of the present. So, relax Stars. Posterity will probably take care of you, will preserve the reputations you have acquired, if not earned. One way or the other. No controlling *that*, you know. The future may find all of us to have been foolish and far from relevant to anything that matters. My own experience with history and historians teaches me that they will not settle for, not without interrogation and inquisition, the official, the Establishment view of things.

Meantime what is there for us to do, those locked and lost in the present (though not without good memory or solid knowledge, not without a *past*, then) who care at all about American fiction? We are appalled (I speak for my constituents, both readers and writers) at the *waste* involved. Waste, including deadly toxic waste, is such a commonplace of contemporary American life. Why and how should literature be spared? So many worthy talents that are lost to us by the waste of the System. But those who survive the school of hard knocks and the great shrugs of indifference (may I, with mild pride, count myself among them?) are tough, hardened. Are not likely to cease and desist in the face of indifference, even rejection. And we need not, shall not cease in the effort, as readers, to seek and find new and worthy writers. Discovery is still a real possibility. And even though people, including writers, appear to be reading less and less, there are more and more literary magazines (coming and going) and presses, places for good writers to appear and to be discovered.

As for the Stars, I believe they are safe enough from any serious literary revolution. We already had one, right after World War II, a revolution which, among other things, raised unknowns like Faulkner and Fitzgerald to the status of Stars in our firmament. And it is already late in this tedious and terrible century, too late for much beyond the usual decadence to come to pass. And, anyway, I can't think of any century which has witnessed more than one serious literary revolution. Thus our Stars will go on being Stars. Happily ever after.

There is one thing we could do, maybe ought to do. In fairness (never mind *justice*) we are entitled to ask more of them. They should be held, feet to the fire, to the highest standards imaginable. Damn near absolute standards. For instance, the contemporary Southern writer (even the achievements of the late Flannery O'Connor) *should* now be measured against the standards of William Faulkner. Our poets should not be allowed to measure themselves against, just for example, Mark Strand and Charles Simic. Compare and contrast them to Chaucer, Shakespeare, Milton, and Byron. See what I mean? And our Stars should never—ever—be permitted to have it both ways. They may not be our lucky lords and leaders and yet, at one and the same time, lay claim upon a common bond they share with us, the many, the unwashed, the majority. They are not just Folks. Never can be any more. And, beyond that, we should agree that no one in the Literary Establishment need be trusted. For trust, unlike so many other things, must be earned.

Once More unto the Breach, Dear Friends, Once More

The Publishing Scene and American Literary Art

> Literary mores no longer place as much stock in the hieratic model of the writer, which is just as well. Unless one is good at self-sacrifice, is endowed with an iron will and a genius-sized gift, it's likely to be a defeating thing to insist on producing Art or nothing.
>
> —Theodore Solotaroff, *A Few Good Voices in My Head*

Once upon a time, not so long ago, trade books published in America were conveniently divided (*segregated* might be a better word for it) by publishers into two basic categories—"popular" and "serious." It was those terms, as much as anything else, Saul Bellow was fighting against when he coined his own opposite poles, "public" and "private." We are talking about, roughly, thirty years ago: the War over with, replaced, of course, by other, smaller wars without ceasing; the last of the original millions of veterans, who had crowded the campuses as never before on the GI Bill and changed American education (among other things) for better and for worse forever more, gone off into their long-deferred "real" lives at last; the paperback revolution that had furnished the affordable textbooks of that era and which had, for a time, revitalized the dozing, yawning American publishing business with the double whammy of fresh new money for the taking and the up-to-date sweaty greed to go out after it. About thirty years ago we had even had a little literary revolution, too, one of those once in a century or so (maybe) overturnings of the statues and monuments of the Literary Establishment and their replacement with a new set of heroes and icons. (I suppose the nearest thing to it was in seventeenth-century England when the Roundheads finally managed to kick ass on the Cavaliers and shut down all the theaters as part of what they hoped was a final solution. Of course, half a century later the theaters were back in business, but utterly different. The old Shakespearean stage was long gone and forgotten.) In our own revolution, for example, Faulkner, Fitzgerald, Hemingway, and even Steinbeck, none of whom could be said to have prospered greatly either in rewards or reputation in the years before the War, were now suddenly declared to be the Old Masters of the first half of this century. (You want to see how highly regarded they were during that first half-century? Go and pick up any old *New York Times Book Review* or *Herald Tribune* or *Harper's* or *Scribner's* or any other literary magazine between, say, 1920 to 1945, and you'll see who the Updikes and the Oateses of the time were, and they were sure not Faulkner, Fitzgerald, Hemingway or Steinbeck. Wolfe, maybe, but his time was brief, brief.) Needless to say certain publishers were simply delighted. And all publishers began sifting through their backlists looking for old timers and unknowns who maybe could be resurrected to the cheerful music of the cash register. And, do not forget, for the first time ever, courses in modern and contemporary literature were now being offered at American colleges and universities. There was going to be some good money there, too, for those lucky or clever publishers who could get their snouts up close to the edge of the trough. "Serious," or to use another synonymous term of the period, "prestige" writing just might pay off in the long run after all.

It is an important condition of modern and contemporary literary art that the most prominent and active American publishers of our times have had, at least as a secondary or "spin-off" goal, the desire to be not only successful but also socially respectable. Money alone could not purchase or confer that reward. It was necessary to publish something not merely worthwhile, but also *recognized* to be worthwhile, at least within the precincts of the New York City where they lived and worked and prospered. See Theodore Solotaroff's essay, "What Has Happened to Publishing," in *A Few Good Voices in My Head* (1987), where he writes "of Jewish newcomers' using family money to establish houses that conformed to their desire and drive to play an important cultural role in New York, much as their counterparts were doing in Vienna, Berlin, and London." We could make too much out of the special limitations, partly self-imposed, both ethnic and regional in American commercial or "mainstream" publishing. But there is a tension there and a different purpose. Insofar as Solotaroff's observation is accurate—and there is no good reason to question his authenticity—it depicts a curious cultural and social scene, at once strictly regional, of small space, and international. Looking not west of the Hudson to the huge area and population of the nation itself (which appears to figure chiefly in their calculations, *dreams* if you prefer, as a source of raw materials, including writing, and of potential customers, *natives* if you would rather, caught in a classically colonial paradigm), but east, across the Atlantic to the example of European urban culture. This particular upward social mobility is not, then, an example of the *American* dream and has only a commercial need to be in touch with the larger and wider American dreams and aspirations. He said it, I didn't; but in large part it helps explain how the inordinate influence of the New York City community (as it sees itself, of course) on serious American literature came to pass.

In the meantime, "popular" literature, preferably best-sellers, could keep the old cash flow flowing, pay the piper, and take care of overhead—which later included the salaries and expense accounts of people employed in the business who, if they weren't getting rich, were at least living comfortably.

It all seems so sweet and innocent and so very long ago. So long before the arrival of the "Blockbuster," and the chain bookstores, and all the latest, improved means of persuasion and advertising and publicity, of the conglomerates which could afford to pay for all this. Before, also, the sudden upsurge of "creative writing" in hundreds of institutions, which soon led to hundreds of jobs for poets and fiction writers. Who could be modestly supported by the patronage of the colleges and universities, provided they published and in places with enough "visibility" to bring credit on themselves and their patron institutions. And provided that they picked up enough good reviews in the right places. The "right places" being mainly and chiefly the media centered in and around New York, thus, in a serious sense, making these American educational institutions, coast to coast, curiously dependent on the good will and attention of one particular region with its own mind-set and special interests. And there was also an exponential increase in the number and variety of possible grants, awards, fellowships, and prizes able to be acquired if not exactly earned by writers.

Along with all of this came, hand in glove, the social twins who always arrive to accompany awakening ambition—corruption and conflict of interest. What had once, and recently enough, been a lonely and savage struggle for simple survival was radically altered, at least for some, becoming the perhaps even more ruthless and brutal battle for the fruits of personal ambition. The poets turned out to be the worst of the lot. No surprise there. They had endured the toughest times. Only the well-to-do could really afford to write poetry. Those who were not rich enough by inheritance or, by privilege, firmly set (like Williams and Stevens, for instance) in a lucrative profession, went under. Like poor old Maxwell Bodenheim. But now you could earn a half-decent salary as a teacher with a prospect of maybe tenure or even, maybe, an endowed chair someday, provided you minded your p's and q's, acted more or less the way a poet is supposed to act, and picked up enough outside support and recognition to justify your very existence. Given the prospect of comfort and a kind of junior executive security for poets, it is hardly surprising (though not in the least praiseworthy, either) that the poets in large numbers began to behave toward each other in ways which would have embarrassed Iago and to pull insider tricks and stunts which would make Ivan Boesky blink and blush. The fiction writers were only marginally better behaved, perhaps because there was/is more scrutiny devoted to them. They still have some readers and the prospect of reaching a few more. Some of them are doing rather well. Ann Beattie, for example, who only teaches from time to time when she really has to, is quoted in *Publishers Weekly* (December 25, 1987) in a statement which less than a decade ago (and even allowing for inflation) would have aroused some hearty horse laughter among the brotherhood and sisterhood of working writers: "If I tried to support myself solely by writing short stories, I'd have an annual income of under $10,000 a year." It has been at least half a century in America since anybody came close to making that kind of money from writing short stories. The poets don't even read each other (not even when judging or reviewing each other's work), so who cares what they do or don't do? Those among the poets who have (somehow, as much to their own surprise as anyone else's) arrived at the top of the little heap are willing to live with things just as they are. If people start to *read* them, who knows?, they might easily be toppled from eminence and replaced by others whose names and whose works are mostly unknown. To them at least.

By now, you will have guessed, we are already located in the big middle of the here and now. And we are supposed to be talking about the publishing scene, not writers. Problem is, *truth* is, most of the writers (practically anybody you have ever heard of) are involved in a close symbiotic relationship, *cozy* you might say, with the publishing world. Without the acquiescence and tacit support of the writers (especially the most successful ones), the whole creaky system might collapse. They can fool you, though, the writers. Take PEN for example, forever using our dues to battle against some forms of overt censorship here and there, against racial separation and segregation in South Africa if not, say, Kenya or Ghana, firmly committed against torture everywhere in the world except in certain Eastern Bloc nations, and mostly keeping their own mouths tight shut about the inequities and injustices, trivial and profound, perpetrated on the American public by the same folks who give writers their advances against royalties and publish their books. Whatever the price is, it doesn't include a vow of silence or even very much self-sacrifice.

The writers are far from blameless, and they must take a good share of the blame, not only the publishers, that there is so little place for genuine experimental writing in America. By Americans. If you happen to come from another country and have to be translated out of another language and into English, you are *expected* to be a little bit off the wall.

What has happened most recently within the old system of American trade publishing is a series of slight but significant changes, chiefly during the past five years. One item is a new category, a new usage—*literary*, as in "a literary novel." A literary work has no pretensions (or hope) of somehow becoming a Blockbuster; possibly, though, it may become a best-seller. Blockbusters, the ultimate best-sellers, are the bread and butter, meat and potatoes

of contemporary commercial publishing. The whole system is organized around the Blockbuster. But a great many of the type,
widely advertised and expensively promoted, given every chance,
have proved to be duds. Nothing is more costly or absurd than a
Blockbuster which has arrived on the scene with all the excitement of a soggy firecracker. For a little while the routine was to try
to line up several potential Blockbusters per season and hope that
one or two caught on. This proved to be very wasteful; and whereas
American commercial publishing is nothing if not widely wasteful, it was too much so for the limited resources of most publishers. Over the past few years the publishers have tended to spend
more time and money and planning on fewer potential Blockbusters. For the rest of their line, many have discovered that a "literary" book will do just fine. You get a lot more attention and review space (which, at the least, can be considered as a form of
cheap advertising; like the publication of poetry, for instance)—
more so than before, because reviewers, given a choice, prefer to
review literary works rather than most of the Blockbusters, which
don't need to be reviewed, anyway. A true Blockbuster can't be
helped much by good reviews. And bad reviews? Think of Samuel Goldwyn's famous reaction to criticism: "It rolls off my back
like a duck." More to the point, the literary book is, almost always,
more economical. Doesn't call for an enormous advance. If good
things develop, fine and dandy. If bad things accrue, why the publisher can quickly dump it, cutting losses (and they are usually
minimal losses anyway) at a dead run. And once in a while, it is
believed, a genuinely literary work can, in fact, achieve a noteworthy financial success. Can even become a bona fide best-seller.
On November 30, 1987, *Washington Post* book critic Jonathan Yardley took positive note that serious writers were beginning to show
up on the best-seller lists. He cited Gail Godwin, Toni Morrison,
Tom Wolfe, and Scott Turow. He did not mention some others
whose books had, earlier in 1987, found places on the various best-
seller lists, writers like Philip Roth, Saul Bellow, Gore Vidal, John
Gregory Dunne, Walker Percy, Larry McMurtry, Kurt Vonnegut,
and Pat Conroy. Important thing to keep in mind is that (surprising as it may be) from the point of view of most "mainstream"
publishers and the national book critics and reviewers, these writ-

ers are all equally "serious" and "literary." One should also be aware that the term *literary* has been stretched, perhaps to its extreme, to include even such things as movies, widely distributed and advertised feature films. For example, the *New York Times* (January 7, 1988) discussed *Broadcast News* as an example of the type—"The Making of a 'Literary' Film."

In some ways the fact that writers who at least began their careers as "serious" and "literary" artists can now produce profitable work for commercial publishers has had a negative impact on contemporary writers. The positive values, if only as a vague source of hope and of good morale, are obvious. But in many cases these people are merely the token literary artists on the publishers' lists. Which is to say there is usually not a whole lot of room left on those lists, or in the publishers' special mind-sets, for many new people. Or for any *rediscoveries*. This latter is, ironically, the most difficult category of all, because the publishers have by now established a deep and serious interest (it's their investment, after all) in keeping the accepted Literary Establishment intact, as firmly settled as can be. Just as, at the end of World War II, rediscovery and revisionist history were worthwhile (therefore almost inevitable) in practical, pure and simple financial terms, so from now on it would be a serious problem, in those same terms and for an entire linked chain of beings living off the literary plankton—publishers, their stables of writers, reviewers and literary journalists, critics and academics—if the Establishment were, at any point, threatened with any significant change.

Because of what happened to Faulkner, Fitzgerald, Hemingway, Steinbeck, etc., a whole generation of American writers came along, believing that nothing in literary history was carved in stone, set in concrete. They learned the wrong lesson from their own immediate past; for now nothing seems so solid, secure, and untouchable as the literary pantheon as it is perceived by its supporters. The sense of revision and rediscovery has been transferred away from the contemporary scene and turned onto the redefinition of the Canon. (For a popular discussion of this, see "U.S. Literature: Canon Under Siege," *New York Times*, January 6, 1988.) The motives here are, of course, political and social as well as personal. (The personal element is for feminist and minority critics, for example, to find things to write about and to build profitable careers upon. And it is always somewhat easier to be an instant, natural-born gender or ethnicity expert than to be the master of an extensive and approved canon.) Thus, in terms of revisionism, Hawthorne and Melville and Cooper are far more vulnerable than, say, Carver or Barthelme or Beattie. These latter are, at this time, contemporary midlist authors. That is, they do not lose a great deal of money for their sponsoring publishers; but, at the same time, they do not, not directly at least, make much for the publisher either. Their star status is partly a matter of acknowledged quality and excellence and partly a matter of publicity and promotion. The ratio of these characteristics to each other would be an interesting subject for debate if there were any place (other than this one) for even discussing such things. Never mind. I expect most readers are willing to grant those three, and others, a measure of literary excellence even if they do not necessarily take them all to be self-evidently head and shoulders above, superior to any number, a goodly number, of others among their contemporaries. The most interesting thing, here, is that unlike Roth, Bellow, Walker Percy, etc., who somehow (though not without support and supporters) earned their status in the hierarchy, the next batch of writers (here merely *represented* by Carver, Beattie, Barthelme, as if by a decent law firm) were simply awarded that status by their publishers at the outset, their installation being confirmed by continued publicity.

The inevitable next step was to see if a writer could be championed by a publisher and turned into an early best-seller. What would happen if a publisher took a book by a "serious," "literary" writer and offered the kind of massive and expensive support that is usually reserved for Blockbuster authors? There are a number of recent examples of this kind of scheme. The rise to a certain kind of notoriety of Jay McInerney (*Bright Lights, Big City*) is a result of this kind of attention. So is the career of writer Richard Ford, whose two most recent books, the novel *The Sportswriter* and the collection of stories *Rock Springs,* have been given the full contemporary publicity and promotional treatment by his editor (himself much publicized)—Gary Fisketjon. Between them, Ford and Fisketjon have succeeded in giving the writer a maximum "visibility." However, Fisketjon concedes that sales have not been, except in a strictly relative sense, extraordinary. Ford is certainly well known, a "name" now, and, as well, has received the kind of prominent and prompt review attention that most American writers, even among the finest and most famous, never come to know. But the full apparatus of modern "exposure" could not quite bring out book buyers and readers in the numbers (yet) which would justify the expense and effort. More impressive, more extraordinary, and, finally and in a deadly serious sense, far more dangerous to the declining, somewhat ambiguous integrity of American literary art, has been the story of the "Brat Pack." This is a story which also involves Fisketjon, as a principal mover and shaker, among others of the so-called Baby Editors who came into the limelight (a prominence once reserved for the likes of Maxwell Perkins and Saxe Commins) in the mid–1980s. Their latest task and challenge was at once somewhat more daunting and more cynical: to take a little group of writers—in this instance Bret Easton Ellis, Jill Eisenstadt, Tama Janowitz, and some others, all more or less in the shadow of Jay McInerney—writers of extremely limited literary talent, and somehow to sell them to the great unwashed American colonial reading public as literary celebrities and (maybe, all in due time) as at least Spokespersons of Their Generation, if not as major literary figures and influences. What this involved was publicity, the beauty of it being that (at least in the view of the Baby Editors and their cohorts) today, as we drift into the inevitable decadence that haunts the ending of every century, it does not matter in the slightest whether the publicity be positive or negative, good or bad, the desired results will be more or less the same. The first stage proved remarkably successful. In a very short time any scholar worth his salt could have quickly put together a checklist of severely, often outrageously negative reviews in prominent places by prominent reviewers of the latest literary works of the Brat Pack. These could have then been added to an even longer list of articles about these authors as personalities, celebrities, *characters*, and, as well, as social symbols of this and that, of something or other, in every kind of magazine you can think of, from the *Georgia Review* to *Vanity Fair, Gentleman's Quarterly, People,* and the *New Yorker.* Conservative critics raged, the chic and trendy had campy good fun; but everybody mentioned the Brat Pack and usually spelled their names right. At first it was merely a whole lot of publicity and (again) seemed to have no real effect on sales or reading habits. But, at last, by the end of 1987 the masterminds, the Baby Editors, had begun to sell some *books* on the basis of all that publicity. Whether anyone actually read or will read them remains to be seen. The important thing to note is that this late in our sad and bloody century when, it would seem, all the world would be at last more or less immune to the coarser, cruder, more vulgar and more obvious forms of hype, some cynical young people of less than (zero?) serious accomplishment could prove P. T. ("This Way to the Egress!") Barnum right as rain.

Truth is, these children of our century's old age did not invent anything. Literary journalism was already in its place and functioning, like many other forms of contemporary journalism, more as a matter of images than any reality whatsoever, more as a matter of personalities and newsworthy events than matters of art and life. Mailer, of course, had seen this whole thing coming, plugged into the power of it, and danced his little shocked and shocking Boogaloo in *Advertisements for Myself.* But it is hard to believe that even *he* could have imagined a literary journalism which would (in 1987) devote space, energy, even some thought to such questions as the matter of Joni Evans departing from Simon and Schuster (and, simultaneously, divorcing her boss and husband there, Richard Snyder), going on to replace Howard Kaminsky (who seems to have been fired over something about a party in Frankfurt—who knows? who cares?) at Random House. Then there was the hue and cry and the counterattacks of the book reviewers when, against overwhelming odds and well-laid plans (it seems), Larry Heinemann won the National Book Award for his novel *Paco's Story.* Much more space was spent on this argument than was ever (so far) allotted to reviews of the novel. And there was so much else to write about, to think (?) about. There was the big J. D. Salinger lawsuit. There was the final departure of Shawn and the arrival of Gottlieb at the *New Yorker.* The rising and falling of certain smaller nations, some minor wars and famines attracted less press attention than that little episode. There were public accounts of odd little literary quarrels. See, for instance, "Big Fight Among the Little Magazines" (*New York Post*, June 22, 1987), which tried to detail and make some sense out of a battle between Robert Fogarty of *Antioch Review*, Gordon Lish of the *Quarterly*, and Ben Sonnenberg of *Grand Street*. In a roundup of important events and happenings of 1987, "Updates on '87" (*Washington Post*, December 31, 1987) spent some time (as it and the *New York Times* had earlier spent a good deal of time and space) considering the sad fate of a *book proposal* (!) by Joan Braden. (If you can publicize and review book proposals, who needs to bother with books?) Equally important to the *Post* was the case of Shere Hite, "The Sean Penn of the 1987 literary circuit," whose latest opus, *Women and Love*, was one of the most prominently reviewed and publicly discussed books of the year. In fact, this may have been a moderately important story, for this was a case which ran counter to the Brat Pack Caper. In spite of everything, it failed to live up to plans and expectations. A "Knopf insider" was quoted: "The general expectation is that publicity, good or bad, generates sales. On this title, publicity generated sales but not to the magnitude it should have."

The peak of literary journalism in 1987 was probably Rust Hills's "*Esquire*'s Guide to the Literary Universe" (*Esquire*, August). Where Hills jumped aboard the bandwagon to celebrate the likes of (yes!) Gary Fisketjon. Whom he declared ("The President Ordains The Bee to Be") to be "the only young editor in the business who has the power—and the inclination—to publish his contemporaries." Presumably Hills means people of Fisketjon's own age. Notice that there is no mention, not the slightest hint of quality or excellence. Merely contemporaneity.

And that, ladies and gentlemen, is where we find ourselves as we stagger forward into the last decade of the century. What can be said of the American publishing scene in our time? That it has, in almost every way, reflected the vices and virtues of the society of which it is an odd part. That, at times and almost in spite of itself, it has allowed artists, master artists, to surface and to endure. That the great corruption, if not simply danger of the last half of the century, has been the attempt on the part of the publishers to *create* (by fiat as much as fact) its own gallery of stars and master artists. That this last, while not an outright failure, for there are fine and gifted writers who have been championed by their publishers, is nevertheless not likely to improve the lot or situation of most American writers, either the discovered or undiscovered.

Nevertheless—witness the incredible persistence of many small presses, the surprising success of many small regional publishers (Algonquin Books, for example)—there are other forces at work. Not the least of these is a strong new kind of regionalism in the nation, which, at the very least, goes counter to the effort to govern and control the whole country's taste from one great, dying city. And not the least force for the possible change, if not destruction of the (already) Old Order of things is technology. Even imaginable technological changes could easily constitute a revolution. But we are on the edge of almost unimaginable and surely unimagined changes which seem likely to make the whole present system of American publishing as quaintly old-fashioned as a medieval market fair. Let it come down, as the man said to Banquo.

Meantime, as if by magic alone, so many good and gifted, old and new American literary artists of all kinds carry on, often quite outside of the system. Perhaps it is appropriate to summon up magic at this point. It was no Brat or Baby Editor, but a genuine literary artist, R. V. Cassill, who has seen clearly a thing or two in a long lifetime and who said of our time: "I think we are at the end of an age, and the magicians have always appeared at the ends of ages."

Tyranny by Sloth

The original occasion was the tenth anniversary banquet of *Chronicles* magazine on December 2, 1987. A talk, then. It is my own and my own voice, but, as you'll see, soon my invisible and fictional companion, John Towne, came with me and couldn't keep quiet. I apologize in advance.

When I say that I thank you for asking me here to speak to you, that I thank you I am here, I have to confess that I am flying in the face of the latest status ritual practiced by many of my colleagues in the scribbling professions. The latest thing, as you may already have learned (I am a slow learner and also somewhat out of touch), is to prove your high place in the hierarchy of contemporary American writers by *not* showing up for scheduled and promised appearances and events. The greater luminaries simply don't arrive. At the next aspiring level, the basic idea is to cancel out, offering no good reason or proposing an obviously implausible one, about twenty-four hours prior to the event. And now that the word is out, there are many places, particularly in the status-conscious groves of academe, where their disappointment and shame and contempt are clearly visible, as if etched, if and when you actually arrive at the right place at more or less the right time. It means they have been snookered one more time into wasting some of their limited resources on an obvious second-rater.

Of course, in the literary world other coincidental funny things have been happening lately—interesting mix-ups, for example. My Charlottesville neighbor Ann Beattie swears to me that she was recently flown out to a school in Ohio for a visit and a reading (and good money) and realized, after she got there, and no joke, that everybody thought she was Anne Tyler. The name on the posters and the programs was Anne Tyler. The name on the check proved to be Anne Tyler. She was introduced as Anne Tyler. Ann Beattie grinned and went through with it, although for some reason she chickened out and read from her own work and not Ms. Tyler's.

In another recent incident—every chairman and toastmaster's recurring nightmare—novelist Nicholas Delbanco, professor at Michigan and one of the most elegant and eloquent of introducers, was asked, on about ten minutes' notice, to fill in for a colleague (who had been taken suddenly ill) by introducing Margaret Atwood to an expectant audience. Or so he understood his assignment. Quickly he prepared a few notes. Then he ran across campus to Rackham Hall, rushed on stage and up to the podium where he offered up a fulsome, deep-voiced, and impeccably suave introduction of the life and works of Ms. Atwood. Turned then, smiling, to greet her as she came to the podium. Only to discover, to his almost unspeakable dismay, that he was looking directly into the familiar and glowering face of Margaret Drabble. . . .

Anyway, for better and for worse, here I am. I am not, however, completely alone. I have brought along with me my invisible and fictional companion, a character named John Towne, out of a novel of mine called *Poison Pen*. Not because I want to inflict him upon you. Not at all. But mainly because I can't trust him, left alone and behind in the pages of his home. Better I should keep an eye on him.

For those of you—the overwhelming majority, no doubt—who don't know him and never heard of him, let me just quote a few (honest to God) journalistic descriptions of the fellow:

Publisher's Weekly: "a vulgar scapegrace"
New York Times Book Review: "a low life crank"
National Review: "a coke-befuddled redneck"
The Washington Times: "a man of *unsavory* character"
Charlottesville Daily Progress: "a character of exquisite vulgarity"
Village Voice: "an academic charlatan of the lowest order . . . an exceptionally sleazy picaro"
Book World: "a full-time con artist, misanthrope and lecher"
Chicago Tribune: "a lecherous, misanthropic, failed academic"

They didn't even like him much down home in my native Southland. Here's the *Geensboro News:* "a loathesome, racist, crude and gruesome creep."

Well, you get the idea. An interesting consensus of reactions. One thing about Towne, he's got a lot of advice to offer.

For instance, true to character and form, he wanted me to build this little talk around something that interested *him*, namely the truth and consequences of a headline and story in the *Charlottesville Daily Progress* (October 25, 1987): "Aging Sexpot Van Doren Tells All." Towne finds it especially exemplary of the inward and spiritual truth of our times. He is particularly fond of the following paragraph, which he takes to be a better than average example of the fine-tuned complexity and subtlety of contemporary morality:

"Was the casting couch a Hollywood fixture in those days?"

" 'Yes, I found myself on it—but I only did it because I wanted to,' she said. 'I never went to bed with anyone I didn't want to. I had opportunities, but I didn't do it. Had I done so, I might have had better parts.' "

Well, Towne has got a point. It is pertinent. I mean if Joe Biden had been an actress instead of a U.S. Senator, he might have sounded exactly like that.

"Surely you don't plan to talk about *literature* and the (pardon the expression) literary life," Towne argued.

I agreed. Partly because in one aspect of one thing I find myself more or less in agreement with him. Towne's hydraulic law of uniform corruption—that is, that corruption everywhere seeks its own level and that, thus, all aspects of our life and world, at any given instant, are equally corrupt—seems to have some real truth to it. A corollary to the law, however, is that it doesn't apply to the literary world, which is unquestionably on a completely different level of corruption. Indeed, sad experience teaches me that it is hard to imagine any social unit as riddled with corruption as the American literary scene. My own personal opinion, on the basis of anecdotal evidence, is that next to the American Academy and Institute of Arts and Letters, the Court of the Emperor Caligula would look like an early session of the Council of Trent.

More serious, however, is the fact that to the mundane practices of misinformation and disinformation, as widely practiced by our press, which at least has the general goal of national destabilization to justify its ways and means, the literary folk (whose mostly unspoken consensus is so ironbound as to ignore all political differences and cross the boundaries of social class) are dedicated to rhetorical games played at the expense of the full dimensions of the truth.

For example, although there have been some debates concerning matters of form, aesthetic arguments, in the world of poetry, serious questioning or discussion of any of the serious issues of our time have been almost completely absent in American poetry since the deaths of Pound and Eliot and Frost and most recently John Ciardi.

Saddest of all, nobody seems to miss this. Or them, very much.

I collect whole notebooks of splendid little examples, of which here is only one, only a typical and very recent one. Here is John Gregory Dunne in his piece "This Year in Jerusalem," in the December issue of *Esquire*:

> Surrounded by soldiers as I waited to pass through the metal detectors and security check, I was struck once again by the way the Israeli military was woven into the country's social fabric. In the United States, soldiers are those weird looking young men we usually see only in airports, this one with his hair too short, that one with the tattoo and the mottled complexion and the flat hill accent, the black lance corporal here, the Hispanic Pfc. over there; in other words, no one we know. At the trial that morning the soldiers had the sentient mainstream faces so rarely seen in the contemporary American services.

Of course, all this is layered in appropriate and protective kinds of irony. A baklava of clever observation. He doesn't really mean all that. Forced to a final wall, he can always admit that he really doesn't mean anything. Meantime, however, in the form of an entirely typical piece of contemporary literary rhetoric, you have an aside, passing as an observation, a matter of opinion told as a fact as it were. And which, is, in fact, a very lightly encoded cryptogram, a cheerful little message sent to other true believers, slightly disguised as a commonplace, unexceptional stereotypical comment about our volunteer armed services, offering a gesture of gratuitous, if relative, contempt for our country and its people, paid for by a little tip, a shrug and a pourboire of self-contempt . . . *"in other words, no one we know."*

I sometimes honestly think that a certain kind of liberal, equally the *literary* liberal, uses the overt profession of personal guilt as justification for an almost murderous contempt of fellow man.

All the assumptions behind Dunne's deft little aside are so familiar to us as to be more or less harmless if we notice them at all. They stand like crumbling statues in a weedy, overgrown public park or garden. Not neutral, mind you, but more or less harmless . . . unless and until you allow yourself to consider the possibility that the relentless and largely unquestioned documentation and consumption of such distortions of reality can add up sooner or later to what constitutes a killing dose of poison. Meanwhile, though, it all has a certain sly charm. Even the little instances of pure and simple ignorance are socially if not rhetorically redeeming.

I said *largely* unquestioned. Not completely. We are here on this occasion to celebrate the existence and survival of *Chronicles*, which asks some questions and answers others which would otherwise be ignored.

And that is what I really should be talking about and what we should be thinking about: questions and answers in the unceasing search for the truth.

Whenever I go to work in the morning and go through the entrance of Old Cabell Hall at the University of Virginia, I pass under some words of Thomas Jefferson: "Here we are not afraid to follow Truth wherever it may lead nor to tolerate any error so long as reason is left free to combat it."

Some words of Jefferson ought to be my theme. Here Towne butted in and argued.

"Don't talk Jefferson at them," he said. "You give them Jefferson, they'll give you Sally Hemmings."

"Hey," I said. "I am not speaking at a Norman Lear testimonial."

"Lucky you," said he. "But it's all pretty much the same old thing."

"We'll see."

"Well," he said. "If you have to talk about Mr. Jefferson, go for it. Don't give them the sweet violins."

I tried my best to explain to him that in my own Episcopal Church even the *hard sayings* of Jesus Christ have now been put on the back burner, if not actually banned. How can I give them the iron fist of Thomas Jefferson?

"Here's how," he said. "As an example of exactly the kind of thought or idea which ought to be part of any full and free discussion or debate about ourselves, but which is not, because we are these days so concerned about monitoring our thoughts, even as we permit ourselves the crudest possible luxury and license by using the worst words our language allows."

"Look," I said. "Here we are living at a time when everything you can think of has been weighted with political symbolism and significance. Even baseball teams (it was racist to wish for the Minnesota Twins' win in the Series); *musical instruments*—if you listen at all to what might accurately be called Radio Daniel Schorr, I mean National Public Radio, you know that the flute and the acoustic guitar are the instruments of compassion and that compassion is a virtue exclusively reserved for the left and especially for those who most publicly assert that they have compassion; even the care and cure of dread diseases are politically weighted. Fabrics, clothing, and hair styles, bottles of beer and soda pop—it's a political mine field out there. How can I possibly say anything that will catch attention and mean anything?"

"You want me to attract their attention?" Towne asked.

In the end we compromised. From radically different points of view we both agreed that if our way of self-governing were to survive much longer—and by the way, we even in our absolute privacy allowed ourselves to consider whether a survival of our ways and means of self-government is a hopeful or a baleful prospect; for *ourselves*, I mean; never mind the multitudes outside of our particular traditions and history, for whom all democratic forms are at the least exotic—anyway, we compromised on the choice of a single passage, one example among many, from the words of Thomas Jefferson, one which carries the imperative necessity of the full and free debate of issues and assumptions to a logical, if honorable extreme. . . .

Here, then, are his words, taken from a letter written in Paris and dated November 13, 1787 (a wink or two beyond two centuries ago). You probably remember them well enough: "God forbid we should ever be 20 years without a rebellion. The people cannot be all, and always, well-informed. The part which is wrong will be discontented in proportion to the importance of the facts they misconceive. If they remain quiet under such misconceptions, it is a lethargy, the forerunner of death to public liberty. . . ." (I skip a little):

> What country before ever existed a century and a half without rebellion? And what country can preserve its liberties if the rulers are not warned from time to time that their people preserve the spirit of resistance? Let them take arms. The remedy is to set them right as to the facts, pardon and pacify them. What signify a few lives lost in a century or two? The tree of liberty must be refreshed from time to time with the blood of patriots and tyrants. It is its natural manure.

No question but that is a *hard* saying. No question, either, but that it is complex, thorny with prescience and pertinence, and I think eminently relevant to our very times and this very occasion tonight.

But before we go into some of those things, try to imagine, for a moment, the uproar and outrage which would follow if any contemporary public figure, at any point in life, early or late, and in any form from letter to the editor to a diary note, had ever said such a thing.

The only one I can think of who could get away with it is Joe Biden. Because everybody would correctly assume it was just plagiarism, anyway.

Thomas Jefferson said it and seems to have meant it, too, though some of the terms he used meant different things then than now. Take tyrant, the concept of tyranny, for example. For somewhat more than two thousand years, on up through and including the times of Thomas Jefferson, tyranny was defined and equally applied to the overzealous exercise of rigorous justice without mercy and to the squandered blessing of reflexive and thoughtless mercy without the context or foundation of rigorous justice. Thus any leader or statesman, from the citizens of the Greek city states, through every kind of emperor and monarch, absolute or benevolent, on through the rebellious generation of Jefferson, would surely and easily define our contemporary American social situation, with its elaborately formulated, indeed *codified* absence of any system protecting the rights of the law-abiding citizens and their civilization from predatory assaults, as clearly, unequivocally tyrannical.

And, as such, it would have always been deemed worthy of the strongest possible kind of resistance.

The most usual and immediate response to this passage that I have received from reasonably thoughtful and thoughtfully reasonable people is that we must consider the relativity of historical context. That in the period (brief or long, depending on your own historical scheme) since Jefferson we have come to value the sanctity of human life, have come to view life, in and of itself, as precious. Certainly more precious than our ancestors viewed at least the lives of others.

This is an answer, a position which might be regarded as simply and brutally laughable, coming as it does out of this bloody, bloody century, this century whose appropriate image is of rivers, Amazons, Mississippis, Congos of human blood. Century in which even the Holocaust, defined by both intent and execution, can only be claimed to be one enormous genocidal example among many, first among many parts . . .

It is certainly not becoming, and it ill behooves anyone from this twentieth century to regard Jefferson's statement as evidence of a more bloody-minded disposition or blithe disregard for the lives of others than our words and acts.

Indeed, once the idea of hypocrisy has been introduced, a good, strong case can be made that Jefferson's approach, even taken by a literal mind, is closest to that of a good general, Patton, for example, whose own casualties (*and the casualties he inflicted*) were always minimal precisely because his tactics were sudden, ruthless, and anything but tentative.

Thus I can see that it can be decently and honorably maintained that certain complex and confusing issues troubling us in these times probably should have been settled in the streets, sealed in the blood of patriots and tyrants, rather than vaguely resolved in legislatures, courts, or in the press.

As to the sanctity of human life in our own country, we must never allow ourselves to forget that in fact a good many years ago we settled for the deaths of roughly sixty-five thousand people—

men, women, and children—on our highways as statistically acceptable per year. Sixty-five thousand is a number our society has somehow agreed to live with. I don't need to remind you that that is, of course, more than the total number of American dead in all the years of the Vietnam War.

Do you suppose they would consider putting up a series of black walls in honor and memory of all the dead drivers, drunk and sober alike, of America?

A possibly more plausible argument, one that is frequently heard from intellectual sources, is that (with perhaps the exception of Israeli preemptive and retaliatory strikes on terrorist targets) warfare as an instrument or extension of national policy, even the policy of self-defense, is no longer really feasible.

Unthinkable is, I believe, the correct adjective. That there are wars going on, here and now, within and between most of the nations of the earth is a fact beyond the interest of most of these advanced thinkers.

I am reminded of the celebrated 1960s, when rape seemed statistically likely to become a new national pastime, and women were advised not under any circumstances ever to resist a rapist. Exactly the opposite advice is freely given in courses and seminars nowadays. I am reminded of the Navy Shark Repellent in World War II, a colorful dye which, while it evidently had no effect on sharks one way or the other, at least allowed a brief feeling of safety and security *before* the jaws clamped down.

Never mind.

Let us return to text. To Jefferson. Clearly, despite all his good wishes and even high hopes for some measure of domestic tranquillity, he envisioned the quality which he conceived of and called liberty as enduring only in a state of constant, unrelenting testing. Interrogation by means of full debate and argument where facts are assembled and known and where reason, itself, is allowed to be and run free. Absent those conditions, he likewise clearly believed (at least on this occasion) that it was meet and right that genuinely significant issues should be sealed and settled in blood.

That, if need be—no, more accurately, *when* need be, for he simply assumed that, come what may, ignorance and misconception were inevitable companions—that when need be we should be ready, willing, and able to die for and kill for our principles.

But let us be pragmatic and try to get at the heart of what he was saying as it may possibly apply to us.

One cannot (to use that lovely *media* phrase) *rule out* the possibility, now or ever, of bloody acts of resistance and rebellion (in whatever form) in the United States. What, after all, was the seizure of federal prisons and hostages in Atlanta and Louisiana but a clumsy act of rebellion? One cannot ever rule out the possibility. But since the race riots of the late 1940s and the late 1960s, although we have had plenty of violent events and incidents, large and small, we have witnessed no full-scale, real and honest rebellion. And for the present such a thing seems highly unlikely.

Which may well mean that, in Jefferson's own terms, we live at a time when the love of lethargy has at last replaced even the hope of preserving liberty. Maybe . . .

Or it may mean that, for the time being, resistance and rebellion must take place on the other fields where our great life and death issues are being settled.

Settled, for better and worse. Not well or deeply discussed. Many things are discussed, if only lightly debated, but next to none of the great and deep questions are being asked.

This whole problem, which ought to have attracted our attention and, at the very least, aroused the passion of intellectual anger, has been most passionately discussed *not* by any American thinker of any persuasion, but by the great Russian writer Aleksandr Solzhenitsyn, and only on one occasion—his baccalaureate address at Harvard in 1978.

You will remember it. And I hope you will refresh your memory of his words by seeking them out again. . . .

His observations are remarkable, subtle, profound, and, I think, as accurate and prescient as they are controversial. May I quote from a couple of paragraphs?

There is yet another surprise for someone coming from the East, where the press is rigorously unified; one gradually discovers a common trend of preferences within the Western press as a whole. It is a fashion; there are generally accepted patterns of judgment and there may be common corporate interests, the sum effect being not competition but unification. Enormous freedom exists for the press, but not for the readership, because newspapers mostly give emphasis to those opinions that do not too openly contradict their own and the general trend.

Without any censorship, in the West, fashionable trends of thought are carefully separated from those that are not fashionable.

Nothing is forbidden, but what is not fashionable will hardly ever find its way into periodicals or books or be heard in colleges. . . .

It continues . . .

It earned Solzhenitsyn immediate and rabid denunciation by the press he criticized. Gentle and wimpish liberals suddenly discovered the "America-Love-It-or-Leave-It" standard and applied it directly to him.

Time has only allowed the uniform derogation of Solzhenitsyn by the press to slack off a little bit. One week ago the *Washington Post* ran a lengthy feature, "Solzhenitsyn and His Message of Silence." If you were to read the article, you would have discovered that his *silence*, in this case, means that he turned down an opportunity to be interviewed by the *Washington Post*. They don't suggest that he is crazy up there in Vermont. But they do at least imply that he is keeping a low profile for a self-serving reason: "It has even been suggested that, if Gorbachev means what he says, the work of Aleksandr Solzhenitsyn might be published in the Soviet Union for the first time in more than two decades. Some of his fellow émigrés believe Solzhenitsyn is silent for that purpose too: that he not jeopardize the best chance for his return to the motherland, in word if not in deed."

A bullet wound would, of course, be considerably more painful. But I doubt if firing a bullet at him could be a more *hateful* act than writing those words.

As long as they can kill their opposition with words, why waste bullets on any of us?

World of words, that's where the battle—the ceaseless war of rebellion and resistance against intellectual and spiritual lethargy, and for the sake of liberty—is going on.

Things have not improved much, if at all, since Solzhenitsyn spoke. Indeed, the stereotypes he noted—the sculptural museum of modern group-thinks—have acquired the patina of dignity since then. Whole topics have been declared to be off-limits, beyond all legitimate discussion or even historical reconsideration. In history and the so-called social sciences, and even (alas) in the stricter sciences, especially medicine and biology, it is now widely accepted and understood that evidence which weighs against fashionable contemporary political and social positions is to be suppressed, or at least modified and limited so as not to offer any ammunition to the skeptical opposition. I can recall that once upon a time we laughed at science under Stalin, never dreaming that most of its practices, if not all of its excesses, would come to pass here.

In literature there are such inhibitions as the prevalent critical notion that even for the sake of verisimilitude, fictional characters must not be allowed to maintain views, prejudices, or, indeed, use words which offend stereotypical contemporary standards. Or if they do so, they must be known to be unredeemably wicked and must be *punished* for their sins. . . .

Even the exalted arena of Shakespearean criticism is not safe from this kind of agitprop scrutiny.

If I may be so bold as to second Solzhenitsyn's proposition, I would have to tell you that I have only recently returned to the twentieth century from a couple of decades spent living as an expatriate, an alien, in the sixteenth century. And it is my best and considered judgment that then and there, in Tudor England, when the consequences—and *legal* consequences—of asking certain questions, voiced opinions, even (at times) thoughts and intentions, were deadly serious, there was probably more honest, deep-digging, and far-reaching debate and dissent than we have experienced in this free society for more than a quarter of a century.

Even under the rigors of almost absolute monarchy they were not afraid to debate not only current issues but also, maybe more important, first principles.

Of course, they had at least *some* of the same problems and concerns. Here, for example is Sir Walter Raleigh writing in his *History of the World:* "How shall the upright and impartial judgment of man give a sentence where opposition and examination are not admitted to give in evidence?" He then quotes from Lactantius. "They neglect their own wisdom who, without any judgment, approve the invention of those that forwent them; and suffer themselves, after the manner of beasts, to be led by them."

To which Raleigh adds his own observation, coming amazingly close to the words and views of Jefferson: "By the advantage of which sloth, dullness and ignorance is now become so powerful a tyrant, that it hath set true philosophy, psychic, and divinity in a pillory."

We are gathered to honor not the voice, but the various and sundry voices of *Chronicles*. Which, as it happens, is one of the very few and very precious forces actively engaged in the war against lethargy.

It is with words, with ideas, with facts, with questions, and, God willing, with passion that the good fight is being fought.

We are much beleaguered, more so than we would like to admit, if only for the sake of sanity. We need each other. And I am proud to be here and to be a part of all this and all that.

John Towne's cynical laughter echoes in my inner ear like a car horn in a tunnel.

"You'll be sorry. You and your big mouth!" he says. "One thing about the American Establishment, regardless of race, creed, color, country of origin, gender, or sexual preference, they will never forget and forgive."

"So what?" I say. "I never wanted to be on the Supreme Court, anyway."

Winning and Losing

This was a talk made to the new members of Phi Beta Kappa at the University of Richmond.

This is a festive and happy occasion, a celebration, really, of something rare enough in our time and our society, involving both recognition and reward. Your newly earned keys won't open any real doors or real beer cans, but they are more than merely symbolic paraphernalia. Or, put it another way, their symbolism has all the impact of the real and the true. Did I say *rare*? I meant it. This is a society that greatly rewards such things as an ability at slam dunking, a talent at posing in a bikini bathing suit, or singing (well or badly, no matter) the twenty-five words or less that, according to Iggy Pop, constitute the entire vocabulary of rock and roll. And this is an age and a society which join to offer equal recognition (like the rain that falls indifferently on the just and the unjust) to Nobel Prize winners and to naughty politicians, preachers and their casual girl-friends or boyfriends as the case may be. A society in which fame and notoriety are, very often, exactly one and the same.

In the face of all this, you are entitled to take some pride in the undeniable fact that you are being here and now recognized and rewarded not for your image as intelligent and successful students, but for the real thing, a measurable accomplishment, achieved over an extended period of time against the odds of many tempta-tions and distractions. Not the least of these being the society's special relentless contempt reserved for intellectual powers and for anything that remotely smacks of elitism. Which is to say— never mind that we live in an age, at a time and a place when honor, though it may or may not be valued, is not rewarded—you have nevertheless achieved something honorable and worthwhile. I am happy for you, and happy to be invited to be here to help you celebrate, all the more so because when I was awarded a Phi Beta Kappa key at Princeton University, before most people here to-night were born, I was not able to attend the festivities.

I hope you will pardon me—even as I rejoice in your good fortune—if I use the brief occasion to talk with at least moderate seriousness about some moderately serious things. I don't want to be like the gloomy fairy godmother who appears at weddings and christenings in so many fairy tales and spoils the fun with bad news or with unpleasant magic spells. But I do want to take and to use this opportunity, while you are all still basking honorably in the limelight of your achievement, to talk briefly about the general topic of winning and losing.

Maybe another justification, above and beyond fairy tales and myths, is, more simply, to try to tell the truth. With the full knowledge that to tell the truth, in the words of the poet and Nobel laureate Czeslaw Milosz, is like firing a revolver in a crowded room.

You have just, here and now, won something. Something we can all agree is both important and valuable—praiseworthy. Of course, you did not do so all alone; nor, for that matter, were you free to act, to do the larger part of it yourself. The same genes which gave you your height and weight, color of hair and eyes and kind of nose, gave you the basic foundation of intelligence (and, indeed, much of the interest and energy to exploit that intelligence) which enabled you, by dint of hard work or effortlessly—and only you can ever know and judge the truth of that—to do well enough in your academic work to find yourself sitting here.

Should we be proud of our genetic makeup and program, of what comes with our carcass? It's a serious question, though in a sense it is already answered. People who have inherited great physical beauty or, for example, athletic prowess of one kind and another are (in my experience and in yours) almost invariably as proud of the fact of themselves, as vain of and about it, as if they had exercised some large part in the creation of their most admirable and enviable attributes. By the same token, I notice that people who are sincerely proud of their genetic gifts are correspondingly more vulnerable. The beautiful people must live in the fear of their coming of age more than you or I do (I allow for the exception of all the beautiful people here among us). Which I suppose is only just. Part of the point about Job—I speak of Job from the Bible, someone we come back to, as we have to in any honest discussion of winning and losing in this world—the point about Job is that he had so much to lose. It is bad enough to be down and out, stone broke and suffering from the effects of boils and a lot of bad advice from your fair-weather friends. But it is even worse when you used to have, in abundant excess, all the good things the world has to offer. Job could hardly blame his bad luck on his genetic makeup, and it was more than mere genes that kept him from cursing God and thus allowed God to win the bet with Satan, a bet that Job, neither before nor after, knew anything about.

Can we be proud of our genetic makeup? Well, to an extent we are proud of it whether we are entitled to be so or not. To an extent what we are celebrating here is the fact that, at least as far as intelligence is concerned and can be measured, you have the good luck to possess good genes.

We should bear in mind the reverse, the corollary to our inevitable pride in our particular gifts. Which is that we do not, as a rule, condemn to shame those whose genetic makeup has rendered them either outwardly and visibly handicapped or inwardly and spiritually bereft. We have reached a stage of development, at least in the Western nations, where, as a matter of general rule, we do not blame or punish others for their genetic flaws. We do not, usually, believe that crazy people and crippled people are the way they are because they want to be that way. And yet somewhere, and not very deep, not much more than skin deep, we sort of assume that others somehow chose the face and body, the mind and gifts they are stuck with. It's as if they went through some vast K-Mart of human physical and mental possibilities and made a whole lot of bad choices. So, at best, we are secretly critical of others for their bad taste in being themselves. Perhaps—if gene splicing and genetic engineering continue to develop at the present rate—in a generation we shall be able and entitled to criticize others for the faces they choose to wear.

By the way, I wish I had some statistics to prove that there are three words most Phi Beta Kappas never hear—"Attention K-Mart Shoppers." But I'm afraid that the opposite is true. Always has been. Here is a poet, Theodore Prodromos, more than fifteen hundred years ago, as translated by David Slavitt:

Is this a life, I am weaker, paler
than any apprentice, and older, and curse
in all my learned languages learning.
I pray for coppers, dream of gold.
Study, study! Study my purse.
Learn if these notes might be good for burning.
I am master of hunger, doctor of cold.

In spite of that bleak prospect, you are lucky. Luck had a large part in your being here. Not just the luck of genetics, but luck on a much simpler level. The flu at just the wrong time; a banana peel at just the wrong place; luck of the draw, luck of the examination question for which you happened to be prepared, happened to be able to answer. There are plenty of gifted and intelligent and hard-working students who are not here tonight and who will never have Phi Beta Kappa keys because of bad luck.

Should we then be proud of our good luck and scornful of those whose luck is thin?

Here a split in our richly diverse and plural society is very evident. Most of those who come out of WASP culture—though it really has to be expanded to include most of Northern European culture—most Americans who are descended from Northern European culture tend to be very cautious about celebrating the results of any good luck. John Riggins of the Redskins made many touchdowns yet almost never allowed himself the indulgence of a victory dance in the end zone. Why? It is most often suggested (usually by critics from other cultural roots, to be sure) that it is a matter of WASP inhibition, inability to express emotion. I am inclined to believe it is much deeper than that. It goes beyond the ideal concept of Christian humility as well. It goes way back to something pagan and fearful, a notion that the gods and demons and forces of this world are deeply offended by human pride, especially pride in good luck (which is, after all, an unearned gift) and that once offended, the gods and demons like nothing better than teaching all kinds of unpleasant, and often uncomfortable, lessons in humility. Add to this primitive fear and wonder the whole long, deeply ingrained Judeo-Christian tradition and you can understand why it is almost instinctive for the WASP, at any moment of triumph, and there have been some, believe it or not, to try to keep out of the spotlight. The WASP tradition of public modesty is not a false modesty when you consider that it is the unseen audience of gods and demons to whom this is directed. Gods and demons are not interested in true or false. They are concerned with ritual forms, in this case, the ritual form of humility. And, as every thoughtful WASP knows without even thinking, time is on the side of the angels and devils. They may not punish or reward you then and there, but whenever it pleases them.

There is an interesting example of exactly this. In our time, for the first time in roughly four hundred years, we have lots of people living to be very old. Many in their eighties. Well over 100,000 over one hundred. One thing geriatric medicine has discovered is that injuries of youth, broken bones, for instance, but in fact all kinds of wounds and injuries, return. Old aches and pains which lay dormant for half a century and more suddenly reassert themselves. The wounds of youth are thus visited upon old age. If you think about that, you can begin to understand how some of our ancestors could imagine that angels and devils had the last word. And think of Jacob, the Jacob of Genesis, in one of the most beautiful and enigmatic stories in the Bible, wrestling an angel all night long and winning the angel's blessing. You remember it:

> And Jacob was left alone and there wrestled an angel with him until the breaking of the day. And when he saw that he prevailed not against him, he touched the hollow of his thigh; and the hollow of Jacob's thigh was out of joint; as he wrestled with him. And he said, Let me go, for the day breaketh. And he [Jacob] said I will not let thee go, except thou bless me. And he said unto him, What is thy name? And he said, Jacob. And he said, Thy name shall be called no more Jacob, but Israel: for as a prince hast thou power with God and with men, and hast prevailed.

Jacob prevailed, as no mere man before or since, and was blessed by an angel. But he was also crippled by it.

We call it paying the price nowadays. And, along with your good genes and your good luck and your hard work, you have also paid a price for your success, though like a credit card debt it may not come due except gradually over more time than you can imagine.

That is to say, with this honor, this recognition of your past accomplishments, you are now committed and obligated to the future. You are rewarded for what is known and then, as if the past were a door shutting behind you, you are pointed directly toward the future. Which is, by definition, the unknown, the unimagined. What can be known and imagined is not really the future, but only an extension of the present. And it is out of the present that the greatest threats arise.

If I were really the gloomy fairy godmother at the party, I would feel it necessary to point out that, if things go along as they have been, neither better nor worse, one in four of you will be the victims of violent crimes. One in four will die of cancer, unless a miracle cure is found. Just so a number of you here will, unless unanticipated answers are found to some extremely complex questions, die of AIDS. Traffic, which regularly kills sixty-five thousand Americans and cripples four times that number every year, will certainly get some of us here. Think about that for a moment—the average, that is the acceptable number of annual traffic deaths, exceeds the American casualties of the entire Vietnam War. If they put up a wall in honor of dead drivers, it would probably run all the way from Washington to Richmond.

I mention these things not to be depressing or discouraging, but to make the point that it is in the present, the very dangerous present, that you must live out your lives. And that it will take all the wit and cunning and intelligence and good luck you can muster for you to endure and maybe prevail.

Bear in mind that your mind will all the while be assaulted by an unceasing barrage of clichés and stereotypes, by misinformation and disinformation and outright lies. From all sides. From all interested parties. Not least, in fact most often, from the very media of communication of information in all forms.

Those of you whose intellectual bias is primarily scientific have the fearful consolation of Nature's sublime and utter indifference to anything at all beyond the working out of its own inimitable and very often chaotic and mysterious laws. An awareness of your infinitely small place in the Big Picture can, at the least, allow you to shrug off the slings and arrows of bad fortune and take the blessings of good fortune as happy accidents to be savored while they last.

Those of us whose training and tilt are toward what we claim and hope are the humanities do not deny (how could we?) the validity, both bleak and bright, of the scientific vision. But we like to add some other dimensions to it. Out of the long-lived and persistent Judeo-Christian tradition and the wisdom of Greece and Rome, we have a sense of other patterns and laws, not contradictory to Nature's impeccable, if enigmatic equations, but parallel to them. What Jews and Christians and Greeks, and even some of the best of the Romans, have been telling us all for a couple of thousand years, and indeed much longer than that, telling us in many ways and shapes and forms, is that life—even the good life, perhaps especially the good life if, as is the case so often in our America, it is based more on comfort and self-esteem than our goodness—life is always tragic. There may be much or little comedy, but the end of it, the summation is always tragic.

When Thomas Nashe, Elizabethan poet, wrote his celebrated six-stanza "Song," sometime in the 1590s, he was being neither cynical nor depressing but was offering up an unexceptional description of reality which would raise the eyebrows of nobody before or since except maybe our contemporary clowns, like Hugh Hefner, whose whole business and philosophy are based on denying the obvious.

Here is Nashe's most famous stanza:

> Beauty is but a flower
> Which wrinkles will devour:
> Brightness falls from the air,
> Queens have died young and fair,
> Dust hath closed Helen's eye.
> I am sick, I must die.
> Lord have mercy on us.

Many of you will remember, in one form or another, some of the ancient words from The Book of Common Prayer, in The Order for the Burial of the Dead.

From Job and Timothy: "We brought nothing into this world, neither may we carry anything out of this world. The Lord giveth, and the Lord taketh away. Even as it hath pleased the Lord, so cometh things to pass: blessed be the name of the Lord."

Or, in the familiar beginning from the Book:"Man that is born of woman hath but a short time to live, and is full of misery. He cometh up and is cut down like a flower; he flieth as it were a shadow, and never continueth in one stay."

Argue with that at your peril.

To say that life is tragic, that all our lives partake of the pattern of tragedy, is not, as you no doubt learned from your teachers, necessarily disheartening. For the pattern of tragedy implies—no, includes—the promise of justice. Even though we go around continually asking for and seeking justice, in a world and a society riddled by ineradicable injustices, we may not even recognize it or want it when it comes. But come it will, like it or not, ready or not, most likely, in the image out of Scripture, like a thief in the night.

One problem for the student of justice is that justice is on a different time scale, like geological time or astronomical time, than the little flare of time (like a match in the dark) we call a human lifetime. Which means, chances are you won't see the working out of much justice in the present. Except in crude, cause-and-effect ways, the larger pattern is unavailable to you in present time. Until very recently, wise men looked to history to indicate the patterns of justice in the world. Given time, things can work out in interesting ways.

Here is one. A fairly simple one, even a fairly amusing one:

In 1579 a Scotsman named James Hepburn, who was Earl of Bothwell and, among other things, the last of the husbands of Mary, Queen of Scots and, thus, for a time, King of Scotland, died in poverty and squalor and dishonor in a dungeon in Denmark. Before he could be buried there were some worldly problems to be attended to, the principal one being to determine his status, his correct rank and title. He had been, in fact and deed, King of Scotland, his face on official coins, his signature on lawful documents. But there had never been, for various reasons, a service of coronation. The question was, then, whether or not he was really a dead king. In a custom as familiar then as now, a committee was formed to deal with this matter. And in the interim, Bothwell's body was mummified and placed, in shriveled indignity, in an oak chest in a little parish church in Denmark. In 1979, four hundred years later, the committee turned in its final report. They concluded that Bothwell was, indeed, King of Scotland, and his mummy was then buried with full royal honors. Denmark—and so far only Denmark—lists James Hepburn, not James Stuart, as the sixth King James of Scotland, adding one name to the long list of Scots kings.

Who says there is no justice in this world?

All human skulls are grinning, but if ghosts are also allowed to laugh at the living, then Bothwell must have enjoyed some hearty laughter in our year of 1979.

As for ourselves, we should at least be careful of what we choose to laugh at. In one of the great speeches of our age, in 1978, Aleksandr Solzhenitsyn told a Harvard commencement some truths nobody there wanted to hear. And was vilified for it by our free and easy press.

Such matter of fact and inarguable statements as this remark— "Even biology knows that habitual extreme safety and well-being are not advantageous to a living organism"—were taken as attacks on the very spirit of contemporary liberalism in America. We have become very sensitive. Much that he said fell on deaf ears, including these simple comments about life in the U.S.A.:

After the suffering of decades of violence and oppression, the human soul longs for things higher, warmer, and purer than those offered by today's mass living habits, introduced by the revolting invasion of publicity, by TV stupor, and by intolerable music. . . . The fight for our planet, physical and spiritual, a fight of cosmic proportions, is not a vague matter of the future; it has already started. The forces of Evil have begun their offensive—you can feel their pressure—and yet your screens and publications are full of prescribed smiles and raised glasses. What is the joy about?

A good question. One which you and I must ask daily and seek to answer.

But here and now, we are entitled to a little joy. We celebrate the honor of something well done. We salute you and each other. The keys we have received, you and I, are as much promise, a promise you and I undertake, as they are indications, like medals, of good service, of work well done. To accept your key you promise to use your gifts in a continuing search for the truth; and to the extent that you seek and search truly, your role will inevitably be more one of service to others than self-aggrandizement. The truth is that the key, like the garter of the Knights of the Garter, is a badge of service and humility and thus can be worn with honest pride. And that is what the joy is all about here and now. If, as everything teaches us—all the great books, all the great teachers and all the history of the world—if we are not doomed, but destined to fight losing battles, we are nevertheless free to do so with courage, with joy when joy is appropriate and sorrow where it is not, with the full, unstinting expense, the giving back from the gifts we have earned and been given, gifts signified by the honor which has been offered you and which you have accepted.

I want to wish you good luck. And I want to encourage you, and myself, with some words of a very great twentieth-century poem, "Four Quartets," by T. S. Eliot:

> Do not think of the fruit of action.
> Fare forward.

Literary Biography in Our Time

The grandiose title of this piece should not (cannot) disguise the fact that it is, in fact, that shaggy beast, the chronicle review. In this one, done for the *Sewanee Review,* the following books were listed and (briefly) discussed: Matthew J. Bruccoli, *James Gould Cozzens: A Life Apart;* Andrew Field, *Djuna: The Life and Times of Djuna Barnes;* Russell Fraser, *A Mingled Yarn: The Life of R. P. Blackmur;* Joan Givner, *Katherine Anne Porter: A Life;* John Haffenden, *The Life of John Berryman;* Ian Hamilton, *Robert Lowell: A Biography;* Andre Le Vot, *F. Scott Fitzgerald: A Biography;* James Matthews, *Voices: A Life of Frank O'Connor;* Hilary Mills, *Mailer: A Biography;* Marie Rudisill (with James C. Simmons), *Truman Capote: The Story of His Bizarre and Exotic Boyhood by an Aunt Who Helped Raise Him;* Eileen Simpson, *Poets in Their Youth: A Memoir;* and Judith Thurman, *Isak Dinesen: The Life of a Storyteller.*

I.

The craft of literary biography is sorely tested by some deeply inherent if not insoluble technical problems. There is no escaping the truth that most writers, good and bad alike, lead reasonably dull and sedentary lives, even those who have conveniently managed to die young. Of course there are some famous exceptions, but they are few and far between. The rest—the overwhelming majority—are most alive when they are single-handedly facing the tundras and steppes of blank paper armed with nothing more than a pen or pencil or maybe, these days, with a word processor. No matter what their equipment, however, they just have to sit there (Hemingway and Thomas Wolfe, to be sure, *stood there*) like intelligent bumps on a log, brooding and scribbling. You will surely have seen "The Writer" in the movies, a nice-looking, healthy, and engaging person played by Jason Robards or Robert Redford, for instance, or perhaps Jacqueline Bisset. We can tell they are serious, hard-working writers because they are shown hunting and pecking at a manual typewriter, and they tend to crumple and scatter a lot of wastepaper on the floor, proving that there's more than inspiration to the writer's craft. From that montage scene we dissolve through to the writer being awarded the Pulitzer Prize or the Pullet Surprise or what-have-you. And then, if we are in the hands of smart screenwriters and canny directors, we will never see them *writing anything* again. Still it isn't that the life of the writer is so unredeemably boring except perhaps in the flashing visual context of the silver screen. It is rather that the writer is, in the simple and irrefutable medieval sense, a widow to this world, a contemplative. Of course there are conventional ways to dodge the issue. Some of these have been chosen here. F. Scott Fitzgerald is more fun to write and to read about than most of his peers. Djuna Barnes and Isak Dinesen were eccentric to the point of exoticism. From time to time Berryman and Lowell were certifiably crazy. Mailer and Capote are . . . well, public *personalities.* Frank O'Connor not only was wonderfully *Irish,* but he also led a fairly trashy domestic life. To write about R. P. Blackmur or James Gould Cozzens must have been much more difficult.

In every age both serious and popular biographies of contemplatives have been produced, but these have mostly dealt with saints and mystics and martyrs. These biographies were devoted to worthy and exemplary lives. Even in this odd age of ours, which sometimes celebrates Art as if it had replaced Religion, as if the aesthetic were demonstrably mankind's highest level of spiritual experience, precious few of our writers can qualify for hagiography or can count even as secular worthies. And therein lies the second serious problem facing the literary biographer. It is not so much a problem for the late biographer of established reputations from the fairly distant past. For the most part we tend to be only tacitly judgmental or defensive when considering the lives of the likes of Chaucer, Shakespeare, Milton, Dryden, Keats and Shelley, etc. But along about the middle of the nineteenth century—with Dickens, say—we begin rigorously to judge the dead by the standards of the living, as if history were a progressive continuum and as if, for instance, the special intellectual systems of Freud and Marx could be applied to everything indiscriminately, fore and aft in time. Next, entering directly into our own troubled times, we discover that we are considering people who (unlike more mundane makers and doers) were extraordinarily inactive and remote from large and critical events of the times, and who are generally characterized by almost obsessive self-absorption, self-indulgence, and pure and simple, if ruthless, selfishness. In general they are, one and all to a greater or lesser degree, small-minded, mean-spirited, ambitious, and envious, incredibly ignorant of almost everything beyond the immediate precincts of their vocation, and largely indifferent to everything that does not touch upon them directly, that does not happen within their self-imposed cloisters. In general they prove themselves to be hopelessly inept in coping with quotidian reality, a clumsiness that might well be vaguely charming if it did not usually also involve the inflicting of brutal injuries and injustices upon others, equally upon loved ones and foes, the innocent and the guilty. Each obviously possessed genuine literary gifts, and a passionate commitment may at the least be inferred from the record of the exploitation and development of those gifts through a lifetime. Most outward and visible evidence of passion in their lives is directed toward a uniformly intense careerism together with an urgent desire to satisfy some of life's significant and common appetites—sex, booze, and drugs often loom large. Ill-health, both mental and physical, appears to be not so much the effect of their chosen style of life as an aggravated and inevitable accompaniment to it.

On the whole, then, it is safe to conclude that, abstracted from the little theater of their true gifts and literary accomplishments—all of which are manifest in the works of art themselves, and fortunately do not need the extraneous support of a wealth of biographical data—the lives of most modern and contemporary writers are neither especially worthy nor noteworthy. Even their gifts and accomplishments, unlike those of the shadowy and towering dead, remain in question, at hazard. Unlike the biographer of, say, Shakespeare or Chaucer, the biographer of a prominent contemporary writer must preserve and defend (and perhaps expand) the particular position the artist has earned or otherwise acquired in the shifting literary hierarchy. Or, in the unlikely event that the biography of someone relatively unknown or ignored by the literary establishment would actually be written and could actually find a willing publisher, then the biographer must challenge the assumptions of the status quo and must also make a strong case for his subject. Either gesture of the biographer—acceptance of the present fashions of the establishment or an attack on them—requires a rhetoric and strategy which can slide easily into sophistry. It is a wonder that anyone of sound mind would undertake such a formidable task. It seems to be an equal wonder that our hard-pressed publishers would encourage the form. Yet they do. When asked recently *why*, some publishers offered several reasons: that biography is traditionally important to them, at once a pleasure and a justification in an increasingly nonliterary line of work; that literary biography is an outward sign of corporate solvency and good values; that literary biography can serve to generate renewed interest in the works of the writers in question; that there is still a public for biographies of which there exists a smaller subgroup which (oddly) finds the lives of literary types as interesting as the lives of generals, politicians, movie stars, ball players, celebrities, criminals, and other common public figures; that our libraries of all kinds and sizes still tend to buy literary biographies, whether or not they have bought or would buy the works of the subjects. A good many more people are interested in reading *about* John Berryman or Robert Lowell than are ready to read their poems. In short, publishers feel better about themselves for publishing some literary biographies; and they have a fair chance to break even, perhaps even to turn a little profit, with these works. The odds are much more favorable than they are in the case of publishing poetry and fiction, even the poetry and fiction of the subjects of the biographies. Because of all these things, together with the required expense of time and money in research and writing, biographers are usually awarded decent advances against royalties, often a good deal more than the authors they are writing about ever earned. Any biographer stands a better chance to earn some rewards for his labor than any poet and most novelists. And, of course, for those biographers involved in the huge corporate enterprise of academe, promotion, tenure, salary raises, even office space can derive from this legitimately scholarly and critical effort.

Another of the biographer's basic problems, one peculiar to our own laws and society, must be mentioned. If a biographer is to have full and free use of the pertinent letters, manuscripts, and other papers of an author, he must have the cooperation of the author, if the author is still alive, or more commonly, he must pass muster with the author's estate and literary executors. Even under ideal circumstances, therefore, all literary biographies are to some extent controlled, indeed censored. In addition, because of a rash of lawsuits, both serious and frivolous, the lawyers, especially the publisher's lawyers, nowadays must clear any material that is published. The lawyers tend to anticipate all possible dangers, often with a firm and heavy hand. An extensive story in the *New York Times* ("Protests Delay Steinbeck Biography," August 4, 1983) treats the kinds of problems arising from the power of a writer's estate and, separately, of a publisher's legal staff to shape—and in this case to delay—the appearance of a biography. Jackson J. Benson, Steinbeck's authorized biographer, is quoted as saying: "In mid-May, suddenly, at the very end, after I had turned in the proofs, suddenly Viking's lawyers and lawyers for the Steinbeck estate said that there was a chance that members of the family might be offended by certain parts of the book." The story goes on to discuss the fact that certain changes were required, ending with the observation that "Mr. Benson said making the revisions 'has just been a terrible ordeal,' but now, he added, 'I just want to get it published.' "

All literary biographies dealing with contemporary writers are to some extent "authorized." I mention this because Hilary Mills's *Mailer* was widely described as *not* being an authorized biography. Mailer may not have actively participated in the process; but, by the same token, it would have been impossible for the biography to have been prepared and published without Mailer's tacit cooperation—if only through the cooperation of his close friends, who allowed themselves to be interviewed and quoted. That some emphasis was laid upon this book's "unofficial" character, thus implying that it might not be in any way controlled, leads me to infer two things: first, that there is an "authorized" biography arranged for and scheduled, one which must be protected; second, that this biography was seen by at least *some* of the principals as part of the orchestrated campaign to publicize *Ancient Evenings*.

The claim of being "unofficial" was made at least in part in the hope that the befuddled reader might believe that the book offers up facts that Mailer himself might have preferred to consign to oblivion. In any case the extent of control over the raw materials of any literary biography, a control which can easily extend to actual censorship and almost always involves a cultivated inhibition on the part of the biographer, can only be guessed at, for it is an utterly private transaction. Just so, when there are papers in libraries, the libraries reserve the right (and possess the legal powers to enforce it) to grant or to deny permission for scholars to use and to publish from those materials. What this comes down to, no matter what it may be called and no matter how justly and fairly the power may be exercised, is *manuscript approval*. The results, then, even under ideal conditions, are a diminishment of candor and a complex additional burden laid upon the biographer who, though he may be fully honest in his use of the raw materials (we must remember that it is impossible for others without the same free access to precisely the same materials to measure the biographer's integrity), cannot wish to *appear to be* less than fully candid. This desire to demonstrate frank honesty, in conditions where that virtue is at best doubtful, tends to create curious distortions in which trivial faults and inconsequential flaws are given full status as "warts and all," as if to camouflage, if not to compensate for, the absence of serious critical inquisition.

The long and the short of all this is that every contemporary literary biography has to be taken as being tainted. Certainly none can be trusted without the exercise of some real and reasonable reservations.

II.

Eileen Simpson's *Poets in Their Youth* and Marie Rudisill's *Truman Capote* are memoirs that present important biographical information and materials. *Truman Capote*, a joint effort by Capote's Aunt Tiny and a well-tanned, neatly bearded Berkeley Ph.D. named James C. Simmons (the dust jacket tells that he "has published one book and over thirty articles in connection with his field of study, and has also written 150 articles specializing in travel, wild-life, and history"), reads almost as if it were fiction, appropriately like some of Capote's fiction. Whether this account is true or false, or a little of both, its effect is to create an image, adding at least some dimension to the conventional public image Capote had lately cultivated. It shows, as the mildly campy jacket promises, a "bizarre and exotic boyhood, set mostly in Monroeville, Alabama, and presents a charming portrait of this artist as an odd young man who managed to survive family troubles and tragedy which could easily have crippled a weaker man, one who went on, through will and discipline and dedication as much as a wealth of natural talent, to turn light on the shadows of his early life." Quite aside from the veracity of details, there are some strong points and solid arguments here. One is that Capote has used and transformed much that was real in his life and made art out of it. Another is the emerging portrait of a strong-willed, powerful survivor, much tougher than the fey and slightly lisping character familiar on television talk shows. Indeed, except for James Gould Cozzens, Capote may be the toughest of this bunch.

Eileen Simpson's book, gracefully written and candidly personal, concerns people who are now taken to be more significant literary figures than Capote: Delmore Schwartz, R. P. Blackmur, Robert Lowell and Jean Stafford, Randall Jarrell, and, of course, chiefly her own first husband—John Berryman. Allen Tate appears here and is involved also. Tate is, curiously, at the center of a much larger inclusive circle than Berryman; and he appears, sometimes briefly but always influentially, in the separate biographies of Lowell, Berryman, Blackmur, Djuna Barnes, Katherine Anne Porter, Frank O'Connor, and even F. Scott Fitzgerald. *Poets in Their Youth* is warm, sympathetic, understanding (Mrs. Simpson is a psychotherapist), and finally very sad. For these poets, one and all, came to sad or early endings. This is a book about beginnings, however, telling how these gifted poets, wholly dedicating their lives to poetry, came together over a time at a number of places; how they prospered and succeeded and then, under many outer and inner pressures, began to disintegrate. And because Mrs. Simpson tells the truth, as she experienced and remembers it, the story is more about the building of careers, literary careerism, than about anything else. The first two paragraphs on the first page compare and contrast not the art but the reputations of Schwartz and Berryman. "At the age of twenty-six, Delmore was famous in the literary world," she writes. "John's career, by contrast, had barely begun." It becomes clear—and all the more so since their gifts and achievements are demonstrated elsewhere and can only be assumed here—that what interested them most was recognition, that alchemic alloy blending fame and rewards. Recognition seemed to them a real possibility and a distinctly worthwhile goal, one for the sake of which they would apparently stop at nothing and one which would ultimately prove, even at peaks of later success beyond their early imagining, never to be quite enough, never quite fulfilling. The full-scale biographies of Lowell and Berryman bear out in weighty detail the implications of Eileen Simpson's story, here encapsulated in her discussion of Lowell's elegy for his old friend Berryman: "They had been students, teachers, veterans of the Cold War; had gone to Europe, daydreamed of a drink at six. And though Cal doesn't say so, they had had their breakdowns and incarcerations, talked to their psychiatrists about their seductive mothers and ineffectual fathers, won the prizes, been in *Life*, put their eyeglasses in a shoe at night so they could find them in the morning." They had also, of course, written the poems, many of them "confessional" and coming directly out of experience, which would win them "the prizes" and provide an occasion for their photographic images to be published in *Life*, poems which will have to shine on (or fade) regardless of the benefits of either photographs or prizes. What comes through clearly, and is sadder than the brief chronicles of these talented young people, is a sense of profound weakness (against which Capote looks to be, in his survivor's agility, as hard as nails) in these poets who had almost all the wrong values and who demonstrated an integrity almost exclusively limited to the actual making of their poems. These people wrote the best of their own poems almost in spite of themselves, as if their gifts overmastered them. Since they were all—but each differently—dedicated to uninhibited manipulation and self-advancement, it is sad to realize that in a deep and secret sense they were compelled to doubt their own finest achievements and to distrust their successes as being based more on "image" and good luck than on reality. We can see how they got exactly what they wanted and how the sweet taste of it turned to ashes for them. It is a very old story, of course. What is new about it is the still largely unexamined question as to what extent this pure lust for recognition was the result of their freely embracing the self-same goals and values as our society, a society they considered themselves liberated from by vocation.

Of all the careerists treated here, Norman Mailer, as he is found in Hilary Mills's *Mailer,* emerges as at once the cleverest and most successful—therefore, in those terms, the most interesting character. Yet, as depicted, his life and career raise a difficult question applicable to all these others. If, in truth, his outward and visible life is a kind of crazy quilt, a flourish of masks and charades, what are we to make of the work, the art in whose name and for whose sake he (they) summoned up all the craft of Proteus? Can we believe in the truth of the work even as we come to know the fictive and ambiguous life of the maker? St. Matthew treats the same perilous question: *Ye shall know them by their fruits. Do men gather grapes of thorns, or figs of thistles?*

III.

Of the two fat and richly documented biographies, Ian Hamilton's *Robert Lowell* is the best *written.* Sentence by sentence it stands as the best written of the whole group except for Fraser's *A Mingled Yarn,* which aspires to something more and more complex than the others. A poet himself, Hamilton is convincing in showing what experiences Lowell's poems came out of and the process of how they came to be. In that sense it is a fine critical biography as well as a life story. Ironically Berryman's life is more obviously interesting and complicated, but something (maybe it is simply style) works in Hamilton's favor. Like several of the other biographies, Haffenden's *Life of John Berryman* offers the device of a full "chronology" of the life at the outset. This can be very useful when it is properly exploited, can work to free the main text from the restrictions of purely chronological exposition. Yet none of these books, except for Fraser's, moves significantly in that direction. In the others the "chronology" works like an outline overture, and the danger of repetition is not overcome.

Both Hamilton and Haffenden are British, as is Joan Givner, author of *Katherine Anne Porter.* Several of these biographies are by writers of nationality and background different from their subjects'. Le Vot, of course, is French, and his *Fitzgerald* is in fact a translation. James Matthews (*Voices: A Life of Frank O'Connor*) and Judith Thurman (*Isak Dinesen*) are purely and simply American. Of less significance than occasional errors of fact—which newspaper reviewers have noted and in some cases have made too much of and which anyway are the responsibility as much of editors as of authors—are the finer, subtler, deeper differences (sometimes distortions) which come from a different point of view and an alien social texture. In some cases (for example Le Vot, who has next to nothing factual to add to the Fitzgerald story, but a great deal of useful judgment and nuance and, since he was writing for a French audience, a good deal of worthwhile explanation of basic material) the essential ignorance of the stranger can be beneficial. James Matthews loves Ireland and things Irish more than most natives could. That love gives his life of O'Connor both energy and authority, in spite of sentimental moments and, perhaps, an inevitable desire to be well regarded by the Irish literati. To judge Judith Thurman's *Isak Dinesen* is more difficult, but the author apparently has assimilated the complex cosmopolitan milieu of the Baroness Blixen. This is a work of authority, made stronger by occasional judgmental interventions by Thurman. In some of the others, however, try as the author will to compensate for this weakness through care and the weight of an accumulation of accurate information, there are real faults. Lacking a born and bone-deep understanding of a society, a reflexive awareness of the rough edges and textures of it, the biographer either can try to ignore the social aspects of the story or else is forced to accept his subject's view of the society as authentic. Most of these biographers have followed the latter method, with more or less success. With Lowell, Berryman, and Porter, there is another kind of problem. We share the same language, of course, and many of the same traditions, but our social system, especially our sense of social hierarchy, is quite different. Most Americans are hopelessly confused by our class system once they stray beyond the boundaries of known or native regions. Haffenden and Givner have not been able to be accurate in placing their subjects socially. Yet social status and social aspiration had much to do with the motivations of both Berryman and Porter. Hamilton's task looks much easier: no question that Lowell was a Boston aristocrat. Yet Hamilton seems, at times, as befuddled as Lowell himself by the sheer size and plurality of this large, unruly nation and by the fairly limited and diminishing part that old Bostonians, whether princes or paupers (the Kennedys, of course, are *new* Bostonians), have played in this nation's story for at least a century—a slow decline in influence probably beginning about the time that the Massachusetts Bay Colony ceased to be a viable and terrifying institution.

Maybe more interesting than subtle deficiencies is the fact that these biographers and their publishers seem to have felt neither reluctance nor inhibition in undertaking the study of the lives of writers from other cultures and societies. It may be true that the imaginative leap from one life (and point of view) to another is far more difficult to bridge than any difference between cultures. Moreover, any life story retold out of the distant past is likely to require more imagination than is needed to adjust to differences and distinctions between two coexisting contemporary societies. Again that thin and probably frivolous book on Capote stands apart from all this, for what is accomplished there is the acceptable re-creation of a tribal culture that is as real as that of a good novel. And it is done by the ways and means of the novel and therefore offers a truth more accessible to the imagination than the more rigorously factual. The other books, except for Eileen Simpson's memoir and parts of Fraser's evocation of R. P. Blackmur, are heavily freighted with apparatus—with notes and indices and charts and bibliographies and extensive acknowledgments, with all the outward signs of sweaty hard labor—and there is no denying them the authority which hard labor awards. Even the proofreading of these volumes must have been a most difficult chore. Yet something is missing, something of the spirit which *giveth life*, something which can be communicated best by voice and tone, by rhythm and texture, by means of the magic of a sensuous affective

surface. Am I suggesting that something closer to fiction or poetry, in form and content, might be a better form for biography?
Perhaps. . . . But, if so, we have not yet seen a full model of that
form except in some autobiography. Maybe pertinent is Frederic
Prokosch's *Voices: A Memoir,* which gives us brief personal anecdotes involving dozens of writers, including completely memorable appearances by Berryman, Lowell, Isak Dinesen, and F. Scott
Fitzgerald. Any one of Prokosch's recollections could be fabrica-
tions, and because the writers are so typically themselves and
speak as if they wrote their own dialogue one cannot suppress
suspicion; yet in an aesthetic context with brilliantly vivid surfaces they are most deeply alive.

Except for my expressed qualifications and at times my over-
powering sense that these works have been checked and double-
checked by publishers' committees, there is nothing seriously
wrong with any of these books. *Katherine Anne Porter* has been
(justly, I think) taxed by some reviewers for certain distortions
and misunderstandings, as has Andrew Field's *Djuna*. This is a
risk, and a real likelihood, when there are others alive who know
the subject and take different views. We tend, again justly, to defend our friends from strangers and, even more, to defend our
own perceptions of our friends from inquiry. The Princeton community (another link between several of these biographies) seems
to have taken umbrage at the picture of R. P. Blackmur in *A Mingled
Yarn*, the more so since many people there contributed to it by interview and correspondence. There can be no good answer to the
objections of those who knew the subject well except to remind
them that, for better or for worse, the biography is not really addressed to them.

IV.

My favorites among all the full-scale biographies considered
here are Matthew Bruccoli's *James Gould Cozzens: A Life Apart* and
Russell Fraser's *A Mingled Yarn: The Life of R. P. Blackmur.* I admire
them mainly for different reasons, for they are very different. But
they have a few basic qualities in common besides sharing the same

publisher, Harcourt Brace Jovanovich. Both authors are compelled, by circumstance, to build a case for their subjects—to justify, as it were, the attention given and received. In the case of Cozzens— much attacked, perhaps maligned, late in his long career—Bruccoli must seek to defend him, as well, against misapprehensions and reckless charges. In both cases, then, the biographer must create a basis of accurate fact from which to build a story. In each case, though differently, the subject was influential within his own circle (Blackmur especially with, among others, the whole stable of poets of *Poets in Their Youth*), but each was also withdrawn in shadow, outside of his work less known, even by friends, than many other literary types. These two were as private as active men of letters can be in our time. Each life is a sad story: both men were riddled with real frustrations and bitterness, tormented by bad health, and their lives ended not with any young and theatrical gesture but with a slow, painful, bravely endured dying. Both stories concern that best loved (in the popular mainstream) condition—maturity, with its sober balancing of debits and credits, its measured gains and losses. Finally, both of these books demonstrate (again differently) a dedication to the power of accumulated and carefully selected and arranged fact. Two basic kinds of facts, both really essential to any formal biography but both only irregularly evident in the other biographies, are deftly developed here—the fact of physicality and the facts about money. Both Fraser and Bruccoli keep attention focused on the health, good and ill, the physical being, of their subjects. Their only rival in this is *Isak Dinesen*, in which Thurman must concern herself with chronic syphilis and anorexia nervosa. But in a real sense money is the key to the story of so many American literary artists. So much is done or happens because it has to, because of profit and loss. Without regular reference to credible numbers—actual advances, sales, grants, income versus actual costs and expenses—the whole financial story loses credibility. In that sense, the business sense, the world of these other biographies might as well be Oz. In most of these literary biographies most of the time, as in almost all American literary biographies that I have ever seen, it would scarcely be a serious violation of reality or decorum if Rumpelstiltskin appeared, from time to time, to spin gold out of straw so that everyone could eat and travel to Rome or London. In Fraser's book, and especially in Bruccoli's, you are aware of the financial truth all the time.

Bruccoli's book is a triumphant structure of found facts. This gives it great authority, enough to overcome the fact (for the reader) that the style is at its best moments transparent. There is not much pretty writing here except where Cozzens himself, a skilled and complex stylist, is being quoted. To which criticism the answer can be that the biographer's choice here is architecture, not interior decoration, that the case for Cozzens gains credibility through being presented in a plain style. Fraser takes the opposite tack. Dealing with an artist and critic with a knotty mind and a famously gnarled style, he seeks to write not in allusion to or imitation of that style but at least in expression of the density and subtlety of it. The danger, not always avoided, is of a kind of showboat virtuosity, of elaborate overwriting. But there are enough stunning passages where it works, where the style is worthy of the subject, to outweigh the flaws and to make the gamble worthwhile.

Each of these biographers has done well. Bruccoli and Fraser have, it seems to me, done about as well as the form itself allows or deserves. Whether the conventional form of the biography can do justice to a literary artist of our times remains in doubt. It will remain so until a more adequate and inclusive form develops—if it does.

My Silk Purse and Yours

Making It, Starring Norman Podhoretz

This is the earliest piece by a long shot in the whole book. It is also clearly dated. Podhoretz has gone a long way, in his own way, since *Making It* (1968). My piece no longer applies. And it is also the only explicitly negative criticism you will find here. I don't have anything against negative criticism, just that it seems a waste of space and time and energy and trees. There are too many good books that get lost or ignored. *Making It* was not a "bad" book. I seem to have thought it was unintentionally funny in many ways that our late twentieth-century world is unintentionally funny and unbearably sad.

Nothing personal, Norman.

Also, to be fair and more or less honest, I ought to admit that I like the title of this piece. And since that has also come to be the title of this book, it really has to be here, doesn't it?

I.

I desire that all men should see me in my simple, natural, and ordinary fashion, without straining or artifice: for it is myself that I portray.

—Montaigne

Norman Podhoretz's *Making It* is a fascinating piece of work. Candid as he can be, he lifts the long Victorian skirts of that lady sometimes called the Bitch Goddess of Success and once upon a time known as Dame Fortune. He sneaks more than a peek. Framing his anatomy of ambition and the American lust for success in the form of an autobiography, Podhoretz seeks to make his story an *exemplum* of the gospel he preaches. It is a story of and for here and now; and only Norman Podhoretz could have done it. If it raises more questions than it answers, that is the purpose: to make us admit those questions exist, to meet them without shame, and to grope with him for answers.

A highly readable account of one young man's search for his identity. Recommended for adult readers.

II.

Not many girls enjoy posing in the nude and it must be admitted that co-operation is mostly for the purpose of earning fees.

—Andre De Dienes, *Best Nudes*

Mr. Norman Podhoretz
c/o Random House Inc.
457 Madison Avenue
New York, N. Y. 10022

Please Forward If Necessary

Dear Norman,

Hope this reaches you all right. Mail service these days leaves something to be desired. And you never can tell about publishers. Here today and merged with Dow Chemical or something tomorrow.

I enclose a blurb from the *Hollins Critic*. Not that you need it. Your book seems to be getting attention in the right places, and mostly they are good reviews. Except maybe that one in *Life* where John Aldridge came on laughing and scratching and slipped you a mickey in a cup of good cheer. But you know old John. He's still trying to top Daniel Defoe's *The Shortest Way With Dissenters*.

So anyhow you are getting reviews. Sure they are riddled with reservations, but they add up to praise in the end, which is better than the end of a boot. And, ironically, this is a tribute to the kind of power you have learned to live with as the editor of *Commentary*. Of course people in power have to put up with a certain amount of flattery, even if it's only the dubious flattery of being taken at face value. But it's like saluting officers, which they taught you in basic training. Now that you're an officer, too, don't sweat, you've got it made. The time to worry is when they stop saluting. When that happens, it won't be subtle. You'll know.

Not that I am making a big deal about this review in a humble organ of limited circulation and modest means. I am not in favor of humility or false modesty any more than you are. The meek are the real secret troublemakers. All they want to do is inherit the earth. But, let's face it, this is the provinces, the sticks, the boon-docks. Far from the bright amazing center of culture you write about, the pleasures of court life, masques and masks. Take it for what it is, then, a "get well" message from the remote reaches of the Empire (O far from the Empire City!). At least maybe you'll be amused. And if, between parties sometimes, you get hung up in idle or in pensive mood, remember what the hangman says when he slips the noose over somebody's head—"Wear it in good health."

You may be wondering. Maybe you have even asked yourself: "What's with this crank whom I have never met coming on with a big, fat, cheerful 'Dear Norman?' " I am glad you asked that question, Norman. It is true you don't know me from the Man in the Moon. And I don't know you from Jason Epstein or even Jason Podhoretz, a minor comic character in a novel called *The Exhibitionist*. Of course, I have read some of your work. And even way out here I have "heard things." But I never pay attention to malicious gossip. I could argue, if I felt hostile, that as a self-confessed celebrity, you have got about the same right to privacy as, say, the Playmate of the Month. But don't get me wrong. My reason for the unwarranted familiarity is that it seems like the thing to do in a literary way. It seems fitting and proper, decorum as it were, to call you Norman in response to the experience of reading your life story. Not that I really feel I know you any better than I did when I picked up the book, admired the prestigious jacket, good cloth binding and paper (excellent production job) and the photograph on the back. But I feel like I *ought* to know you better. Sort of a poor man's Categorical Imperative. . . . But there is a more relevant reason. It is a literary allusion. You like to play with literary allusions too. I can tell from your book. So maybe it is a bad habit and tends to stunt intellectual growth, but we both had the same kind of liberal arts education and can't help ourselves. Anyway, years ago I ran across an article by Diana Trilling. I recall it began with "Dear Norman" too. Man, was I out of it! I was half way through before I figured out it wasn't Norman Vincent Peale.

So it is with a glow of nostalgia that I am bold to address you by your first name. Please, sir, do not misconstrue it as an attempt to pretend to a familiarity it is not my privilege to possess. Be big about it and don't let it bug you. At least I didn't call you "Norm."

Best wishes. Have to run now. Have to write a review of *Making It*. Say, if you want to read some really *good* recent books I recommend: *Feel Free* by David Slavitt, *Killing Time* by Thomas Berger, and one you should take a good look at—*A Bill of Rites, A Bill of Wrongs, A Bill of Goods* by Wright Morris.
Yours truly,
George

P.S. Is it true that Bennett Cerf thinks he is the Alfred Knopf of publishing?

III.

They had always known that I would turn out to be another Clifton Fadiman.

—*Making It*

Making It is described by its publisher as "a confessional case history." In one place the author says it is "in a way, a letter," and in another he says that it is "a frank, Mailer-like bid for literary distinction, fame, and money all in one package." All these descriptions are helpful in defining the qualities of this book. It is a confession in the form of a case history, with some of the ease of the epistolary style. The confessional quality is adroitly established by a series of allusions to St. Augustine. This, too, purports to be a story of conversion. The realm of confessional literature, from the Epistles of St. Paul to such recent examples as Norman Mailer's works and George Plimpton's *Paper Lion*, is explicitly alluded to and used functionally in much the same way as certain writers have used the epic tradition in mock heroic works. The book is addressed to several groups of readers: one personal to the author and beyond critical scrutiny; one semipersonal, the named and unnamed figures of the New York Literary Scene whom the author designates as The Family, the real wheeler-dealers, shakers and movers of the intellectual milieu to which the author belongs; and last, the larger group, you and me, Reader, to whom the book must be addressed if the author is going to get all the fame and money he says he is after. He wants distinction, too, though whether anyone can give him that is debatable. He seems to feel distinction is the inevitable handmaiden of the other two, tripping along like Charity with Faith and Hope. He also seems to feel that power in America exists as a result of the coupling of fame and money. No question about that, I suppose, unless one starts wondering if power can be conferred at all in the same way fame or wealth can be inherited, stolen, earned, or received. In any case, the book is simultaneously addressed to several audiences. Since the apparent form of the book is nonfiction, this presents some artistic difficulty for the author. Consider the problem of exposition. Members of the elite, The Family, can be expected to know most of the details of their own history and, as well, the author's part in it. He runs the risk of boring them to distraction, a risk he compensates for by offering his original interpretation of the meaning of The Family and its history. No doubt this is of considerable interest to that group. And he even makes it interesting to us who have no knowledge upon which to evaluate the merit of his notions. The passages concerning The Family offer some of the most energetic writing in this book. Added to the author's enthusiasm for the subject is the explicit sincerity of his belief. He cares about them and he shows this. Therefore the larger audience is invited to care too, insofar as they can care about the narrator.

In autobiography there is always a problem of the credibility of the chief witness for the defense—the author. When matters of truth and innocence, fact and guilt are involved, the reader necessarily arms himself with a device for which Hemingway had another name, here called the divining rod of skepticism. Unlike Norman Mailer in *Advertisements for Myself,* the author does not include representative examples of his literary work. Perhaps he assumes a widespread awareness of them, but this is unlikely, for it would indicate a very advanced stage of self-delusion. Maybe he decided this rhetorical risk was less than the danger of losing the attention of The Family. But I am inclined to credit him with the bold intent of "making it," this book, all on his own and by its own merits. Nevertheless we still have the problem of the "credibility gap." In fiction the reader is free to believe, disbelieve, and to suspend disbelief. This freedom, acknowledged, becomes a strength for the novelist. But in nonfiction we are less free. We can take it or leave it. Thus autobiography starts at a disadvantage, because no man, be he ever so loathsome and evil, is without some self-esteem. Even Crabby Appleton, the villain of *Tom Terrific*, enjoys the crackling self-deception that he is the meanest man in the world and "rotten to the core." But this hyperbolic estimate is not fully shared either by Tom or by Mighty Manfred, the Wonder Dog, despite Crabby's assaults upon their sense of justice and fair play. Meaning that all confession is assumed to be a statement by the author of his own case in the light that pleases him most. We automatically mark that this book is not the work of an elder who can prop his weary shanks upon the pillows of a lifetime's reputation. This young man still has a lot to lose. He is most vulnerable by his own admission. And he asserts that he cares a great deal about being a winner. The Family, though depleted and dwindling in power, is still alive and kicking. His own admiration for that group and pride of belonging would incline one to doubt that he would risk their wrath while he retained a measure of sanity. He has plenty of reasons for being untrustworthy.

IV.

Slum child, filthy little slum child, so beautiful a mind and so vulgar a personality, so exquisite in sensibility and so coarse in manner.

—*Making It*

This book does not exist in abstraction from literary tradition or the scene which it proposes to celebrate by paradoxical encomium. I asked the best critic of American Literature I know of, William R. Robinson, to give me a one-paragraph statement on the background of American autobiographical writing. Robinson is able to take a dare, and here is what he wrote:

Mythic autobiography, the major indigenous narrative form in American literature, originates in the Puritan diaries, where divine intellect regarding an individual's spiritual destiny is sought amid the obscure omens of personal events within the physical world. Melville generalized this focus upon the juncture where the divine manifests itself through nature into a theory of art when he asserted that art is a meeting and mating of opposites. But this theory and such inside narratives as *Billy Budd* and *Moby Dick* issuing from it had been preceded by Emerson's Transcendentalism of the Puritans' symbolic drama within the single, separate person; and they were later philosophically justified by William James's vigorous defense of the "I," the interior life, as the only true place where we can find real fact in the making. As James saw it, then, the American imagination grabs hold at the precise moment where the transformational event takes place, which occurs from the inside out, so its truth can only be observed there, inside, while, miraculously, existence erupts from being. It bears witness to and exemplifies creation, the individuating process whereby, having gathered its powers at its source, purified of whatever would weigh it down, whether matter, guilt, or egotism, the imagination leaps free. Thus, whether practiced by Cotton Mather, Thoreau, Whitman, Hemingway, Henry Miller, or William Carlos Williams, to mention only the established literary figures, this form affirms as the supreme value for man the individual liberated from necessity and free to act joyfully and for good in the world. Without a doubt and vigorously, it indeed celebrates fact in the making.

The tradition of "mythic autobiography" persists. But in the present situation all the forms of nonfiction thrive while the novel keeps on dying and dying like the lead soprano in certain Italian operas. From *In Cold Blood* to Paul Holmes's *The Candy Murder Case: The Explosive Story the Newspapers and T.V. Couldn't Tell*; from *Paper Lion* by George Plimpton to *My Own Story: The Truth About Modelling* by Jean Shrimpton; and not to forget that the more successful works of fiction in our time base much of their appeal upon "authenticity." For example, there is much in common between *The Exhibitionist* and *The Confessions of Nat Turner*, both bestsellers. In terms of popular appeal, both are blessed with the illusion of authenticity. In one we are led to imagine that we are privy to the inside story of Jane Fonda. In the other we are encouraged to think we are getting the lowdown on the Walter Mitty dreams of James Baldwin. The essential difference in the two books lies in the fact that some people enjoy the titillation of "bondage" stories and violence while others prefer simple sex; that some prefer to escape the problems of the present by blaming them on the past (thus sharing their problems with the dead, practicing, as it were, intellectual necrophilia) while others escape from their own hang-ups by reading about movie stars who have hang-ups too.

In short, the literary situation could not be better for *Making It.* The distinctions between fiction and nonfiction have become meaningless. It is possible that nobody can distinguish between truth and fiction anymore and nobody cares. In which case this autobiography with its large credibility gap is well timed. I prefer, however, to take a more charitable view of both the author and the public. I am a Democrat and cautiously egalitarian. Even though Norman Podhoretz makes a shattering assault against any possible equality among men, I like to imagine that the public is not so stupid as it allows its manipulators and managers to assume. If we ever let them know that we know the score and have been keeping it all along, our leaders might become subtle and dangerous instead of being merely mischievous. It is possible that the public has simply recognized that the only mode of our times is fiction. From Walter Cronkite to Walter Lippman, from Norman Vincent Peale to Norman Podhoretz, all are equally purveyors of entertainment, more or less entertaining.

Therefore *Making It* is, in truth, a modern novel and should be treated as such. When it is treated as a work of fiction, it becomes a more interesting book. And it is spared from the greatest danger that besets the author of his first confession. As Henry Sutton puts it: "The confessional pretends to candor but generally misses the mark: X confesses to pederasty and Y to treachery and deceit, and we forgive them these sins, and easily; what we cannot forgive—X, Y, or anyone—is the sin of boring us." By examining *Making It* as fiction we at least mitigate the circumstances of ennui.

V.

I was supposed to be endowed with exceptional intelligence, and yet it took me hours to learn how to lace up my new combat boots efficiently, it took me days to learn how to reassemble my rifle in the required time, and I never learned how to adjust a gas mask properly. What was my kind of intelligence worth then?

—*Making It*

Making It brings together a number of kinds of fiction. Basically a classic example of the bildungsroman of the nineteenth century, it includes such diverse contemporary types as the Jewish novel, the College novel, the Army novel, the American-in-Europe novel, with lesser elements from the novel of espionage, the roman à clef, the works of Horatio Alger, to name only a few. It is then extremely *literary*, which is perfectly in keeping with the concerns of the protagonist. There is clever use of the conventions of the Pornographic novel, for the protagonist asserts that the hunger for success has replaced sex as "the dirty little secret," and by imagery and analogy he keeps this notion continually present in the story. Not that the protagonist *sublimates* his sexual energies. He refers to any number of girls, in passing, with whom he has enjoyed some intimacy. He mentions a wife and children too, though most often in the Baconian sense as "hostages to Fortune." There is one girl who stands out from the faceless crowd of others, an English girl whom we learn is blond. The protagonist admits that he loved her for a time. Otherwise, however, love does not enter into this story at all.

The protagonist, now a successful literary critic, remembers his life and adds some commentary to show its meaning. He tells how he grew up in Brooklyn, went to school and got along fine until a teacher, Mrs. K., whose unpleasant motives he now understands, pushed and prodded him toward "achievement." She wanted him to go to Harvard, but he went to Columbia (while simultaneously studying in the Jewish and traditional Seminary College) and then to Clare College, Cambridge. Blessed with the benefits and cursed with the deficiencies of the best in liberal arts education, and having acquired some good "connections" through such of his teachers as Lionel Trilling and the irascible F. R. Leavis, he set out to be a critic. He was beginning to make his mark when he got caught in the Draft. Basic training was a horrible shock, but he managed to survive and wound up with a soft berth overseas. Once he got back, though, things moved along swiftly. He made a name for himself, writing things for *Commentary*, the *New Yorker*, and other magazines. After some ups and downs he finally made it as editor of *Commentary*. Along the line he was taken in, almost formally, by The Family. As the book ends he has got it made and is glad of it.

The life described, while enviably tranquil, would hardly seem of interest to anyone except the protagonist himself. He never has much trouble and never fails to get what he wants. Probably the nearest thing to a crisis (excepting basic training, which he sees as a *trauma*) came when he wrote a sassy review of *The Adventures of Augie March* by Saul Bellow. This could have caused him real trouble, but ironically, it served to his advantage. It was his key to membership in The Family, who, it turns out, were just waiting around for someone to give Bellow a bad time. In short, *outwardly,* there are no problems and no suspense unless you happen to be the protagonist. And at the time he is remembering all this, in comfort and security, he knows how it will all turn out anyway.

Yet it is not a simple and straightforward success story, because the protagonist is not a simple man. Inwardly it is a story of turmoil and a series of "conversions." Simplified, his dilemma is: what to do with his success? His own background rendered him more or less unable to aspire to the things of this world. Overcoming inhibition, he went on to get an excellent education and to win prizes, awards, and the first and best fruits of it. Only to discover that the principles cherished by the liberal arts rendered him unfit to do anything in the world and especially rendered him unable to enjoy the ends of ambition when they came to him; for both success and ambition were suspect, particularly in terms of the egalitarian ideals that the society paid lip service to. Through some soul-searching he finally came to an adjustment, realizing that riches, fame, and power are not in and of themselves bad and that everyone else is "doing it" and "making it" anyway, no matter how piously they otherwise pretend. And, as a critic, he was able to turn his own discipline to work for him, to come to an understanding as to why this conflict in his own mind, a *typical* American conflict as he sees it, came to be there. The epiphany for which he had prepared himself came when he went to a conference of Big Shots at a place named Paradise Island by its wealthy owner. Symbolically, *it,* too, had been converted from its original status and name—Hog Island. There the protagonist saw and felt, helped by good rum and the pleasant surroundings, the true meaning of The Good Life. And he saw that it was good. And he resolved never again to be ashamed of wanting it, any more than he would be ashamed of his sex drives. The understanding which he reached, concerning the egalitarian ideology and its consequent negative view of success, has broad implications. It is more than the hypocrisy of the living. It is a deliberate confidence trick, fine print in the complex social contract of the U.S.A., designed by the WASPS to keep the post–Civil War immigrants and their descendants at a decent distance from the banquet table. Now, however, thanks to him and others, the word is out, the con game is exposed. Thus the protagonist can hope his story may serve to inspire others. In this sense there is conflict in the story and some narrative suspense. A suspense not ending with the book, for the protagonist, having committed himself to his goals, becoming as the Elizabethans would have said "a child of Fortune," is ripe and ready for whatever the future may bring. Since Dame Fortune is reputed to be fickle, that could be anything. The possibility is left open for further adventures as he rides the Wheel of Fortune up or down.

But *Making It* is more subtle than that. There is another level to be considered. And this requires some examination of the first-person narrator. We must consider whether he may not very well be an example of that figure who haunts the pages of contemporary fiction—the anti-hero.

As the protagonist sees himself, his gifts are intellectual. There is no indication that he has the slightest doubt concerning his intellectual accomplishments. This makes him a very positive character. Of course it is "in character" that he would not bother to demonstrate the rock foundations of his certainty. Nevertheless, there are certain clues. Evidently trusting in the power of redundancy, the protagonist *tells us* over and again that he is an exceptionally smart fellow. And to doubters and shruggers he can point to certain accomplishments that have won him applause. And from time to time he offers us some examples, in synoptic form, of his critical judgment at work. Unfortunately these are not always dazzling examples of mental acrobatics; indeed, as presented here, they are uniformly unimpressive. Sometimes we are given examples of his reasoning powers. Not even the most sympathetic reader will be as pleased by these examples as the protagonist is. His views of history, the arts, modern life, etc., are a string of clichés, largely derived from the authority of rather well-known popular books, brilliant, if at all, only in the way that the signals formed by ships' flags are brilliant to behold. In this sense, there is a redeeming thread of humor running through the whole book, though the protagonist himself is nothing if not serious minded.

Led on by these clues we begin to notice that the protagonist has other serious flaws. One of these is that practically everything in the story is *abstract* to him. Even his physical descriptions of things and places, which are all too rare, are clearly out of books, perfunctory and lifeless. The protagonist is presented as immune to all sensuous effective experience in life as well as in the arts. He would appear to have experienced little or nothing of the joyous dance of the five senses and, it would *seem*, doesn't know what he is missing. Always (perhaps a true Seminarian, despite his "conversion") when faced with a new experience he cites the authority of books. And when he feels that the books did not prepare him for an experience, he blames the books. There is a touching innocence here, for it never occurs to him that he may have read the wrong books, or that he could have read them without understanding or imaginative engagement. A superior example: he notes that while waiting for his draft notice to arrive ("Greetings, Norman!"), he busied himself preparing the now-celebrated Bellow review. One of the books he read was *Dangling Man*. Which, though he offers no evidence of knowing this, is *about a man waiting to get drafted*. In one ear and out the other? Not quite. . . . In another place he offers some observations upon the limbo of waiting to be called. Anyone familiar with *Dangling Man* will see where his "original" observations came from. With few exceptions all the books he mentions are widely known, indicating nothing special about his reading habits as compared with anyone else's. In fact, on the evidence he gives us, it would be impossible to conclude he is "well read" at all. Perhaps this is merely a rhetorical device; he alludes to those things he can be sure his reader will know. On the other hand it may be a wonderful sort of *style*. One thinks (to be bookish) of Jay Gatsby, who never descended to the vulgarity of cutting the pages of his elegantly bound sets of books.

Beyond that, with the exception of a very few who have briefly captured his admiration, people are merely names when they are named at all. There are some golden names all right, and well dropped; but the protagonist will allow them no life. They are objects to him. Even his parents are given short shrift, and the death of his father serves mainly as an occasion for him to defend continuing on at the Seminary, not out of belief, but out of a deathbed promise that he eventually breaks in any case. Girls are just "girls"; sex is just "sex." He shows an ability to analyze the motives of others, almost always to their disadvantage; and he is especially sharp in perceiving the dark and unpleasant motives of his "friends" and any who have done him a good turn. Conversely, when subjecting his own motives to scrutiny, he is willing to ascribe the best and most favorable interpretation. Though he subjects himself to rack and thumbscrew, he always comes out smelling like a rose. He is, in fact, without awareness of the point of view of other human beings. The sentimental attribution of motives is, after all, a very different thing than consideration of another's point of view.

This becomes downright peculiar when we consider his endorsement of the uses of power. Power is predicated on self-interest and depends upon the exquisite awareness of the self-interest of others. Power cannot afford to be sentimental. It becomes unstable, dangerous, and ceases to be power at all. It becomes evident that he means *privilege* when he speaks of power. And there is a startling irony in his drive for fame and all that the Elizabethans called "honor." As the protagonist presents himself, he has no concept of honor whatsoever, a lack which would seem to preclude the possibility of achieving any kind of stable fame. He is at great pains to prove that he is a phoney and so is everyone else around him. Phonies in a Barnum and Bailey world. But, paradoxically, there is no relief from self-doubt here. Instead of rejoicing in the Brotherhood of Phonies or the Phonyhood of All Mankind, he still feels somehow "different" from, *alienated* (to use his word) from everyone else.

And though he is a writer and writes with some perception about the mysterious process of writing, he opts for only one *kind* of writing, the product of pure and simple inspiration. Just as "research" and scholarship are pejorative terms and, in his view, inhibitions to intellectual excellence, so labor and skill in writing are contemptible to him. He mentions *skill* in opposition to "authority":

Authority in writing need not be accompanied by consummate skill or any other virtue of craft or mind, for like the personal self-confidence of which it is the literary reflection, it is a quality in its own irreducible right, and one that always elicits an immediate response— just as a certain diffidence of tone and hesitancy of manner account for the puzzling failure of many otherwise superior writers to attract the attention they merit.

The way I understand this is that the protagonist comes out for invoking the Muses and winging it. Which is great unless, like the protagonist, you want to be a *professional*. Because a professional can't afford "writer's block" or he is out of business. Like Bart Starr, he has to play in bandages. But our hero, here in *Making It*, suffers long and hard, he says, from writing blocks. He sees this book, his confession, as a big breakthrough. Well, it has its ups and downs, but the Muses conned him if they let him think it swings. As for *authority*, well, the protagonist has got the words, but he can't carry the tune in a galvanized bucket.

All this adds up to an extremely unreliable narrator. Who can neither be trusted nor trust himself. And thus it brings immediately into question his bigger assertions. Like the fact that he ever had any experience of "conversion" at all. What I see is that at every stage he hedged his bet, by leaving himself as a hostage behind. Therefore there are many of him—a boy in Brooklyn, a Seminarian ("sermons" is a word he uses again and again), a student still hoping that Trilling or Leavis or Hadas or please *somebody* will give him an A+; a poor, bewildered, uncomfortable draftee being yelled at by a mean old sergeant, a Cambridge gentleman, sipping tea while his Gyp builds up the fire, etc., etc. The book, intended to exorcise all his ghosts, in fact invokes and summons them.

In any case, we have a protagonist who knows neither himself nor the world, who seems crippled in *feeling*, vulnerable in pride and arrogance, able only to love himself, and *that* in moderation. Almost blissfully unaware, you might say, maybe able to be *happy* because his self-deception is almost total.

Even in this, the covert level of his character, we are not yet near the naked truth of him. The protagonist gives every indication of seeing himself in this same unflattering steel glass. And, like a patient under analysis, reveals most by that which he tries to conceal. He is, then, desperately, urgently insecure. He wants to feel joy, but he cannot. He wants to be able to love and to be loved, but he cannot because he despises himself and feels unworthy of love. He wants to be a poet, his long lost childhood dream, and is unable to convince himself that he has any right or "authority" and has managed to stifle the poet by creating insurmountable frustrations. He says he wants fame, power, wealth, and, even social position. But it is painfully clear he does not want these because he is deeply terrified of responsibilities and dangers. Truly powerful men love danger. And they love to gamble. Even as the protagonist commits himself to Fortune at the end, he tries to hedge his bet, in full, certain, and sad knowledge that Dame Fortune is always most cruel to those lovers who mock her by this transparent device.

VI.

I will get Peter Quince to write a ballad of this dream: it shall be called Bottom's Dream because it hath no bottom.
—*A Midsummer Night's Dream*, IV.ii

What does all this have to do with the real live Norman Podhoretz in person? It is not only possible, but also necessary, to distinguish between the character of the man in the book, which can be known, and that of the man who wrote it, which cannot. We make this distinction with no difficulty in the works of Henry Miller, never really crediting the author with the sexual exploits of the character, Henry Miller. Podhoretz asks us to do the same thing. The result of this divorce is to make for a much more interesting and praiseworthy book. For, without denying the literal sense of the book, one is directed to consider the *sentence*, in the Chaucerian use of that term. The medieval literary critics, taking their model from St. Augustine (just as Podhoretz does), were extremely sophisticated. They recognized that all literary work has meaning, its own form of *allegoria*. Their basic three-level reading of a work is helpful here. The first two levels of the character of the protagonist are so contradictory as to approach *enigma*. Enigma, as a figure, indicates that the meaning of the work is outside of literal interpretation. Thus, though *Making It* appears to be a simple-minded fabliau, it is more complex and more fabulous. The "real" Norman Podhoretz, the author of the book, has created an allegory of pilgrimage. But it is a *false* pilgrimage. The protagonist arrives at what is clearly Babylon and is fooled by the "Welcome to Jerusalem" signs. There he is, up to his knees in the Slough of Despond and trying to make the best of it because all the maps say this is The Delectable Mountain. In his innocence he wants to believe and to do right. Innocence is the key to the character. He is the bumbling naïf of great satire. Echoes of *Candide, Rasselas, Joseph Andrews*, etc.

The meaning is then clear: "Take a perfectly ordinary innocent guy, a guy like me (or you, hypocrite Reader), and let him believe in the ideals of the society and do his best to live by them, and look where he ends up—*Nowhere*! And look what he becomes—either a figure of fun or a pathetic Frankenstein monster."

Put it this way. In selling Norman Podhoretz a sow's ear and letting him think it is a genuine silk purse, the society conned him. Just as Huntington Hartford tried to con the suckers by calling Hog Island a Paradise. It is a shell game, ladies and gentlemen, and (he's *so* right) you can't win even at the charity bazaar booths run by art, religion, education, etc. The whole society is one big seamless garment. And the goals of all, by definition, look exactly like sugar lumps, but turn to bitter ashes on the tongue. Even the man who is lucky enough to find out before it is too late that he is supposed to be a winner and that it is "all right" to win, even *he*, laurels of victory on his brow, is revealed to be another loser. Either a pathetic bum of the month or a clown in cap and bells. Take your pick. Nobody wins. There are only alternative ways of losing.

Unless . . .

Unless a man can learn this and has the courage and ability to play both roles at the same time. To clown it up (like the Fool in *Lear*) or to put on sackcloth and ashes and then, amazing, begin to dance for joy in memory of Isaiah's truth, that the oil of joy is for mourning.

As a child Norman Podhoretz dreamed of being a poet. The

protagonist tells us he failed. Perhaps the real Podhoretz succeeds, though. For the truth of this book, disguised as it is from the protagonist, is poetic, a statement of the eternal paradox of man's goals in the only world he knows for sure, the one he lives in and will die in. As the protagonist of *Making It* is always saying, if he had not come along, we'd have had to invent him. And so we just did.

B. S. Johnson
The Poetry

Bryan Stanley William Johnson was born in London and spent most of his life there except for some periods during World War II when, together with other London children, he was evacuated to the country and, much later, in 1970, a period during which he served as Gregynog Arts Fellow at the University of Wales. His father was a bookseller's stockkeeper, and his mother had once worked, in the early 1920s, as a servant in Chester Square in Belgravia. After World War II, Johnson finished school, then found work as a clerk in a bank. But in 1955 he went to King's College of London University, graduating in 1959 with an honors B.A. in English. He taught high school and was a sports reporter for a time. In the early 1960s he became an editor of the *Transatlantic Review*, which then had its chief editorial office in London, and served as coeditor for poetry for that distinguished magazine. In 1964 he married Virginia Ann Kimpton, the Virginia of the novel *Alberto Angelo* (1964), the Ginnie of *Trawl* (1966), and they had two children. His literary awards included Gregory awards for *Travelling People* (1963) and *Poems* (1964), the Somerset Maugham Award (1967), Grand Prix at both the Tours and Melbourne film festivals for *You're Human Like the Rest of Them* (1971), and the Granada Poetry Prize (1971). On November 13, 1973, he was found dead, a suicide, in his house in Islington. He had killed himself while his wife and children were away from the house. The London *Times* obituary of November 15, 1973, identified him as "one of the most naturally gifted writers of his generation," adding, "He was also one of the very small number to commit himself wholeheartedly to the experimental presentation of fiction." He was also described, with accuracy, as "a combative but immensely likable man."

With the poetry of B. S. Johnson we at first appear to be dealing with the challenging, if not altogether uncommon, situation of a gifted, prolific, and influential literary artist, most of whose major work was done in other forms and whose influence as poet would seem to have been distinctly less than his undeniable impact as an unusually successful and highly original innovator in prose, an important member of the generation of postmodernist, "self-reflexive" novelists. A glance at a list of his published books shows ten works of prose against two slender volumes of verse, only one of these, the first, *Poems* (1964), having been published in America. And added to the predominance of other work above and beyond the poetry are three plays, three screenplays, nine television scripts, a Third Programme radio script, and several miscellaneous anthologies which he edited or coedited. All this was achieved in a twenty-year span of productivity, for Johnson was only forty when he killed himself.

Measured by quantity or judged by and in terms of critical attention paid to his work, the poems might be taken as the left-handed exercises of a novelist or, in any case, as his minor work in the sense that, say, the poems of William Faulkner or Joyce Cary or James Joyce, however accomplished, are mainly interesting for their relationship to the central creative work of those artists. Of course anything that a major literary artist does with words is of interest, but the poems of these three masters, in and of themselves, are probably of no more consequence than, for example, the novels of James Merrill and Louis Simpson. B. S. Johnson was certainly the first and foremost among the British novelists to adapt and assimilate the technical exploits of Jorge Luis Borges, Samuel Beckett, Bertolt Brecht, and others. His model from the past was Laurence Sterne's *Tristram Shandy* (1760–1767). His efforts were often criticized in Britain, but he had serious champions also, for instance, Anthony Burgess, who described Johnson as "the only living British novelist with the guts to reassess the novel form."

Johnson managed in his own singular kind of novel to combine a directly autobiographical impulse, an unflinching re-creation of the truths of himself and of his times as he perceived them, with complex and highly artificial strategies associated with the experiments of postmodernist fiction. Johnson did not like those two words, *experiment* and *fiction*, applied to his work. "Certainly, I make experiments," he is quoted as saying, "but the unsuccessful ones are quietly hidden away. . . ." He constantly set the term *fiction* against what he said was the chief aim of his own work—

to tell the truth. This is emphatically argued in *Aren't You Rather Young To Be Writing Your Memoirs?* (1973): "I am not interested in telling lies in my own novels. A useful distinction between literature and other writing for me is that the former teaches one something true about life: and how can you convey truth in a vehicle of fiction? The two terms, *truth* and *fiction*, are opposites, and it must be logically impossible." The later novels use his name and the names of others, real people and places. But the naked truth is often distanced by such devices as the peepholes in the pages of *Alberto Angelo* or the presentation of *The Unfortunates* (1969) in a box that contains separate sections of varying lengths, which may be arranged and rearranged by the reader in almost any kind of order.

Beyond Johnson's overshadowing reputation as an innovative novelist, taken together with the almost reflexive distrust demonstrated by poets toward those few whose talents are more general and various, there are other things which have at least permitted his poetry to be slighted if not ignored. His poems are few in number (thirty-one in the first book, thirty-two in the second), and they were slow in the making. Johnson acknowledged this, more as a fact than as a problem, in a statement on the jacket of *Poems Two* (1972): "While I am reasonably (even over-) prolific in other forms of writing, I manage so few poems that it is seven years or so (as it was with my first volume) before I have enough to form a collection." And the poems are, superficially at least, less overtly innovative than might be expected. They are, generally, short, tight, direct in statement, and, though often, especially in *Poems Two*, free and easy enough in style, they are still basically formal in structure and rhythm. Outside of the context of his work as a whole, the poems might be taken as at worst inhibited, at best mere exercises. But Tony Curtis, in "The Poetry of B. S. Johnson" (1976), has persuasively argued that the poems are so clearly related to all Johnson's other work that they may not be taken out of that context. They are, in an unusual and functional sense, part and parcel of the same canon.

Moreover, for better or worse, Johnson's poetry had a place in his theory of the development of contemporary literary art. If the new novel was the proper vessel for truth now that storytelling (fiction, "lies") had found its proper home in film and television, then poetry, also a form for truth, had redefined itself. As he wrote in the introduction to *Aren't You Rather Young To Be Writing Your Memoirs?*: "But poetry did not die when storytelling moved on. It concentrated on the things it was still best able to do: the short, economical lyric, the intense emotional statement, depth rather than scale. . . ." Finally, another factor working against him, Johnson's poems are, in the context and fashions of contemporary British poetry, original enough, perhaps even *deviant* enough, to be somewhat outside the operable critical standards which could so easily be used to place and to rate the work of others. Johnson's line of development was from the more formal, more *written* voice to a daring version of the vernacular, an adroit colloquialism (both in matter and manner) more familiar in the work of certain American poets than in the work of his countrymen. Among his British contemporaries, D. J. Enright has achieved something similar in *The Terrible Shears* (1973).

With the publication of *Poems Two* Johnson proved that he had found a voice as a poet, a voice not limited by the fashions of the times. It is a daring voice in the sense that the risks of his kind of poetry are great. The greatest danger is flatness, that by incorporating the texture and rhythms of spoken prose into verse, the verse itself will become prosaic. Johnson avoided this trap by keeping his poems tightly brief and by demonstrating, as he had done again and again in the prose, that he was gifted with a perfect ear for the flexible spoken language. How easy and supple are these lines from "The Poet Holds His Future in His Hand":

> Tonight I looked at it: I don't often
> it performs its two functions well enough
> in return I keep it reasonably clean
> but quite by chance I look at it tonight
> and there were several dirty marks on it
> I of course looked harder: and they were veins
> underneath the skin, bloody great black veins!

The final poem of *Poems Two*, "Distance Piece," even rudely ripped out of the structure and context of the book, is a dramatization of his method, wherein the opposition of spoken and written language is (briefly) overcome as the two are, finally, married:

> I may reach a point
> *one reaches a point*
> where all I might have to say
> *where all that one has to say*
> would be that life is bloody awful
> *is that the human condition is intolerable*
> but that I would not end it
> *but one resolves to go on*
> despite everything
> *despite everything.*

It may well be that the greatest influence on the formation of Johnson's poetry—as, indeed, the selfsame situation allowed him to exert a considerable influence on other poets—was his position, beginning in 1964 and continuing until his death, as poetry editor of the *Transatlantic Review*. Founded in Rome in 1958 by J. F. Mc-Crindle and George Garrett, the *Transatlantic* was located first in New York, then in London. Although its circulation in the United States was only average for a major literary quarterly, it was widely circulated throughout the British Commonwealth and in Europe, having the largest circulation of any English language quarterly in the world, easily overcoming its chief international rivals the *Paris Review* and *Bottghe Oscure*. From its inception the *Transatlantic* was unusual in a number of ways. It offered no reviews or criticism, only fiction, poetry, and occasional interviews. It published more poems than any other major quarterly, sometimes devoting half an issue to poetry. And its editorial policy was determinedly and deliberately eclectic. Poetry of all kinds and poets of all schools and cliques were welcomed. When McCrindle moved to London in the early 1960s, taking the *Transatlantic* with him, he hired Bryan Johnson because, as McCrindle allowed, only in part facetiously, Johnson was "the closest facsimile I could find" to George Garrett. Both were about the same size and coloring. Both wrote novels and poetry. Both were editorially open-minded and wished the magazine to be a place where literary quality had next to nothing to do with fashion or reputation. The extent of their success (or failure), as they coedited the poetry, with Johnson at the center assuming the chief responsibility, remains to be measured by others. But it is simply a fact that poems came in from poets of all kinds all over the English-speaking world—by the thousands. No question but that editorial weariness, and sometimes ennui, must have slowed Johnson's own production as poet; but, at the same time, he was closely in touch with what was happening in English-language poetry, more so, probably, than any other poet in England or America at the time. In that sense he was, inevitably, an extremely sophisticated reader of contemporary poetry, and in part as a reaction against his own fine-tuned sophistication. Johnson was led to develop his direct, sometimes brutal, always subtly colloquial style. Just as his novels were sometimes defined and criticized as "anti-novels," so his poetry could be called "anti-poetry" in the sense that he felt and saw a need for a certain kind of poem that interested him and that no one else was seeking to explore and develop. By the end, he had become so much the leading, shaping *character* of the *Transatlantic,* that after his death Mc-Crindle was unable to imagine continuing the magazine without him and so closed it down.

Johnson's suicide, coming as he arrived at the peak of his artistic powers, surprised many people. But his poetry, the place for his most intimate truths, shows that life against death was always a wrestling with the outcome in doubt. Despite stiff upper lip and gritted teeth, despite *courage*, despair, for the world, for himself and his decaying and rebellious body, for those he loved and hoped for, overwhelmed him. The last blow, indirectly, was the slow death of his mother from cancer, something he wished to re-create in a complex trilogy of which only the first volume, *See the Old Lady Decently,* was finished and published posthumously in 1975. The weight of this sad knowledge and experience is much present in *Poems Two*, in poems such as "Where Is the Sprinkler Stop Valve?," about how best to urinate on and kill a fly in a urinal—"you cannot beat the random element as in cancer, as my mother knew." Or in the simple, savage "Food For Cancerous Thought":

> The small betrayals
> eat us all away

> the work done for less
> than the minimum
>
> the lickerish glance
> at another girl
>
> the long snack taken
> just before a meal
>
> but we shall
> be eaten away
> anyway.

Where he might have gone as an artist, what might have become of B. S. Johnson in his full maturity, is purely and sadly speculative; but the *Times* was safe enough and true enough in its obituary, which praised him highly for his accomplishment, in asserting that "one could say of him, as of few writers at forty, that his talents might still have taken him anywhere."

A Few Things about Fred Chappell

Surely from at least the time I first went to teach at The University of Virginia (the fall of 1962, then), I was fully conscious of the talent and aware of the work of Fred Chappell. And I had already concluded what I still believe now—that he is one of the best writers of my generation. About which conclusion a number of things need to be said right away. Fred, of course, is seven years younger than I am; and the way that generations come and go, are announced or announce themselves, issue manifestoes and publish farewell addresses in these so-called postmodernist days, Fred may honestly and well feel that he is part of another generation. If so, fine. Still, I am stuck with the old-fashioned, more leisurely, quarter-century concept of generation, and so I can claim him for mine. It is sufficient to remark that we are both children of the Great Depression, both of us Southerners by blood and birth and choice. And there is even some particular overlapping of the sense of place, for though I am (that rare being then and now) a native of Florida, I had kin there and spent a lot of youth in the western North Carolina mountains, close and all around Fred's birthplace and stamping ground. Maybe the only significant difference between us in the experience of that seven-year gap is that I spent some of it away in the U.S. Army, killing time. It is a minor difference in kinds of experience which surfaced only during the late days of the Vietnam War when Fred was a good deal more trusting of and, shall we say, sensitive to the confessions and tales of both outgoing recruits and homecoming veterans. And about all that who knows? He may have been right and I may have been wrong. No question but that he was more open than I. It's just that I had long since lost that particular innocence. Had logged too many hours of hearing and swapping tedious stories ("war stories," we always ironically called them) with other G.I.'s not to be profoundly skeptical of a whole lot of what I heard from the next generation of soldier boys.

II.

It is hard to believe that *It Is Time, Lord* did not appear until 1963, because by 1962 I had certainly concluded that Fred Chappell was not only a very gifted writer, but also a famous one. This has since become a kind of joke between us: how my boss at Virginia, the inimitable Fredson Bowers, instructed me to busy myself and get famous writers to come to Virginia (as cheaply as possible) to give lectures and readings, to visit classes, and to gain "visibility" for the English Department. How one of the very first ones I invited was Fred Chappell, who came up from Greensboro and did everything very professionally and wonderfully well and only told me long years later that it was, in fact, the first public reading he had ever given in his life. For me, he was not only famous then, but remained so for so long, for so many unchallenged years, that his little confession could not begin to dislodge the original thorny (mis)conception. One of the reasons I simply assumed that Fred was famous came from what William Blackburn told me. In 1961, as I recall, I made a visit to Duke (it must have been my second visit there) at the invitation of Blackburn. When the true history of the literature of our age comes to be written, especially of our Southern literature, William Blackburn will have a solid place in it, more than in footnotes. For this gentle and gifted man taught some wonderful writers, helped them to begin to find their voices; among them: Mac Hyman, William Styron, Reynolds Price, James Applewhite, Anne Tyler, and many others, including Fred Chappell. Bill Blackburn was a dedicated bourbon drinker and so was I in those (O, lost) days. One spring night in 1961 we sat up late at his house, drinking deep and talking about life and art and swapping "literary war stories." At some point I was just uninhibited and bold enough to ask him if he would venture an opinion as to who was the finest of all the gifted students he had taught and known.

"Fred Chappell, without any question," he replied. "Fred has the greatest gift of all of them. Of course, whether he will ever manage to do anything with all that talent, and whether he will ever be *recognized*, remain to be seen. . . ."

I had already read both poetry and prose by Fred Chappell in literary magazines, including the Duke *Archive*, and I was already thoroughly impressed with his talent. But from that moment, the moment Bill Blackburn named him to me as his best student, Fred was famous. And he would be, ever after, in my book.

Of course, Fred Chappell really was and is famous, in every sense of that word, in France, ever since Maurice-Edgar Coindreau's elegant translations of *It Is Time, Lord* and *Dragon*. I take some furtive pride in the fact that I was at least one of the several separate people who urged Coindreau to go and have a look at the work of Fred Chappell when Coindreau was looking for a good and gifted young Southern writer to translate.

Within certain circles, especially in the South, Fred has long been recognized as one of our best and most variously gifted literary artists. Allen Tate held Fred and his work in the highest esteem and was not in the least hesitant to say so. Eudora Welty, Robert Penn Warren, Randall Jarrell, Peter Taylor, and Reynolds Price, on the record and off, in public and in private, have been strongly supportive. Wright Morris was an early fan. And many younger writers have expressed enthusiastic appreciation. The first really significant critical piece about him was the April 1973 issue of the *Hollins Critic*, by poet and novelist R. H. W. Dillard. In the decade since then Fred Chappell has steadily gained recognition and more and more appreciative readers. By now his literary reputation is (deservedly) national. It especially pleases the ironist in me that some people, some of those people who are wheelers and dealers, players and brokers of what Robert Frost named "the literary stock exchange," are at last able to permit themselves to display a knowing nod and perhaps a little flash of the light of recognition in the eyes when Fred's name is mentioned. In fact, Fred, by dint of hard labor and unmistakable achievement alone, without any boot or apple polishing, politicking or hustling or swaggering self-aggrandizing, has cracked the toughest and most defensive little elite in the American literary scene—the Poetry Mafia. I am not fixing here to name any names. They are mostly Yankees and a very litigious crowd to boot. And I would hate to find myself and/or the *Mississippi Quarterly* hotly pursued by lawyers and nuisance suits. Suffice it to say, then, since the undeniable and overwhelming impact of *Midquest*—brilliantly brought along, one book at a time, then all together in one volume, by LSU Press—there has been a place set for Fred Chappell at the high table of American poetry.

Prose writers already know him well as one of the most interesting and intelligent (and intellectual) novelists alive. Each of the novels is different in structure, strategy, and style. All may be studied with profit by his peers. But not so many may yet know his brilliant and equally various short stories in *Moments of Light* and many magazines or in the marvelously realized memories of childhood and youth in the forthcoming *I Am One of You Forever.* But they *should* know him as an extraordinary story writer. And I hope and expect they will. I have not even mentioned his critical pieces and reviews, as yet uncollected, which are marked by exactly the same intelligence, integrity, sensitivity, clarity, and brilliance which inform all his other work. There are not many American writers who try to do all these things these days. Some, and they are a precious few, dabble in more than one form. Fred Chappell is no dabbler. He is a genuine man of letters (in the Robert Penn Warren tradition) whose work is important, indeed outstanding, in whatever form he is working in and with. Moreover—and I feel certain that some of the critical pieces here are bound to indicate this truth—all of his work is closely related. The forms, themselves, are distinctly different, true to themselves and to their inherent characteristics; but the pervading sensibility and the dominant voices are clearly the same. There are only a few American writers who are really talented in more than one form or genre. And of these there are only a very, very few of whom it may truly be said that they are equally talented in all forms. Fred Chappell may well be the only one among these very, very few (he is the only one I can honestly think of) who is also the same artist in all things; that is, brief lyric or novel, each and all are clearly part of a larger whole, discrete and independent, yet none entirely complete without the others.

I leave it to the critics and scholars to do him justice in the strong hope that they will. To publishers (any publisher, for Fred's work has been published by the whole range, from large commercial houses to small presses) I strongly suggest that somebody hurry up and bring out a selection of his critical essays and reviews.

This little piece of mine has been informal and personal. (How else could it be after these many years of admiration and valued friendship?) All of it adding up to an unequivocal statement of appreciation, not less sincere or even objective for being both personal and informal. But in that same spirit I would like to include some more personal observations. For there are aspects of Fred Chappell's character which so inform his craft and art that it is no venture in biographical fallacy to mention them. I have already stressed his integrity. Now, Fred (in the tradition of Bill Blackburn) is a gentle, tactful, emphatic teacher. A superb teacher, in fact. And he brings those same qualities to friendship. But, at one and the same time, writer to writer, he is tough and ruthlessly honest, if impeccably fair, no matter what the cost or risks. Fred is not always, not by any means, right; and like every good mind, his is a swiftly changing one. But he is perfectly willing to tell you face to face what he feels about your work at any given time. He doesn't like to hurt, but as a critic he will if he has to. And he expects the same consideration. Yet his integrity goes well beyond this level. When he admires or honors something, he is also willing to say so. He will do so in public, in print. Some very well known writers of our generation will not ever review works by their friends for fear that their integrity and credibility might be called into doubt. One Very Prominent Writer, with a very prominent critical podium at his disposal, is reported to have said that he will review the work of personal friends only when his review must be unfavorable, that a favorable review might somehow compromise his reputation. Fred Chappell, absolutely secure in his honesty, will review the work of friends and enemies alike, fairly, and will call the shots as he sees them. Evidently he sees no essential conflict between loyalty and honesty.

(Speaking of loyalty. When Hiram Haydn founded Atheneum Publishers, Fred was one of the first writers he took on. Later, when, as a result of some corporate hanky-panky, Haydn had to resign and move on, Fred moved on with him. Without hesitation or question. Most of the other writers recruited by Haydn stayed put, placing the security of having a distinguished publisher above any loyalty to the man who had founded that publishing house and brought them to it. One cannot blame them for the choice. But one must praise Chappell for his.)

It is not surprising, then, that pure and simple and sometimes extravagant generosity is an integral part of Fred's character. He gives and gives (sometimes foolishly) of his time and energy and of himself, to his students, to his friends and acquaintances, to others, to the (more abstract) world of American letters. I can safely say that no American writer is more active and open in his support of the little magazines, the often fly-by-night places where our literature is born and lives or dies. A complete and accurate bibliography will offer stunning evidence of the contributions Fred has made to the little magazines and, thus, to better conditions for all the rest of us.

One reason that Fred Chappell has been too long receiving the kind of recognition he earlier earned may be his modesty. Fred is a deeply modest man, though not in the usual sense of that word. In part his is a natural modesty, an animal modesty; that is to say he is as sly as he is shy. And in part his modesty comes from his honesty. Any honest writer of our times, aware of the history and traditions of modern and contemporary literature (and Fred Chappell is the best-read person I know), would have to be honestly . . . *modest*. There are and have been giants. We have lived among them. That Fred Chappell is one of the giants (and this truth is something that even he must, from time to time, suspect, even if he refuses himself the full mindless pleasure of believing it outright) is to be inferred from the fact that he walks softly in the world and allows his work to speak for itself.

Ladies in Boston Have Their Hats
Notes on WASP Humor

This one goes back a little while, to the mid-1970s. It began as a kind of a joke and challenge. At the prompting of a novelist and critic, I was asked to write a piece about WASP humor, if any. . . . Time has passed, and I might do this differently now (if at all). But there were a few things to be said. And I will stand by them.

I.

> I felt a little heavy-hearted about the gang, but not much, for I reckoned if they could stand it, I could.
> —Mark Twain, *The Adventures of Huckleberry Finn*

A man I know who lives in suburban Philadelphia bought a piece of furniture. It was delivered by a cheerful man with an Italian surname. Who looked around and commented that it was a very nice house.

"This house is almost two hundred years old," my friend told him.

"Well," said the furniture mover, genuinely sympathetic, "don't feel bad about it. Nobody would ever know unless you told them."

That, ladies and gentlemen, is a double-barreled WASP joke. Right out of real life. Pretty thin, slim pickings. But it shows and tells a good deal when looked at from all sides.

Probably the funniest thing is the whole idea, the outrageous subject matter of this piece. (And maybe, too, the image of someone trying to wrestle with that subject.) WASPs may be funny, indeed are commonplace figures of fun in a great deal of contemporary literature. But the notion that there are distinctive, characteristic tropes of ethnic humor, forms of wit, comedy, jokes even, which are created by WASPs and may be in some way an influential part of our large and various culture, seems outlandish, absurd enough in and of itself to qualify for a couple of quiet chuckles.

Many of our notions of WASPs and their lives come to us through literature, including theater and film. Much of it is the testimony of witnesses from other ethnic groups for whom the WASP, in abstraction, is at best baffling and most often foolish. The trouble with abstract imagining (a contradiction in terms we all have to live with) is that it assumes an artificial uniformity. In abstraction, all WASPs tend to look and act alike. Take former Mayor John Lindsay. For much of the popular press he was the very embodiment of WASP virtues and vices. A great many WASPs found Lindsay funny, a comic character in both style and substance. For others, especially those who may have shared his apparent political persuasion, he was a considerable embarrassment. But for almost nobody in the WASP world was he an adequate or accurate representative of themselves.

To consider the possibility of WASP humor in contemporary American literature, we have to start with the WASPs' ideas of virtue and vice. And to do that we have to agree on who the WASPs are, what has happened to them, and some of the things they believe or assume. White Anglo-Saxon Protestant covers a lot of territory, literally. There are distinct differences between the eastern and New England WASP and the others, scattered all up and down and across the continent. All are white, to be sure, though the Southern WASP shares much, more than he might admit, with the Southern black. All are not necessarily, not strictly Anglo-Saxon, again particularly in the South. In the sense of Protestantism, the religious background and affiliation, the definition has to be wide and broad enough to include the whole range of sects and splinter groups, from the pure and simple Holy Rollers, say, through the maze of middle denominations, to the Episcopalians. Who, though relatively small in numbers (roughly 3.5 million), remain influential by means of the weight of tradition, social position, and the vague general power of their slowly dwindling old wealth. And who, also, within their own very flexible limits of doctrine, offer an almost complete variety of service and liturgy, from witnessing, healing, and speaking in tongues to the last examples of the full-scale Latin Mass in America. Similarly, the whole spectrum of Protestantism would also have to include those sects which are not strictly Christian in detail or doctrine but are, nevertheless, clearly Protestant—the Quakers, for example, or the Unitarians. Any honest picture of the religious variety of the WASPs, particularly those of the South, would have to take account of other and different ethnic groups with whom the WASPs have joined closely in a more than casual ecumenical embrace—the Lutherans, Scandinavian and German, for example, the Dutch Reformed Church, and (perhaps curiously) the Greek Orthodox Church, with which the Episcopalians have often shared churches and services.

About an hour's drive north of Charleston, South Carolina, off the main traffic route and built beside the broad red clay and dust of the King's Highway, among tall pines and silence, stands the old church of St. James Santee. St. James Santee can stand as a symbol for the relatively easy interchange among Protestants of various sects and ethnic groups. Though nominally built as an Episcopal church, it also served all the Protestants in that part of the lonesome Santee Delta, including not only Anglo-Saxons, but also the Welsh, Scotch-Irish, Dutch, Germans, and the French Huguenots. From the beginnings, in that part of the country, there was a great deal of intermarriage and assimilation among all these groups. Family trees in the Charleston area, and elsewhere in the South, usually contain them all and often, too, a sprinkling of the refugee Jews from Spain in the seventeenth century. The separate Protestant sects have mostly remained separate and, in fact, have, as if by some natural law, continued to subdivide and proliferate; but there has always been considerable freedom of movement among them.

The first point, then, and probably the crucial one in the definition of the imaginary abstract WASP, is the recognition that Protestantism, in all its multiplicity and contradictions, is the key to understanding the WASP character. There are, of course, some separate social forces which have worked to create a sort of hierarchy and to put the chiefly Anglo-Saxon Episcopalians at the top of the heap; but the central element of any definition is the common heritage of Protestantism. The Protestant is always a creature of mixed feelings, or paradox. His faith, essentially heretical, individual, and anarchic, is in constant conflict with the very institutions he has created to preserve and foster it. All Protestant groups are basically democratic, if only in the sense of the equality of all believers. Even the grandest of Episcopal bishops is no prince of the Church, but a representative in a way that his Roman Catholic equivalent is not. The emphasis upon faith, an inner state of being and a mystery, eliminates much of the weighing and judging of outward condition and behavior as a spiritual matter. That is to say, the often and justly cited WASP habit of conformity is, by definition, purely a social and secular matter. There is, therefore, a continual warfare within each Protestant between the demands of the secular world and the rigors of his religious experience. At best it is an uneasy marriage. If good works in the world will not guarantee salvation and if apparent wickedness is not necessarily a one-way ticket to eternal perdition, then it follows that the secular and social world is greatly reduced in real significance. Since freedom of the spirit is assumed, then one is liberated to live in the social world with contempt or indifference for it and with as much convenience, comfort, and conformity as conscience will allow. Theoretically, you pay your taxes to Caesar without a big hassle, tip your hat, and go on your joyous way toward the Delectable Mountains. Seen one Caesar and you've seen them all.

Of course, from time to time—in Calvin's Geneva, post-Reformation Scotland, the Massachusetts Bay Colony, for example—the accidental coupling of Protestantism with power or influence has resulted in extraordinary secularization, or at least an unusual identification with secular movements or ideas. Inevitably this breeds rebellion and reforming zeal among the faithful. Witness fairly recently (*Newsweek*, September 29, 1975) the "Appeal for Theological Affirmation" signed by prominent Protestant theologians which, as described by *Newsweek*, "attacked the church's 'surrender to secularism' and to other worldly 'diseases,' from the activist 1960's. 'People were equating Esalen with theology, a marijuana high with a religious experience, and calling masturbation a sacrament,' says co-author Peter Berger, a Lutheran sociologist. 'There was a readiness for a sobering word.' " From the beginning Protestants have been ready with sobering words against the secularization of their spiritual experience, even if, as is the case, there is a strong and continual urge to transfer perceived spiritual values into the social and political (and transitory) realm of the world, the flesh, and the Devil.

Products of Reformation, Protestants can be very serious about reform and even rebellion. Revolution, however, is mostly meaningless, does not engage passionate attention. The American Revolution was, in fact, a rebellion carried out by Protestant reformers; the French Revolution was a more Catholic enterprise. A WASP will be the first to ask you which one worked, which one really accomplished anything. That secular order is best which best protects the freedom of the Protestant to cultivate his faith and follow the promptings of faith and the dictates of conscience. Therefore that government is best which, while allowing this freedom, maintains the maximum possible degree of order, peace, and quiet. The secular order must be as reasonable as possible. Caesar gets respect, to be sure, often more than he deserves. But behind all that is the absence of any passionate commitment. For the WASP the end never justifies the means, because, in the secular world, by definition, the end is trivial.

Philadelphia again. Why not? W. C. Fields and all that . . .

I am riding east on a train from Chicago. Breakfast in the dining car with two Chicago businessmen, neither a WASP, as the train pulls into Paoli.

"Jesus," one says. "The recession must be really bad over here."

What has prompted this observation is the parking lot at the Paoli station, the cars left behind for the day by the commuters on the Paoli Local. Through his eyes I can see that it looks like a junkyard. Rows of cars which are shabby and old without the ostentation of being antique.

"It's a damn shame what the economy is doing to some people," his buddy adds as the train moves on, right down the string of expensive jewels which is the Main Line.

Nothing to say. Nod and sip my coffee. They cannot conceive of the classic WASP custom of nonconspicuous consumption. Not for them, ever, the patched and cuff-frayed tweed jacket, the button-down shirt with a turned collar.

What we are talking about, when we talk about the comic, is vice and virtue and the limits of the flawed human imagination. Presumably the WASP whose reality is inner should possess a full and rich imaginative life. And to a degree this is true, bounded, however, by the simple fact that the WASP must (as must we all) imagine all others as more or less like himself. Therefore deviations from his own code are either examples of deliberate and savage nihilism, or are the result of some defect, some missing element or defective part. In the latter case the WASP conceives that he is dealing with folly. Mostly, then, those who do not behave like him are comic figures.

Take "fair play," one of the English ideals which has survived the long separation from the homeland. The WASP still believes in "fair play" or, anyway, the appearance of it. He applauds examples of apparent "fair play" and either laughs at or detests and condemns its absence. He is not likely ever to recognize, except intellectually, which (as indicated) means superficially to the WASP, that others coming from different ethnic and racial groups are so disadvantaged in the context of our culture that any rules of "fair play" are, de facto, unfairly loaded against them. "Fair play" prevents WASPs from being efficient and successful muggers. Urban mugging, since it is generally a group or team enterprise in which the victim is, among other things, outnumbered, is particularly offensive to the sensibility of the WASP. The argument that any mugger would be a fool to risk personal safety or efficiency in the name of "fair play" won't wash with WASPs. The WASP admires Robin Hood and the highwayman straight out of Alfred Noyes, but condemns the muggers as both cowardly and subhuman. Vince Lombardi's passionate declaration, that winning is the only thing, is at once meaningless, vulgar, typical, and a little sad to the WASP, who sees the game, any game, as an idle, perhaps amusing recreation, mainly an orderly form of physical exercise. Certainly not as something in which anything of value can be won or lost. Wasps make wonderful losers. For one thing, they are trained by tradition and heritage never to quit or to slack off, not even when further effort is senseless and destructive, until some final official gong or whistle sounds. At which point they will gather and give a jolly cheer for the opposing team and then walk away, having gained or lost . . . exactly nothing. Frustrating to the opposition since, because of that, the WASP cannot be thoroughly defeated or humiliated. He won't admit—it never occurs to him—that defeat or victory have changed anything. It should be added that there remains among American WASPs at least the pale ghost of one old-country emotion. Novelist Mary Lee Settle (in *All the Brave Promises*) has described Britain as "a nation whose deepest emotion is embarrassment." Though a WASP may not be truly defeated or humiliated, he can be subtly embarrassed. Which is almost the same thing.

The Civil War was, essentially, the great WASP war. Nothing in modern history, neither World War, equals that war (in a relative and proportional sense) for sustained military savagery. At the war's end one out of ten males of military age in the northern population was dead or disabled. In terms of military casualties that is more severe than anything we know about, including France in the First War. Russia in the Second. In the South the ratio was one out of four, which is worse than anything we know about except perhaps the Roman destruction of Carthage. The truly remarkable thing, in spite of the real or imagined rigors of Reconstruction, is how very swiftly and easily hatred and rancor faded. As if that war had been a kind of game.

Though the American WASP has long since discarded the characteristic English habit of reserve, he retains a deep admiration for something closely related to it. Open or public display of emotion is clear evidence of a defect of character. The sight of Edmund Muskie weeping in snowy New Hampshire, never mind why, was disturbing if not disgusting to WASPs. Nixon's appeals to cheap sentiment were wasted on the WASPs. Truth is, most WASPs voted for Nixon because they thought he was wicked and shrewd, and they believed that was what we needed. It wasn't his wickedness, but his stupidity that turned them against him. The black runningback who crosses the goal line, raises his arms in a victory V, and does the little dance, is amusing. It's the way They are. Not so much naturally uninhibited as lacking some requisite gear or governor of self-control.

When Robert E. Lee was president of Washington College, after the War, he was asked by a parent to pass on some words of wisdom to his child. "Teach him to deny himself," Lee said.

Another familiar WASP characteristic, the emphasis on personal conformity to certain social amenities, to what the WASP defines as good manners, is rooted in Protestantism. For, if we cannot ever truly weigh and judge the motives and mysteries of others or, indeed, much comprehend the motives and mysteries of ourselves, we acknowledge this fact by and through a rather formal code of good manners which protects us from the temptation. Alienation is a kind of social goal, which is, itself, another paradox. On the one hand it salutes and celebrates the ineffable mystery at the center of every other human soul. On the other it denies the possibility of ever being truly honest and open with each other in this world. (Try to imagine a completely WASP consciousness-raising group.) Some common results of the WASP emphasis on manners are, in the best contemporary sense, "counterproductive." There is the usual and regular danger that manners will freeze into the rigidity of the simply genteel. There is the undeniable fact that most others perceive the WASP code of manners as mostly insincere and usually hypocritical. Similarly, WASPs tend to interpret minor violations of the code as much more meaningful than they are. When you speak rudely (if impersonally) to a WASP, when you cut in front of a WASP in a queue, you are denying, in the deeper language of the spirit, that he is a human being with an immortal soul. In effect, you are wishing him dead. Just so, WASPs take the angry rhetoric of militants (coming from anyone but blacks, and sometimes taking blacks seriously, too) as (a) meaning exactly what is being said, and (b) a violation of their own humanity, their honor. In self-defense, the WASP assumes that only subhumans would be guilty of such behavior. So, under appropriate circumstances, the WASP will take you at your word. Given the right circumstances, now or later, he will punish you for it. WASP folktales and myths are replete with stories of revenge exacted for what others might perceive as minor slights.

Politically also the WASP is a bundle of contradictions. The eastern urban and New England WASP (upper class only) is seen by most people, especially other WASPs, as the classic model of the elitist reformer, the "limousine liberal." The great majority of WASPs, in all other regions, are better described and understood as populists. This stance serves to make them inconsistent, uneasy, and conservative. Socially, politically, and above all religiously, they distrust human authority and view all government (Caesar again) as an adversary. Even when, sometimes, they may share a general social goal with their liberal cousins, WASPs are habitually dismayed by the usual means of its accomplishment—the use of the power of government, especially the power of the federal government. The WASP perceives the federal government as distant, alien, and hostile. (See Edmund Wilson's angry introduction to *Patriotic Gore.*) To the populist WASP, the more distant a secular authority may be from his direct and individual involvement, influence, and responsibility, the less that authority deserves more than rudimentary, minimal acceptance. (See Baker's and Blotner's biographies of Hemingway and Faulkner for the attitude of these two masters toward the Internal Revenue Service.) Local issues, or *very* distant ones, are more likely to arouse passion in a WASP than are state or national affairs.

Economically the WASP may be, as his pioneer ancestors were, adventurous, but never truly speculative. The WASP takes a dim view of speculation. For the WASP, the building of an estate (if any) is a slow and cumulative matter. Very conservative. Which may explain why so many WASPs are successful bankers. It also illustrates yet another way in which the WASP has been out of touch with the mainstream of American corporate life in the past fifty years. American business has been chiefly based upon speculation, serious gambling for the Big Hit. The WASP, rich or poor, has been more baffled observer than active participant in this process.

In a literary sense, one should note that very few WASP writers of any kind, moderately successful or clear-cut candidates for the Tomb of the Unknown Writer, have managed even to stumble into a Big Hit. WASP writers of three generations—Faulkner, Wright Morris, John Updike, for example—have had cumulative careers just like WASP businessmen and professionals. This certainly has put them out of touch with the modern American publishing business and, to a large extent, with fellow writers (see Norman Mailer) of other religious and ethnic groups, who comprehend that to succeed in a speculative society you have to gamble constantly and that, in any case, there is small value and little return in a slowly built, long-term reputation. Their answer to the WASP is that reputation and a quarter may buy you a cup of coffee, but it won't pay bills and earn a living, and it isn't likely to gain you attention or one of the prizes until you're too old to care one way or another.

The WASP view of American history is fairly simple and straight-forward. His ancestors—and, like certain African tribes and Oriental peoples, the WASP is constantly conscious of the presence of his ancestors—settled the wilderness, made the colonies, fought and won the Revolution, created the Constitution and the Bill of Rights, protected and expanded the United States, and settled its federal form, for better or worse, with the Civil War. (A spinoff of this latter was the emancipation of the slaves, to whom the WASP sincerely believes his debt was paid once and for all in the spilled blood of a large part of his male population.) After the Civil War ended, there began the great surging waves of immigration to this country. Not many came to the defeated agricultural South, which, once cosmopolitan, was rendered, by comparison, more homogeneous than the rest of the changing country. The immigrants came, from *everywhere*. And the nation was never to be the same. Deep down, however, feeling much like the American Indian whom he dispossessed, the WASP considers all these others as, at best, interesting guests in his country. After all, he feels, though by the exercise of self-control he might not allow himself to say it, the United States is now the second-oldest nation in the world. (Britain, the old homeland, is appropriately the oldest.) He has the deepest roots here. Those who came along later (ignoring the blacks, who certainly arrived among the first), whether a hundred years ago or late last night with wetbacks over the Rio Grande, have their real roots elsewhere. Whatever he might allow himself to think or to say, the WASP was truly baffled that, for example, Earl Warren, child of immigrants (albeit decently Scandinavian ones), would presume to interpret the Constitution of the United States for them. And when, say, a William Kunstler invokes the Bill of Rights in defense of someone, a Yippie named Abbie Hoffman, before a judge on the bench with the same kind of name, well . . . that's another example of WASP humor.

It is not entirely a matter of pure prejudice. For the WASP, like the original Angles and Saxons and the Japanese, is wonderfully assimilative. (Some would say acquisitive.) At least since World

War II he has put garlic in the salad and wine on the table. An improvement, most WASPs would agree, over marshmallows and iced tea. Chinese restaurants thrive throughout the heartland. Even lox and bagels and cream cheese are not scorned. The WASP enjoys Jewish comedians, black singers and dancers, Chinese ping-pong players. But he is more than puzzled that a foreigner (at this writing, Henry Kissinger) should represent his country as secretary of state. He shrugs like a man with a heavy invisible yoke at the incredible slow dissolve of history which has somehow replaced John Marshall with Thurgood.

On the other hand, severely inhibited by his distrust of, if not full-fledged contempt for, the active, secular world, the WASP is more or less resigned to the mutability ("downward mobility") of his worldly fortunes. He shrugs at the prospect of a continuing diminution of WASP power and influence, thus confirming, by chronic apathy, his own bleak prophecy. Faith has given the WASP the strength to endure, but at a price. He loves his country but has no great hopes for it.

II.

The "Gentile" era was ending—Fitzgerald was dead. Hemingway and Faulkner in decline—and the Jewish one beginning.
—Richard Gilman, review of Saul Bellows's *Humboldt's Gift*, in the *New York Times Book Review*, August 11, 1975

The arts, you know—they're Jews, they're left wing—in other words, stay away.
—Nixon to Haldeman, June 23, 1972

Here is another primary WASP paradox, another raging and rumbling visceral contradiction. Not so much anti-intellectual as indifferent to or, more accurately, evenly disinterested in intellectual concerns, the WASP is to be known chiefly by his feelings. They matter. Yet how are they to be known by anyone, since control of the expression of real feelings is an essential element of the WASP social character? This means that one need not pay much attention to what a WASP seems to think about things. Integrity and honor rank very high in the WASP catalog of ideal virtues. But intellectual integrity and consistency are rare and don't count for much. Was Thomas Jefferson a model of intellectual consistency? Most intellectual activity is trivial to the WASP. The passionate and committed intellectual is seen as belonging more or less to the same order of being as, say, a very tall (and most likely black) man who earns his bread and keep by bouncing basketballs and trying to shoot them through a hoop. In a pinch, the WASP prefers the ball player. Intellectual structures, be they ever so elegant, are on the level of the things kids make with their Erector sets. Freud was funny. Marx was some kind of a crackpot. WASPs enjoy Einstein anecdotes (which I'll spare you) that show him as a befuddled human being just like everyone else. They couldn't care less about relativity or the whole intricate course of modern physics. Except as a game. Matter of fact, one system (Copernican or Ptolemaic) is about as good and faulty as any other. Einstein was a gifted clown, a sort of a lovable panda bear with a knack for arithmetic. He sure came in handy when we needed that Bomb, but you couldn't count on one of them to drop it.

Because of the profound place of inner feelings in WASP life and of all the tensions created by the tug-of-war between the secular ideals and spiritual reality, you might conclude that the WASP would be drawn strongly and naturally to art. Not quite. The creation of art is a good thing, of course, a good outlet for women and troubled adolescents and for funny people with funny names. Finger painting and potting, that's about the size of it. If it keeps them happy, no harm done. WASPs aren't oblivious to the appreciation of art. They support museums and orchestras. But they have a fixed and firm disinclination to keep up with contemporary fashions in the arts. Our grandchildren can in leisure enjoy whatever may survive from what is fashionable now. Meanwhile we can get along just fine with what William Faulkner called (on more than one occasion) "the Old Verities."

Literary art is something of a minor exception. It has always been more or less respectable in the WASP world to be a writer, especially a poet, male or female, if you can afford the habit. Maybe it is not as worthwhile, all things considered, as being a professional or a maker and doer of *real things*, but writing is at least not a dishonorable avocation. (Which may explain, by the way, why there have always been so many more WASP poets and writers than WASP painters, sculptors, dancers, musicians.) WASPs read a good deal, but, again, they do not read much that is contemporary except for nonfiction and the purely practical. Since the earliest days of settlement, WASPs habitually have read a generation or so behind the times. Edmund Wilson noted the great popularity of the works of Scott among the Southern soldiery. And WASPs are just now getting around to Faulkner, Fitzgerald, and Hemingway, and are rather enjoying the experience.

One of the things all this means to the contemporary WASP writer is that he knows that, barring some extraordinary accident, he will not be read very much by anyone. The audience, if any, will not be composed of WASPs. It is possible that a serious WASP writer may gain either or both of the rational goals of writing, described briskly to Tolkien as "cash or kudos," but neither of these is likely to mean much, measured by the standards of his own group. This built-in disappointment is a thread, a whole theme, running through John Berryman's *Dream Songs*:

> Fan-mail from foreign countries, is that fame?
> Imitations & parodies in your own,
> translations?
> Most of the relevant prizes, your private name
> splashed on page one, with a photograph alone
> or you with your lovely wife?

All of which can liberate the WASP writer (again, if he can afford the pleasure) in a number of ways. One of which is the freedom to be funny even at the expense of his own group if he chooses. As long as he is working in some recognizably comic mode, he is relatively immune from severe critical reaction from his own group or any other. Dealt with directly and seriously (solemnly), WASP attitudes appear to be offensive to most other people.

Case in point: James Gould Cozzens, a very fine novelist who, because he dealt with the WASP consciousness of his central characters from the inside, dramatically, allowing them to feel, think, speak, and act for themselves, has found himself very roughly treated by literary critics—as if he not only shared, but also seemed to subscribe to, to advocate their stance and quirks. (This reaction is a little strange. No one has successfully accused Shakespeare of advocating the ideas and actions—"Put money in thy purse"—of Iago, or, for that matter, Othello). Because the customs and habits of WASPs strike others as absurdly quaint when not genuinely reprehensible, reviewers and readers wanted to be reassured, by clear lines of demarcation of authorial distance, that Cozzens wasn't speaking for himself.

There is a good deal of wit and irony in Cozzens's work, but his central characters do not usually see themselves as funny. Faulkner has had the same problem—the attribution of character viewpoint to the author, the "mouthpiece" theory—even when the situation and context were obviously comic. Most notably there is the critical reaction to the lawyer, Gavin Stevens, who appears in a number of works. Stevens is not wicked or hateful by any means; but he is often wrongheaded and, as a result, often hopelessly ineffectual in thought, word, and deed. He is a classic WASP example of the farcical effects of overeducation and overintellectualization. Jason, in *The Sound and Fury*, is genuinely wicked (and Faulkner, in published interviews, so identified him), but he is also a clearly comic figure, an archetype of many WASP prejudices and preconceptions. He seems to be acceptable to critics because he is so completely wiped out in the events of the story—gets what he deserves, and with no danger of authorial sympathy. It's worth noting, though, that Faulkner's treatment of Jason is mixed. Jason's burning of the circus tickets was cited by Faulkner as the example of wicked, gratuitous cruelty. Jason's ideas and illusions—for instance, his rages against "the Jews of Wall Street"—are seen as funny. Harmless enough and typical.

Mixed feelings are at once the raw material and the mode of WASP comedy. As a literary form, it could not really begin until American writers found a language and a way to support the expression of the mixed feelings at the center of WASP consciousness.

III.

> I don't trust anybody who isn't capable of nonsense and moments of
> collapse into ridiculousness.
>
> —Richard Wilbur, *The Writer's Voice*

Poetry is something of a special case. It begins by being special
to the imaginary general WASP who, though he may neither write
nor read poems, assumes that poetry is the highest (therefore
more important) form of literary art. One might note that this
assumption has not been seriously questioned by the WASP poets
of our time. Poetry is serious, and most of our WASP poets have
been modestly respectable, not only in the social world, but also
on the literary scene. The extremely influential American masters
of the earlier part of this century were WASPs—Eliot, Pound, Stevens, Frost, Ransom, and Tate, even William Carlos Williams,
despite a slight touch of the Spanish tar brush of which he was
proud. These men were (typically) highly personal, individual,
eccentric (in terms of immediate fashions and conventions), idio-
syncratic in thinking, simply superb at the expression of mixed
feelings, mixed reactions, mixed states of being. Their highly personal views of human and American history were conventionally
Protestant, even in their singularity; and this characteristic remains evident in the work of different and later poets growing out
of their tradition. See, for instance, Lowell and Wilbur, and Berryman's *Dream Songs*, perhaps starting with 217—"Some remember ('Pretty well') the Korean War."

Though none of these earlier masters of American modernism
is usually regarded as a comic poet, each, in his own way, made
rich and various use of the rhetorical devices of poetic humor, wit,
irony, and the comic juxtaposition of mixed, often indecorous feelings. Stevens did so most often and most explicitly, but even Frost,
in his darkest poems, is seldom far from a cosmic grit of teeth
which might be called a grin.

These masters cast long shadows and remain powerfully influential. The next two generations of American poets, including the
present one, are more ethnically and racially inclusive; but plenty
of WASPs are still found in the front ranks—Warren, Wilbur, Low-

ell (despite his period of Catholicism), Jarrell, Merrill, Meredith, Brinnin, William Jay Smith, Dickey, Mark Strand, etc. Each again, is often funny, willing and able to indulge in nonsense and in "moments of collapse into ridiculousness"; but the tradition and reputation of poetry as a proper form for high seriousness, the respectability of it, limits still, for the WASP poet, the complete range of comedy. Raw and rowdy comedy, slapstick and pratfalls, laughing and scratching have come along from people like the Beats. Who, however, except for the father figure, Charles Olson, did not claim the allegiance of significant numbers of WASPs. Some of these later WASP poets may have affected fashionable beards and love/worry beads, armed themselves with bows and arrows and cowboy hats in real life; but their clowning around in poems has been fairly mild, reasonably proper. These later WASP poets (like the earlier) tend to be well born, well educated; some are quite wealthy; you'll even find some in the *Social Register.* Which is to say that most American WASP poets have been and continue to be establishment children whose principal, and perhaps suffi- cient, act of rebellion was to follow the vocation of poetry in the first place. They are often witty, sometimes funny, and are very lively in comparison with contemporaries like Robert Bly and Denise Levertov. But their major concern has been conservative; to preserve and to purify the poetic language of the tribe against continual waves of pollution. Exceptions? Well, sometimes the late Charles Olson was cheerfully slangy in a professorial sort of way. Major exception: John Berryman clowning in the *Dream Songs;* he managed to create a language as mixed and various as his feel- ings and the subjects and occasions of the poems, but always through the mask of Henry, "an imaginary character (not the poet, not me) named Henry, a white American in early middle age sometimes in blackface," who is a traditional figure out of that vanished WASP form—the minstrel show.

There are some WASPs in the new generation of poets, at pres- ent fashionably dominated by a loose group which poet Brendan Galvin has satirically named "The Iowa City Mumblers"; but none of these highly serious young men and women would seem to be very interested in public or intentional displays of humor. I am thinking of the likes of Charles Wright or Stanley Plumly, for example, whose dedicated (if sometimes surreal) solemnity precludes any joking or fooling around in verse. On the other hand, some of the younger WASP poets, including some of the youngest and freshest, like Leon Stokesbury and Frank Stanford, show signs of developing and exploiting a real sense of humor in their poetry. Time will tell if they are able to keep laughing.

With exceptions granted, then, you will find examples of certain kinds of WASP humor, deriving from the inevitable confusions of being both a WASP and a poet, in the poetry of our age. However, the overall strategy of the WASP poets, singly or seen collectively, is very seldom strictly comic.

You must go to prose to look for that.

IV.

There have often been literary Establishments of those with similar tastes and backgrounds who touted each other's work and disparaged that of the outsider. The Yankee Establishment in Concord had no use of Walt Whitman, disapproved of Poe, and shed no tears over Melville's decline. Concord has long since been replaced by Manhattan, where the literary Establishment takes very good care of its own. But as tastes change, Establishments change.

—Edward Weeks, "The Peripatetic Reviewer,"
Atlantic Monthly, August, 1975

And now, following a digressive route, we take you to Boston, where, according to the tedious old WASP joke, the ladies do not buy their hats (like other people) because, you see, they already *have* their hats. And where, once upon a specific time, WASP humor was introduced into serious American literature.

Early in the *Green Hills of Africa* (a book with a good deal of genuine comedy in it, by the way), the character-narrator named Hemingway and called Papa makes his much-quoted assertion to the Austrian interrogator Kandinsky: "All modern American literature comes from one book by Mark Twain called *Huckleberry Finn.* . . . All American writing comes from that. There was nothing before. There has been nothing as good since." True or false (and it's worth remembering that Hemingway's ideas and certainties are much modified by the pattern of experience in the rest of *Green Hills*), the generalization is a good enough starting place. The New England crowd was the literary establishment of America. Uncontested, it seemed, certainly unchallenged since they had succeeded in destroying the South. Where the few writers who survived either wrote for Northern publishing houses or, more honorably and obscurely, wrote for the expendable pages of their own local newspapers. Both Melville and Hawthorne wrote some humorous material. Cosmic humor you might call it. Even Emerson, Thoreau, Longfellow, Whittier, Holmes, and Lowell occasionally lapsed into intentional comedy.

Wherever modern American literature comes from, the beginning of modern WASP humor in serious literature can be precisely dated—the eve of December 17, 1877, in the Brunswick Hotel in Boston, at the dinner given by the editors of the *Atlantic Monthly* in honor of Whittier's birthday. It was on that auspicious occasion that William Dean Howells cautiously introduced Mark Twain to the distinguished assemblage, which included such as Whittier, Emerson, Longfellow, Oliver Wendell Holmes, Charles Eliot Norton, and Henry O. Houghton. Twain, on the verge of being accepted as a sort of junior member of the club, blew it all with his rough and ready story of the miner in the western mountains, "a jaded melancholy man of fifty, barefooted" who had been visited by three literary types calling themselves Longfellow, Emerson, and Holmes. Describing the speech (after all these years) in *Mark Twain: The Development of a Writer,* Henry Nash Smith tells us: "He is reducing exalted personages to a low status and is incidentally concocting a literary burlesque. . . . It is clearly an act of aggression against the three poets as representative of the sacerdotal cult of the man of letters."

Twain had already started *Huckleberry Finn* (in 1876) and, for the time being, had put it aside. After rising to blow his harsh kazoo in the halls of high culture (the gesture itself being typically WASP and one which any WASP, except the victims, would love him for), he went back to it, together with other things—*The Prince and the Pauper, A Tramp Abroad, Life on the Mississippi*—and finished it in 1883. And, if Hemingway is right, modern American literature had begun.

Mark Twain's stance in the notorious speech in Boston, and as well in the ways and means of *Huckleberry Finn*, is exemplary, a model of what to look for in WASP humor. It is a satirical stance first, its special barbs being aimed at the WASP establishment. Which, in the gentle glow of worldly honor and repute, had lost sight of the fundamental and requisite Protestant contempt for Caesar and his rewards. It is characterized also by self-satire, a saving self-mockery. It is often vulgar and vernacular, violating conventions of decorum with a free-ranging style, using the living lingo in surprising contexts. At heart it is populist, not merely announcing us all as the fallen sons and daughters of a fallen Adam and Eve, but simultaneously celebrating the intelligence, sensitivity, and wisdom of the ordinary, often painfully uneducated human being. Who is set off against the pride and authority (ignorance and folly) of the pointy-headed intellectuals. Beneath and behind laughter and absurdity, it is always deeply serious. The reforming spirit is zealous, if disguised. And finally it strives to be joyous (if darkly so), constructed upon the solid rock assumption that this world, the social and the secular world, as distinct and divorced from the individual, invisible, and spiritual world, is flawed beyond repair and well lost.

Its literary antecedents are to be found in the whole Augustinian, patristic tradition, ranging backward, as Augustine himself did, to include Ovid and the great Latin satirists, Juvenal and Horace. In English its masters are the lonely likes of Chaucer, Fielding, Swift, and Byron.

I find myself talking with a gifted and popular writer of nonfiction, author of any number of excellent *New Yorker* "Profiles." Somebody (maybe me) mentions the work of Tom Wolfe.

"I can forgive that guy everything except his insane attack on Shawn and the *New Yorker*. That was really uncalled for. That is really unforgivable."

V.

He saith among the trumpets, Ha ha; and he smelleth the battle afar off, the thunder of the captains and the shouting.

—Job 39:25

Where are we to look for the satiric spirit of Mark Twain among the WASP writers of our own time? Probably not among the reasonably well known and honorable "serious" writers of North or South or any other region. Perhaps a modest case could be made for some of the work of John Updike, who, though seldom funny by any standards, is often an amusing writer. But crucial to Twain's comic stance was the deliberate cultivation of the embarrassing and the inelegant. This stance is almost entirely absent from Updike's work. There may be many personal and artistic advantages to the strict and slick schooling of the *New Yorker,* but comedy, especially of the raw and rude tradition, is not one of them. Except for the uniformly marvelous cartoons, the ghost of comedy does not haunt the haughty pages of the *New Yorker.* Updike's work can be best and most accurately described as a superior and representative example of contemporary establishment WASP writing, his fiction being frequently threaded and laced with humor (especially with little chuckles at others who stand outside the charmed circle) but always also being far too serious for the author to accept the risk of being laughed at. At no point is John Updike secure enough to dare the risk of being taken as . . . plebeian. He would be much more likely to be found as a member in good standing of that distinguished audience at the Brunswick Hotel than to be mistaken as an ally of the artist who was willing to play the fool (and to pay the price for it) in order to make serious fun of them.

Wright Morris still stands tall as a master of comedy, following in the grand tradition of Twain at least in the quirky, screwball eccentricity of his plots and characters and in the special language and style he has developed and magically refined, exploiting the living American cliché until, thus transformed and renewed, it approaches the edges of poetry. And Morris once chose, critically at least, to define his art and aims precisely in terms of *Huckleberry Finn* in *The Territory Ahead* (1958). Of course, none of Wright Morris's novels—not even the wildly funny ones like *Love among the Cannibals* (1957) and *In Orbit* (1967)—is purely and simply comic. All are masterworks of mixed feelings; and, just so, all, even the most persistently serious, contain sharp and clear comedy, splendidly evoked absurd moments. His most recent work, *The Fork River Space Project,* offers, in addition to a very funny plot and sit-

uation (As the jacket copy describes it, it's "about an almost abandoned town and its suddenly vanished population. Were they
taken away by a spaceship or a tornado?"), a narrator who is a
WASP writer named Kelcey, writing under the name of Serenus
Vogel. But most of the characters, the principals in Kelcey's life, as
we know it, are genuine ethnics with names like Dahlberg and
Taubler and Tuchman. And a good deal of the good humor of Kelcey is based upon fundamental WASP bemusement at the habitual eccentricities of alien cultures: "He had a Brooklyn accent,
a cheerful, blue-jowled smiling face. 'You're American?' I asked
him. 'Me?' he wheezed at me, 'I'm Tuchman. Wait till he hears
this one.' "

But all along the way Morris has also been very strongly influenced by the art and artifice, the imaginative *maturity* of the European novel as he takes it and understands it. The result is mixed
feelings about the American tradition. In his most recent critical
work, *About Fiction* (1975), Morris devotes considerable time and
space to exploring the American "vernacular," with all its emphasis on "true-to-life" experience. In this context, and contrasted
with the traditions of Europe, the kind of development from Huck
Finn is seen as severely limiting to American fiction. "Boys who
tell us all—from Huck Finn to Portnoy—we believe tell us the most
about ourselves. The coinage of a language suitable to a boy is at
the headwater of our literature. Portnoy merely reports to us further downstream, where there is more muck and pollution. Only
the vernacular would prove to be equal to this awesome task."
About Fiction concludes with "A Reader's Sampler," a section of
brief comments on some twenty-one works of recommended fiction. The majority of these are by foreigners—Rilke, Mann, Joyce,
Lawrence, Italo Svevo, Isaac Babel, Céline, Elizabeth Bowen, Mal-
colm Lowry, Camus, Max Frisch, and Gabriel García Márquez.
And only one writer in the "Sampler," William Faulkner, is specifically cited and praised for his sense of humor. Morris's own humor and his mixed feelings are conventionally WASP-like, even as
is his emphatic stressing of the high culture of the Europeans over
the vernacular crudities of the natives. And, incidentally, all the
American writers in the "Sampler," with the exceptions of Ger-
trude Stein and Theodore Dreiser, are themselves WASPs. Even

in 1975 Morris appears (with the exception of some kind words, in passing, about Saul Bellow) to be not very much interested in the so-called urban Jewish novel or, indeed, any of the currently fashionable ethnic taxonomies.

The South would seem to be the best place to look for a supply of WASP humor. There is, in fact, a good deal of WASP humor in contemporary southern writing, but it does take some searching for. The whole Fugitive/agrarian school and tradition, from Ransom and Tate and Gordon and Davidson on through Brooks and Warren to Jarrell and Dickey and Madison Jones, is, with the notable exception of some of Ransom's sly and wry little jokes, characterized by an almost urgent solemnity, and by a passionate attempt to avoid the possibility of being accused of vulgarity. Of course, some of the issues professed and defended by the Fugitives/agrarians have been serious enough and traditional WASP concerns as well, particularly their distrust of urban and ethnic culture as against the sturdy ideal of an agrarian WASP yeomanry. But the distinct absence of humor is as much the result of specific social situations as anything else. One situation is the result of the relationship of the Southern writer to the North, especially to the Northern literary and publishing establishment. Even before the Civil War ended serious publishing in the South, it was clear that the Southern writer, to be accepted and respected in the North, whether WASP or ethnic, had to live up to certain preconceptions about Southerners. These assumptions were extensive, subtle and complex; but it is safe to assert that among them was neither the privilege of taking a truly comic satiric stance, at least on many sacrosanct issues which must be approached on reverent tiptoes, nor the easy right to vulgarity. To achieve success in the North, and most of these did so and most of them moved North as well, it was necessary to cultivate an image far removed from that affected by Twain in Boston; all the more so since the basic *ideas* of the Fugitives/agrarians were and are, despite the disguises of civility and the patina of learning, antithetical to the prevailing consensus of liberalism among the intellectuals of the North. You may find professions (do they protest too much?) of a certain outward and visible liberalism in the works of expatriate Southerners like Willie Morris and Larry King; you may even find some jokes here and there; but they will be very safe jokes at very safe targets. The expression of basic WASP feelings and prejudices may well appear, but usually in a context of clear attribution to the consciousness of a character who still has a lot to learn from his betters. Take, for example, this reaction of Robert Penn Warren's Bradwell Tolliver, early in *Flood* (1964):

> The remarks about her mother were made in connection with an easy reference to her own psychoanalysis, a reference which came to Bradwell Tolliver with as much shock as had her use of the vulgar word for excrement. He knew, he thought, what psychoanalysis was, but what he knew was totally abstract. It was something that happened to people in Austria or London, usually to Jews. Everybody knew that Jews like to suffer anyway.

Most WASPs remain extremely suspicious of psychoanalysis and, indeed, the whole discipline of psychiatry, treating both as passing intellectual fads. No psychiatrist will engage WASP admiration as, for instance, a good surgeon does. In this joke, Warren brings together a pair of primary WASP prejudices, the one against all intellectual systems, the other against Jews. But it should be noted that the joke is at the expense of Bradwell Tolliver and is addressed to, accessible to, a different and presumably more sophisticated audience than Southern WASPs.

A second social condition which has been at least mildly inhibiting to the growth and development of a sense of humor among the Fugitives/agrarians is their singular social position within the society and culture of the South. At the time of the Civil War, Tennessee and Kentucky and most of the land west of the Appalachians (with the notable exceptions of New Orleans and the civilized plantation country of the Mississippi Delta) were not unreasonably perceived by other Southerners as being at best a backwoods where it was not still rude frontier country. In the eyes of Southerners with roots in the earlier-settled East and the deep South, this middle South, home country for the agrarians, is *still* somewhat raw and new. Home for hicks and hillbillies. And so you will not find, for example, such highly regarded writers as Andrew Lytle or Peter Taylor taking the least chance of confirming that image by risking much broad humor. These writers insist on being taken as to the manner and the (mythical) manor born. Which very insistence may well be amusing to other Southern WASPs, who, rightly or wrongly, view Peter Taylor's Jamesian Southerners as, in truth if not in fiction, only one generation removed from bare feet and bib overalls and thus more than a little ludicrous for their pretensions to aristocracy; but which will not serve as the structure for much of a joke outside the confines of the old South.

For parallel reasons, one would not turn to the works of such reputable Southern writers as William Styron or Reynolds Price or William Humphrey, each of whom has been justly celebrated for the high gloss of a *lyrical* talent, for the pleasures of anything that resembles rowdy comedy or hard-knuckled satire. It would be extremely disadvantageous to any of these three writers to introduce much WASP humor of the Twain variety into their works, even if they felt naturally inclined to do so. On the other hand, comedy and satire are richly and elegantly displayed in the fiction of Calder Willingham, especially in the brilliant novel *Eternal Fire*, and in his collection of stories and short pieces entitled *Gates of Hell*. In *Eternal Fire* Willingham adds a functional element of humorous self-parody which is almost indescribable, but might be compared to the art of singing a well-known operatic aria *just* off key. . . . This wedding of comedy and satire, including, as in Willingham's example, an echo of Twain's disarming self-satire, is also a vital quality in the fictions of a number of gifted and diverse Southern writers such as William Price Fox, Guy Owen, James Whitehead, and Lee Smith. These writers may not yet be so well known as their more solemn peers, but they are certainly more firmly rooted in the traditions of WASP humor.

So is the work of Truman Capote, when he wishes to be funny. His work in progress, *Answered Prayers*, so far appears to be a classic and savage WASP satire on the Gomorrah-like manners and morals of the "beautiful people."

VI.

"We are," she said, tenderness and sorrow and love all informing her quiet voice, her brown eyes drowning in tears, "we are all moral octoroons."

—R. H. W. Dillard, "The Road: A Story of Social Significance"

I am thinking here of two working contemporary writers, with many things in common and with some clear, sharp differences between them, who can be taken as exemplary of the best of present-day WASP humor and the range of it. These two are R. H. W. Dillard and Tom Wolfe. Near enough in age to be of the same generation, though Dillard is a few years younger, they are both native Virginians of old and honorable bloodlines; each is a practicing Protestant Christian; both are WASPs and comic satirists among other things. Both hold Ph.D. degrees, and they spent their undergraduate years in small colleges not many miles apart in the Shenandoah Valley—Dillard at Roanoke College, Wolfe at Washington and Lee. And each has developed a perhaps surprising (and certainly not widely advertised) area of academic interest and expertise—Wolfe in classical and Renaissance rhetoric, Dillard in bibliography. Despite much in common, there are significant differences between them. Perhaps the most fundamental difference lies in the fact that Dillard comes out of a family tradition which has long been strongly Democratic and populist. His father was for many years the mayor of Roanoke and, for example, was instrumental in helping John Kennedy to carry southwest Virginia in 1960, just as Dillard himself worked vigorously and effectively for Jimmy Carter in the same area in 1976. While Tom Wolfe has not (yet) been counted as openly active in politics, it is clear enough from his works and his known affiliations that his views are much more profoundly conservative and that his kind of populism—for there is always a populist strain in the WASP Southerner—is more paternal than political. The political differences between them, the distinction, may be seen in their attitudes toward Lyndon Johnson. One of the best pieces of writing about the war in Vietnam is Tom Wolfe's "The Truest Sport: Jousting with Sam & Charlie," collected in *Mauve Gloves & Madmen, Clutter & Vine* (1976). It is unusual in taking as its subject the extraordinary courage of carrier-based pilots flying missions over North Vietnam, in particular, one WASP pilot named Dowd; but one of the principal villains is "the Johnson Administration," which forced these pilots to take terrible and often unnecessary risks. Which stance may be surprising enough and WASP-like in its indifference to the prevailing (and, to the WASP, alien) intellectual consensus. But Dillard goes a step further, goes on record, in *The Experience of America: A Book of Readings* (1969), edited by himself and Louis D. Rubin, Jr., celebrating Johnson as one of the most important of our presidents, asserting that "the first year of his administration in his own right saw the enactment into law of more important pieces of social legislation than any similar time in the history of the republic. . . . The pace may have been slowed by the demands of war and the tone may have been different, but the social revolution of 1932 was restored to full and real vitality in 1964."

For Wolfe's view of the domestic effectiveness of the Johnson years, see *Radical Chic & Mau-Mauing the Flak Catchers* (1970).

Of course the primary, if paradoxical, difference between the two lies in the forms they work in. Wolfe, though he may speak as an unreconstructed elitist, writes in the more popular form of nonfiction, specifically in the terms of "the new journalism" which he at once helped to create and define. Dillard, the populist, is a poet, with three published collections, and a writer of fiction with the aristocratic artistry of Borges and Nabokov, both of whom have recognized his work. Dillard's work is frankly difficult. Of his novel *The Book of Changes*, Wright Morris wrote: "I do believe you have written one of the goddamnest books I have ever read from front to back. The writing is a delight. The fancy elegant and resourceful. I have only one question. Should I read it from the back to the front?"

The range of Dillard's WASP comedy, as revealed in his poetry, short stories, and especially in *The Book of Changes* (1974), is wide. On the one hand, he is fond of one-liners, wacky allusions, puns good and bad, and of wonderfully dimensionless cartoon characters with funny names—Sir Hugh Fitz-Hyffen, the eccentric and defective detective; Pudd, the executioner (" 'Pudd,' he hissed, tears of anger on his cheeks, his bald head flashing, 'you are through. As an executioner, you are a nothing!' ") who eventually turns into a magazine; Winslow "Puke" Guffaw, Klansman and (long before Brother Billy Carter) cheerful proprietor of the Honk-E-Tonk; Rastus Coon, who changes his name to Royal Crown and becomes a militant civil rights leader; Cosmo Cotswaldo, scientist and author of *Darwin's Bassoon*; Sara Band, sexy scientist who looks and acts suspiciously like a praying mantis; a cheerful group of strippers with memorable names like Holly Cost, Tricia Vixen, Miss Hurry Cane, Ottavia Rima, Pristine Peeler. At the other end of the spectrum, the jokes are much more complex, based on literary parodies (including a constant element of self-parody) on elaborate narrative and symbolic patterns which, even as they function, satirize many of the basic tropes and techniques of contemporary fiction. And, above all, in the development of what he half in jest defines as his "post-Einsteinian fiction," Dillard loves to use and to abuse the big ideas, the intellectual clichés and counters of our times. Darwin, Hegel, Marx, Fabre, Freud, Einstein, Husserl, Schradinger, Emerson, and William James are familiarly referred to; but then, so are Mayor Richard J. Daley, Fu Manchu, and critic Stanley Moss. The juxtapositions of high and pop culture, of the serious and the facetious, are sudden and violent. The aim, in part at least, is to evoke the familiar WASP reaction of amusement at the intricate predicaments of intellectual life. Take, for example, Cosmo Cotswaldo's explanation, in "The Bog: A Naturalist's Notebook," of the thinking behind his monumental *Darwin's Bassoon*:

> The key, I asserted in my book, to the darkness and despair of our lives for the last century was that bassoon, for it literally shook the fine mind of Charles Darwin into madness and produced the theory of random selection which continues to this day to deny the place of mind in the movement of nature. Think as you will, says Darwin (or rather Darwin's bassoon speaking through Darwin), but for all your effort, all your subtle thoughts, you are of no more value or significance than the ringing of a buoy bell on a rising sea, ringing and ringing, random and mad, or a cattail reed nodding pointlessly in a winter wind, or one of those hideous little dogs with its head bobbing up and down and up and down in the rear window of a battered automobile.

Neither Dillard nor Cosmo (though he is slowly disappearing in quicksand throughout the story) is a nihilist. The key to Dillard's good humor, often bordering on glee and described by one critic as "joyous existentialism," lies not merely in his deep WASP certainty that neither art (his own or anyone else's) nor intellect, any more than good works, shall be our salvation, but also in his firm adherence to the Augustinian tradition of aesthetics and of meaning in literature. St. Augustine is often cited as his touchstone of truth, never in jest. Excepting that Augustine himself viewed the truth of scripture, literature, and the world as joyous, and the alienation of man from that joy most often as a matter of folly rather than tragedy. All of which means that, despite the apparently trendy surface of his fiction, Dillard is in fact closer to Chaucer than to writers like Barthelme or Vonnegut or Pynchon. In a very serious sense, his fiction is satirically critical of the work of these fashionable writers and many others. It is therefore not likely to be very popular with them or their fans. But this does not seem to trouble Dillard very much. He seems to share Mark Twain's courageous willingness to attack the enemy boldly and on his own home ground.

VII.

"Te rog sa-mi aduci inca o patura," he says, his voice fading and falling. "mi-a fost frig." "An Inca, eh?" says Sir Hugh. "And far from home."

—R. H. W. Dillard, *The Book of Changes*

From among the uneven ranks of the new journalists, Tom Wolfe seems to me to be a powerful example of the persistence of WASP humor and comedy in our own times and in many ways Twain's lineal and natural descendant. Wolfe is "well known," more popularly so than most of our novelists. But the particular comic characteristics of his work, and the attitudes behind his comedy, do not yet seem to have been much noticed by either his admirers or his critics. With six books published in a decade, beginning with *The Kandy-Kolored Tangerine-Flake Streamline Baby* (1965)—and all of them, to the envy of any novelist, still in print—he is certainly to be reckoned with. With *The Painted Word* (1975), dealing satirically with the sacred cow of contemporary art in the New York gallery and museum scene ("Cultureburg"), he has managed to touch a painful nerve, to evoke from reviewers cries of outrage, angry catcalls from the otherwise reserved guardians of high culture. The camouflage of comedy in *The Painted Word* is familiar—short-fused jokes, caricatures, the sparkle and dazzle of the language of the speaker, composed half of shards of the latest slang and half of a parodic inflation of classical rhetoric, and all blithely indecorous; the shifty stance of the narrator, at times the wise naïf, plain and pragmatic as Huck Finn, and at the next moment a kind of shrewd Tom Sawyer with his imaginative capacity to transform the ordinary into the grandly romantic; and above all the burlesque of treating a serious and complex subject as if it were simple and trivial, as if it were inherently funny. Behind and within the comedy stands a firm framework of WASP assumptions. Most reviewers have not noticed that *The Painted Word* is funny, perhaps because they sensed the ghostly presence of these assumptions without being able to identify them. It is hard to recognize a profoundly conservative writer who wears such a stylish, thoroughly modern disguise. The general reaction, like the reaction to his series of articles on the *New Yorker* (as yet uncollected in book form), was that this time he had gone too far.

In fact, from the beginning, Wolfe has been going "too far." There is nothing new in *The Painted Word* except its single-minded focus on one limited subject. All he had lacked was the right subject for his satire, something the Establishment really cared enough about to take offense where it has always been intended. One might have supposed that *Radical Chic & Mau-Mauing the Flak-Catchers*, a paradigm of WASP attitudes on race, society, and politics, would have raised a chorus of critical objection. But there, somehow, Wolfe was on safer ground; for his ridicule of the radical chic of Leonard Bernstein and others came after the fact of strong, if deadly serious, editorial criticism by the *New York Times*. Significantly, *The Painted Word* takes as its point of departure a solemn critical article on contemporary art by Hilton Kramer, identified by Wolfe as "the *Times'* dean of the arts" and "critic-in-chief." The target of his satire is the thriving industry of art criticism, personified in a trio of influential critics—Clement Greenbert, Harold Rosenberg, and Leo Steinberg, "the big fish" of "Cultureburg," all three shown (like post office "wanted" posters) in solemn ethnic splendor in carefully selected photographs in the book. This is, incidentally, not overtly and exactly anti-Semitic; WASPs since

John Calvin have prided themselves on not wholly sharing the long-prevalent and active Roman Catholic prejudice against Jews. It is, then, a more secular than theological prejudice. But the point is clear enough: these critics, like Freud and Marx, are intellectual gamesmen and hustlers, an alien if amusing group, not to be taken seriously or at face value. You won't find many of us, of *ours*, making a buck and a reputation out of the latest fashions (shades of the garment industry!) in modern art. The artists themselves, though shown to be exploited by these entrepreneurs, are also depicted as (just like everyone else) greedy, hypocritical, eager to "make it," hungry most of all for success. Both artists and critics are, then, seen to be hypocrites. To satirize these critics, all Wolfe needed to do was to build upon the WASP assumption that most art is trivial and that all modern art is suspect and probably fraudulent anyway, that serious grownups do not produce it, and that those who profit from it are, at best, confidence men (like the Duke and the Dauphin).

But Wolfe's satire is more serious than that, more deeply protesting and Protestant. It is clearly populist. In the second chapter, "The public is not invited (and never has been)," he reduces "the art world" to a minimal elitist group: "That is the art world, approximately 10,000 souls—a mere hamlet!—restricted to *les beaux mondes* of eight cities." The view of American history is, at least implicitly, solidly WASP. He cites, not in this context with any clear disapproval, the reaction of conservative critic, Royal Cortisoz, to the arrival of European modernism in America in the 1920s: "Writing in 1923, at the time of a national debate over immigration (which led to the Immigration Act of 1924), he compared the alien invasion of European modernism to the subversive alien hordes coming in by boat." The narrator is too sophisticated to assert such a thing himself, but it echoes a deep WASP feeling. More to the point, however, are the pictures of human motivation and duplicity among these foolish artists and critics. The WASP assumption of the flawed and divided self is precisely defined in this statement about the intense desire of the artists to be chosen, picked to be lifted from obscurity to the joys of success—"By all means, deny it if asked—what one knows, in one's cheating heart, and what one says are two different things!" The artist, too, like every other "soul," is a creature with a "cheating heart." Finally there is the scene itself, New York, treated traditionally as Babylon suffering under the delusion of being the new Jerusalem.

Whatever Wolfe himself may or may not believe, it is clear that consistently throughout all his work he has at any rate *used* WASP attitudes as the standard against which to measure and to satirize the contemporary scene. Like Twain, he can be savage in the exposure of the forms of stupefacient pretension and hypocrisy that he finds, special lashes being reserved for all the forms of moral hypocrisy. As a divided self, a creature made of mixed feelings, the WASP is extremely sensitive and alert to signs of hypocrisy in the self. It is, therefore, a fairly simple act of WASP imagination to detect and recognize those signs in others. But, like all good satirists, Wolfe has a core of positive standards, usually implicit, against which the behavior of deviants can be compared. There are even some heroes. Among them are people like Marshall McLuhan; George Barris, the artist of custom car design, "absolutely untouched by the big amoeba god of Anglo-European sophistication that gets you in the East"; and Junior Johnson ("The Last American Hero"), the good old boy and racing driver who is presented as admirable for, among other things, his courage, generosity, independence, honesty, lack of secular and social ambition, and the absence of hypocrisy in his social character. These are classic WASP virtues. Wolfe's moral indignation, like Swift's, is tempered into comedy because there is always at least the possibility of reform. "The Old Verities" endure and, measured by them, most human vices are more a matter of folly than of crime.

Manners have always been important to Wolfe. In such essays as "Tom Wolfe's New Book of Etiquette" and "O Rotten Gotham— Sliding Down into the Behavioral Sink" (from *The Pump House Gang* [1968]) and in the earlier piece, "The Big League Complex," he is particularly severe with the absence of good manners among the citizens, high and low, of New York/Babylon. Manners mean, in these pieces, what they mean to the WASP—first, the self-recognition of the flawed self which should lead to humility and, second, the recognition of the divine in others (thus also in oneself) which should lead to charity.

A spy in Babylon, Wolfe has found his place and the subject for his WASP comedy. He can be cheerful enough in recording the decline and fall of New York/Rome/Babylon because the Augustinian image of Jerusalem, the shining city of faith outside of time and human history, is always there for at least his WASP readers. What he may do next remains to be seen. Perhaps the reactions to *The Painted Word*, like the reaction of Twain's audience in Boston, will serve to liberate him and lead him toward wider subjects and deeper comedy. Meantime, however, the work is there, and in it the traditions of WASP humor burn bright and steady like a small pilot light.

VIII.

Then was our mouth filled with laughter, and our tongue with singing: then said they among the heathen. The Lord hath done great things for them.

—Psalms 126:2

In summary: WASP humor—such as it has been, is, will be in our literature—is, on the one hand, inhibited by a complex cluster of beliefs and assumptions deeply held by most WASPs. Yet, on the other hand, it has been and can be liberated by the intensely Protestant spirit which is at the heart of WASP culture. By definition this spirit is rare and lonely, often incommunicable, rooted in faith rather than in works in any form. And a general WASP disregard for works of intellection and art—these seen and felt by the WASP as being a vanity of lesser breeds—works against the production of much WASP humor. When it appears, however, it is apt (like Twain's humor, its finest example) to be complex, incorporating many of the primal WASP assumptions and attitudes (for it is the purest expression of these) even as it ridicules much that is most characteristic of WASP society. Even as it always seems, to one degree or another, not to spare *itself* whipping and ridicule.

WASP humor is, then, a humor based on paradox and born out of painful conflict. It should not be forgotten that the first Anglo-Saxon poet (therefore the true archetype for the WASP literary artist) comes to us as a humorous figure, an illiterate cowherd at the dinner table (like Twain?) ashamed of his inability to play and sing. Who stole away to the barn. Where an angel came to him and bade him sing and even taught him how. An art not so much beyond as *aside from,* separate from all the power and status of Caesar, all the intellectual brilliance of Plato and Aristotle. An angel visits an illiterate, untalented cowherd. It's a funny idea. What the WASP writer, who is true to his heritage, aspires to is the condition of Caedmon, of faith. Here is how it is expressed by R. H. W. Dillard, in the last words of Cosmo Cotswaldo as he slowly sinks to his death in the bog: "I am walking on water. I am sinking in sand. In either case, both cases, I shall be, late or soon, swimming in air."

Afterword

Much has happened since I wrote this essay as a kind of dare or challenge, begun by novelist and critic Earl Rovit. Who suggested that I could write something about WASP humor if, indeed, there were any such thing.

WASP good humor has been sorely tested in recent years and from all sides. Even the safely dead ("dead white males") are not immune from the rage and ridicule of . . . others. Who would have dreamed it *mattered* so much to them?

Tom Wolfe would have and so did Dillard. Both of them wrote and published novels since the time I wrote my little essay. Their works are perfectly in character and in keeping with what went before but in both cases are bold steps forward.

Tom Wolfe had some experience with full-scale commercial success resulting from his book about the astronauts, a regular gang of Junior Johnsons and every one of them an archetypal WASP. Only the late Gus Grissom was intentionally funny, but they were a lively crew. And the book and the movie based on it were hugely popular.

Wolfe's next move was to create the novel, the social novel he had been talking about and toying with for years. *The Bonfire of the Vanities* was even more successful than *The Right Stuff* and sat high up on all the best-seller lists for several publishing seasons and well over a full year.

All along Wolfe had been trying, in a dozen different ways, to tell his fellow writers, particularly the academics and the fiction writers, that they had been missing out by ignoring or, at best, misconstruing the present scene in America. It may be worth remembering that Sherman McCoy, the WASP protagonist of *Bonfire*, was originally supposed to be a writer, not a broker. But the problem, the oldest problem, was how to show him at work. Wolfe needed a more active, less contemplative protagonist.

Perhaps the primary thing to be understood about *Bonfire* is that it is, in the classical sense of the term, a satire, a satirical story. Though satire is intended, always, as a corrective, it does not concern itself with role models. All of the people in *Bonfire*, all the adults and even, to an extent, the children, are one way and another wicked and contemptible. They are all, one way and another, vicious, that is, *vice-ridden*, victims of the vices of the age and the times. Virtue and virtuous characters are conspicuous by their absence. They are defined by not being there, at least in contemporary New York City. The author's ruthless even-handedness, together with the sequence of misfortunes he dealt out to Sherman McCoy, allowed him to treat the *others*, non-WASPs of every kind and shade and creed, as they are seldom if ever treated anywhere nowadays, except, perhaps, in the utter privacy of silent thought. There are some half-decent professionals who pass like shadows through the story of *Bonfire*. But all of the major characters and most of the minor ones are at best contemptible and at worst beneath contempt. The place, New York, is presented as a thoroughly degenerate and dishonest place, corrupt and corrupting, in general and in detail, and so completely out of control.

Amid the pleasures of satire and recognition and the story of the decline and fall of Sherman McCoy, from "master of the universe" to criminal defendant, not many readers or reviewers seemed to notice how all the *others*, the non-WASPs, in *Bonfire*, behaved as if they had been (as in fact they were) scripted by a universal WASP consciousness. From the traditional WASP point of view they are caricatures, funny examples of their kith and kin. McCoy's troubles, meanwhile, derive precisely from taking at face value values and traditions which are alien to WASP culture. His fate confirms the validity of traditional WASP values. To the extent that *Bonfire* is comedy—and except for the deadly serious moment

at the grotesque Bavardage dinner party where Aubrey, Lord Buf-
fing, tells the story of Poe's tale "The Masque of the Red Death"
and brings on a deathly silence, it is all comedy and often wildly
funny—the comedic core is created by having the WASP protagonist abandon his ancient and time-honored values in favor of the
"secular humanism" of other tribes. Combining the strategy of
classical satire with a journalistic fidelity to facts and things of the
age gave Wolfe exactly the qualities he was seeking and at the
same time at least camouflaged his deeply serious intentions. As
he said in his *Paris Review* interview: "You can have a real impact
with fiction provided that you deal with reality, provided you
want to show how society works, how it fits together."

R. H. W. Dillard's second novel, *The First Man On the Sun* (1983)
was not a best-seller, though it remains in print after close to a
decade (at this writing) which is a rare condition in our era, a time
when the shelf life of new books that are not best-sellers has shrunk
to about three weeks.

The First Man on the Sun tells two different stories which gradually become linked unbreakably together. Beginning with the 413th
birthday of Galileo Galilei in 1977 and ending exactly a year later,
there is the author's personal (if not, by definition, private) story,
a sequence of journal entries made during that year by R. H. W.
Dillard, entries involving real people, places, and things and, of
course, the real thoughts and feelings and perceptions of the author. Playing with and against that story, or accounting, of a year's
passage, is a futuristic fantasy, the story of some Irish Solarnauts,
and, a little later, Xhavid Shehu, an Albanian substitute, who will
be sent off into space, launched from Dublin, Virginia (a real place),
for the purpose of landing on the sun. Gradually the reader will
first suspect, then discern, that the story of the Solarnauts is being
imagined and, of course, written by Dillard during the year. There
are relationships, subtle but steadily cumulative, between what
happens in the life of Dillard and what becomes of his Solarnauts.
Midway through the book there is a complete volume of poetry—
"Selected Poems From Sean Siobhan's *Confessions of an Irish Solar-
naut.*" Sean Siobhan is a gifted and original poet who writes in
almost (not quite) the same voice as R. H. W. Dillard. He certainly
appears to have been influenced by Dillard, both in the form of

his poems and in the contents of the journal of January 1977 to January 1978. Meantime, the story of Sean Siobhan and his fellow international Solarnauts can be taken as a kind of parodic, slap-stick version of the same materials Wolfe used for *The Right Stuff.* Both *First Man* and *Bonfires* are, finally, comedies, informed by a Christian vision which is essentially Protestant, differing in the nature of the story and in point of view. If Wolfe's satirical tale is a masque of the red death, a decline and fall of the empire of New York City, Dillard's gentle and charitable book is even more apoc-alyptic from a grand and cosmic point of view: "We are an icy planet," he writes in his final journal entry, "moving from cloud to cloud, ice age to ice age, all across the universe. Or maybe not. Perhaps the sun will see us through, solar wind and forceful light, blazing us a path, keeping us warm and showing us the way. Years from now when what ownership we have on this cold planet, warm planet, will long since have passed, all this will occur, and yet it is happening now, today and tomorrow, and it is our story, yours and mine."

If Wolfe's models are Dickens, Zola, and Victor Hugo, Dillard's are Borges and Nabokov, almost opposite ends of the literary spec-trum. Both are adventurous writers, playing against the grain of much established social and political wisdom. Which is another way of saying that the clichés we live by are often the source of their particular kinds of fun and games. Which is another way of saying that both of these artists, still busy and creative, are mas-ters of (among other things) WASP humor.

II.

Reviews

Knowing better,
we listen and even we believe for a moment,
as Virgil did, and Theocritus, and Daphnis.
Professionals, but they believed they could feel
those rocks getting ready to sing, even taking a breath,
a stronger breath than any of yours or mine.

—Virgil's fifth Eclogue, "Daphnis,"
translated by David R. Slavitt

Short Takes

Short Stories

I have always enjoyed and rejoiced in the art of the short story. From time to time I review story collections here and there. Usually these reviews are in the chronicle form, a lot of titles and a few sentences about most of them. These are newspaper reviews. I have selected mostly the most recent ones, arranged here in alphabetical order by author.

Lee K. Abbott:
Living After Midnight: A Novella and Stories

Good and bad writers have habits, the tics and twitches of style and substance that serve to identify their work as firmly as fingerprints. Very good writers, gifted beyond the limits of the ordinary, have obsessions, are possessed by them; and in their finest hours they transform obsessions into something close to the purity of ritual gestures to be communally shared with readers. In *Living After Midnight,* his fifth and finest collection of short fiction, Lee K. Abbot demonstrates that he is a gifted story writer, one among the few who are our best. *Living After Midnight* is composed of five short stories, all of which have appeared in literary magazines ("Sweet Cheeks," the only third-person story of the five, was first published in *Harper's*), and the title piece, a novella occupying a little more than 120 pages in print and straining to double itself into a novel. One of the pleasures of the novella "Living After Midnight" is that it manages to avoid that inherent temptation. It is held together by chronology and by a pair of central characters, Alex Allan Reed, called Reed, and Carl Malone Hoffman, called "H-man," classic buddies and cutups in student days at Case Western Reserve, who get together again when Reed is twenty-six and divorced and an associate editor for *Cleveland Magazine,* and H-man is at loose ends and on the loose again after some hard times, including jail. They try to pick up where they left off, and pretty soon they find themselves into some heavy-duty doping and the late-night armed robbery of convenience stores, as much for fun as for profit. This is a sad and spooky, not at all predictable, bright and brilliant tale of contemporary grief, misery, and woe.

Reed is the central consciousness (the fabulous H-man really has to be seen by somebody else, and at a little distance, to be believed), and, like many other characters in Abbott's world, Reed has a hot-wired, high ratio, spinning and churning intelligence that runs full out on a wild, dense mixture of high and pop culture (an index of pop figures would not be at all out of place), big ideas, and quick, quirky little jokes. Mechanical imagery is appropriate, for Reed at times thinks in these terms: "Reed had felt that the cogs and bearings of him were scattered there and there and there, and while the car turned this way and that, he scrambled to bring them under control, the wayward widgets he was. He needed these fittings and toggles and gauges." Reed and H-man, like almost all of the characters in these stories, though these two are the most self-consciously verbal, are fascinated by language, with the magic and mysteries of words. Words are things, not signs. Here, for example, is H-man's vision of Thursday in the armed robber's ideal week: "Thursday, on the other hand, was ambiguous. . . . Ambiguity was a slut. Ambiguity could crush your nuts, or make you hum. Ambiguity—a word which had come to the present world via Middle English and Latin, you could look it up—was raunch, pure and simple." And here is Reed's picture of himself as hip journalist: "He was working hard, twenty-four or thirty-five hours non-stop, a lunatic who could give you 150 words on the new giraffe at the zoo. His was a prose of the bump-and-grind kind, sentences that trafficked in words like 'egregious' or 'whip-sawed' to make their point."

The fact that so many of Abbott's characters love to fiddle with words, together with a special kind of self-transcendent aware-ness—"It was over, Reed figured, the movie of his life. He was just waiting for the house lights to come up"; or H-man explaining why he dropped a course: "It was a musical, lots of tap-dancing. The narrator held up a sign, told me to bag natural science"—may be one of the reasons his publisher claims Abbott's kinship to

Donald Barthelme. Also, for other reasons, Raymond Carver. Two writers with very little in common other than integrity and excellence, and next to nothing in common with Abbott except language and citizenship. With the late Raymond Carver, Abbott shares the knowledge, rare in intellectual circles but certainly not unique to either one of them, that ordinary Americans are not necessarily contemptible and that plain people who work for a living can have as much depth and dimension of character and get into as much trouble as anybody else. With the late Donald Barthelme, he shares an irrepressible sense of the fun and games to be played with the forms and clichés of his art, a powerful impulse toward artistic mischief, and, with that, an ever-present risk of excessive cleverness.

But Abbott is his own man. What Abbott shows in all of the stories of *Living After Midnight* is high intensity, tight focus, sustained concentration, prose that, line by line, is alive and singing. Traditional virtues are evident also. Place is efficiently evoked—New Mexico in "Getting Even" and "How Love Is Lived in Paradise," El Paso in "Sweet Cheeks" and "The Who, the What and the Why," suburban Shaker Heights in "Freedom, A Theory Of." Time is exactly rendered. Here the narrator of "Getting Even" remembers an event: "I had switched on the TV—to what the next day's papers would describe as the 'overreaction of the Chicago police department to the demonstrators,' people more or less my own age, protesting at the Democratic party's national convention." Characters seem to be crammed with the excess and detritus of our popular culture. And the style changes slightly, but aptly, with each story. What the tales in *Living After Midnight* have in common, the linkage, is the repetitive use of certain literary devices, sleights of hand which achieve a poetry and (sometimes) a kind of magic. Each story has at least one character driven by an overwhelming obsession. The results, sometimes funny as can be and sometimes sad, are not at all the same. But the quality of these stories is uniformly high. The level of excellence is extraordinary.

Ann Beattie:
What Was Mine and Other Stories

Variety is the dominant characteristic of Ann Beattie's new and fifth volume of short stories. The twelve stories collected here—two of them, "Windy Day At The Reservoir" and "You Know What," long enough to be called novellas—are told in distinctly various narrative voices, the majority in the first person. One, "The Working Girl," is a bright and effective excursion into the territory of self-reflexive metafiction, in which author and reader actively participate in making up the story at hand, and the story is told by the author-narrator. The rest are more straightforward and traditional in outward form; yet each is different from the other in tone and style, the styles perfectly fitting a wide range of characters, men and women and children of all ages and backgrounds. There are several odd and interesting dogs in these stories, and one duck who plays the piano. Though some of these people are privileged, moderately rich and idle, others are hard-pressed to make ends meet. They work for a living at real jobs.

These people may or may not be unhappy and alienated, but they are seldom shown to be all alone. They live in neighborhoods and are involved with a network of other characters. The time is more or less now—Chernobyl and the bombing of Libya figure in the background. Place varies, Charlottesville and Connecticut for example, and is splendidly evoked in "In Amalfi," a story Scott Fitzgerald might envy.

All of the above may surprise readers whose familiarity with Ann Beattie's earlier fiction has led them to place her in some category or other. The category here is brilliant virtuosity, the exciting and energetic moment, that grace above mere craft, when an artist demonstrably and suddenly goes beyond easy expectations. Old gestures are not abandoned, but are more subtly refined. There is new energy here, and a depth of feeling. These stories of marriages failing or holding on, of loves and losses, of memories bitter and sweet, are sometimes bleak but never without a sense of hope. They are tougher and more mature than anything Ann Beattie has done so far. She made a mark and earned a name in the past. Now she is demonstrating a strength for longer distances. Her future, and ours, looks good.

Joseph Epstein:
The Goldin Boys: Stories

When a writer of earned reputation in one field tests his talent within the precincts of a different form—poet writes novel, novelist writes play, playwright goes west to do a movie— we tend to be skeptical, to look closely, wondering how much professional skill will be transferable and if the level of performance will be comparable. Will we have to make allowances? Will the master of one craft become a clumsy apprentice at another? Northwestern English professor, respected editor of the *American Scholar,* and tried and true essayist Joseph Epstein has no problems holding his own as a creator of fiction in the nine stories collected in *The Goldin Boys.* Some readers will have encountered some of the stories separately, for all have previously appeared in magazines, seven in *Commentary* and two in the *Hudson Review.* But now, in sequence and linked to each other by time and place and a number of recurring patterns and concerns, they show us a wonderful storyteller at work, uninhibited by his editorial habits and losing nothing by comparison with his very best work in other forms.

All the stories in *The Goldin Boys* are set in and around Chicago, mainly in the present time, though they deal with generational differences, and the characters (no trendy minimalism here) have backgrounds and long memories impinging on the present. People come and go—there is a remembered trip across the South in "No Pulitzer for Pinsker," and Harry Resnick, imaginative protagonist of "Low Anxiety," even though he has to stay put, vividly imagines far-ranging fantasy journeys in his Chrysler New Yorker— but everything that matters takes place in Chicago. With the possible exception of Count Peter Kinski of "The Count and the Princess" (and he has spent most of his adult life in Chicago), all these people know the city and take a real pleasure in it. Chicago readers will be at once engaged and challenged by routes taken and not taken as the characters drive all over Chicago and the suburbs in a wide variety of cars they care about, live in and pass through ever-changing neighborhoods, eat and drink at familiar clubs and restaurants (there are a lot of memorable meals consumed), shoot golf and baskets, swim and play tennis at a variety of country clubs, and all with an acute awareness of the weather and, too, sooner or later, what is happening on the lake:

> He drove the few blocks down Lake Street, turned north on Michigan Avenue, passing Saks, Nieman-Marcus, Mangins, Water Tower Place, and Bloomingdale's, while on the radio he learned that a local rapist had been apprehended in Michigan, a policeman had been wounded in a shoot-out at a currency exchange on the South Side, and the Dow Jones had fallen again. He turned onto the Outer Drive just north of the Drake Hotel. The lake was green in the coldness of the March day, the waves seemed not merely relentless but aggressive.

One thing all the stories have in common, something the characters share, is not only the authoritative and authentic sense of a place with all its nuances and shadows, but also some of that place's character and energy and the relentless, yes, aggressive sense of change that seems to be a constant. And there are other constants in these stories. Except for the elegantly realized Paula Melnick in "Paula, Dinky, and the Shark," who proves Epstein can empathetically create a fully dimensional female protagonist (truth is all his women characters are alive and memorable and kicking), the central characters are all middle-aged; and, except for Count Kinski, all are Jews. We know what they wear and what they drive and where they went to school and what radio stations they listen to and how they have come this far.

The stories are of a conventional length, but clearly have more weight and density than many contemporary short stories. There are other differences from literary fashion. For instance, the majority of protagonists are businessmen; for variety there are also a mobster and a literary biographer. Epstein's businessmen are not the same, but each is tough, intelligent, sensitive, and imaginative. And they love the work they do. You can believe in their success and just as easily identify with their problems. One of the conflicts, inevitably, is the collision of different cultural worlds. Here, for instance, in "Kaplan's Big Deal," supersalesman Sheldon Kaplan takes a first look at the University of Chicago academics who are colleagues of the woman he is courting: "None of the men had shoeshines; all of the women wore glasses. No one in this room, he imagined, had been much of an athlete or dancer when a kid, or had trouble with the IRS, or was likely ever to call him to ask if he could get them tickets to a Bears game. No, this was not his room."

Language binds the stories also. Five are first-person stories; all are accessible, characterized by clarity and that aptness of style to substance that our ancestors called decorum. The four third-person stories differ in tone according to subject and central character, but all share the good storyteller's habit of pushing the narration as close to first person as possible. This is a kind of magic trick in fiction, but it is the stock and trade of the experienced essayist. Similarly the habit of the pithy and pertinent aphorism is shared by most of Epstein's narrators.

The remarkable, deeply moving title story, an account, told by a friend, of the doomed lives of the gifted (golden) Goldin twins, asks big questions as it deals with the mystery of talent and squandered gifts. This story is a beauty, a little masterpiece, which sets the tone for the whole collection even as it proves that Joseph Epstein's gifts are true and abundant and altogether enviable.

Allan Gurganus:
White People: Stories

It will not surprise anyone who has read Allan Gurganus's *Oldest Living Confederate Widow Tells All* that the author loves to tell stories; and not just that—he loves storytellers and the art and craft of storytelling, too. He takes and shares pleasure in imagining, then bringing forth a rich variety of voices. In his novel and now in the stories of *White People,* Gurganus tries out voices, tries on voices like somebody, half in jest and half in deadly serious concentration, tries on hats in front of a mirror. It's a wonderful kind of hat trick, at once childish and new and strange and old as . . . well, storytelling. Remember Hector trying on his helmet for size, in the presence of his wife and child, just before that great warrior goes out to face Achilles? What I mean to say is that Gurganus is a storyteller in the grand tradition, belongs there; and though he is clearly and fully familiar with the latest gestures of contemporary fiction—constantly shifting tenses, changing points of view, the turning of time forward and backward, and a self-reflexiveness that seems to dare the reader to come forward and help to shape the story—still his stories are strongly traditional in their accessibility, in their amplitude. The whole thing about the influential but fading fashion of what has been called, crudely enough, "minimalism," is not a matter of fat or thin, long or short, but rather a kind of deft shadow play. Minimalism is always less than meets the eye. Worldlier than thou, the minimalist seems forever clever, hardly ever clumsy. It is very hard to be ample and accessible these days and to sound smart at the same time.

In his novel and now in the eleven stories gathered together in *White People,* Gurganus manages to do that gracefully and skillfully. The stories are of varying length; the shortest, "It Had Wings" (an old widow finds a handsome and youthful fallen angel in her backyard and sends him on his eternal way), is four pages; "Blessed Assurance" (an older man confesses a complicated guilt from his youth, when he sold funeral insurance to poor and exploited blacks) is a sixty-page novella, dense and fully developed. Similarly the stories are various in form and content. Settings vary: "Condolences to Every One of Us," though framed in a letter from a lady in Toledo, Ohio, concerns events during a revolution in a remote African country; the mildly Kafkaesque "Art History" is in Eastern Europe before the walls came tumbling down; the highly satirical "America Competes," another epistolary tale, has a scene or two in New Hampshire; the sadly erotic gay story "Adult Art" is set in a heartland urban anywhere; most of the others are set in the author's homeplace—eastern North Carolina. Though they move freely in time, most are set in this century, quite precisely according to generation and decade, for Gurganus has a serious interest in and a good eye and ear for the appropriate quotidian detail, the right phrase for the right time. One story, "Reassurance," is in the form of two letters, one an actual letter by Walt Whitman, the other a ghostly or dreamed (or anyway, imagined) letter from a dead Union soldier, Frank H. Irwin of Company E, Ninety-third Pennsylvania, to his mother, both from the early summer of 1865.

All but one of the stories are dated by the author, five from the

1970s and five from the 1980s, the most recent—"Reassurance" and "Blessed Assurance"—dating from 1989, and arranged more or less chronologically. The stories are various, too, in the places where they first appeared. "Minor Heroism: Something About My Father" was first published in the *New Yorker*. *Harper's* published four stories. Others came out first in literary magazines— the *New American Review*, the *Paris Review*, the *Quarterly*, *Granta*— and a couple of chapbooks; "Adult Art" was published in *Men on Men: Best New Gay Fiction.*

All of this forms a strong first impression of diversity, and yet there is much which binds the stories of *White People* much more closely together than the anthology format suggests. For one thing there are, carefully scattered, the closely autobiographical stories: "Minor Heroism: Something About My Father," "Nativity, Caucasian," "Breathing Room: Something About My Brother," "A Hog Loves Its Life: Something About My Grandfather." These constitute about half the book and involve the author's overt stand-in, Bryan, together with Bryan's father and mother, brother Bradley, grandparents and others. The stories also involve some overlapping of events and information, becoming, thus, dependent on each other and, indeed, upon the sequence in which they appear. They become a continuing story we come back to, the backbone of all the rest. All of the stories, one way or another and pushing the limits of possibility, are first-person stories. They are, therefore, and even in the epistolary stories, spoken stories, composed in and for speech rhythms. They work well, maybe even best, when read out loud. In any case, it helps to listen to them as you read. So, though there are many voices and styles, well executed, there is also, behind them all, an authorial style. It is made up of sentences that are graceful, often witty and funny, always well turned, and not without the spice of continual surprise to save them from predictability. In construction, long or short, Gurganus takes his time, knowing that urgency in a story is a cumulative quality, that suspense builds like the longest journey, one step at a time.

But, all said and done, the unity of this collection stands or falls, works or doesn't, on the basis of its subjects, its themes. Greater or lesser, they are recurring. The conflicts—art versus commerce, love against greed, open-mindedness against rooted bigotry, old versus new and young—are constants. And so is the primary image evoked by the title and sustained throughout, the place of white people in a changing world. Except for Ardelia, in "Breathing Room," "our lifelong helper, cook, and company," and the marvelously realized (and terribly important) Vesta Lotte Battle of "Blessed Assurance," all the characters in these stories are white people and suffer on account of it. The stories are linked by a color symbolism. Whiteness is associated with sickness, pain, blankness, rigidity. And, in "Breathing Room," the sixth grader, Bryan, learns what this adds up to from his teacher, Miss Whipple: "If a group cannot bend, it fails to grow—it loses out to heartier and therefore worthier life forms." Clearly here and elsewhere, and sometimes with more than a little sentimentality, the author is making a statement. But he is too Southern to be rude or insistent about it. When it comes to this statement, like any other, you can take it or leave it. Trust these tales and through them you will come to know and enjoy the teller, who can tell his stories as well as anyone alive and kicking in our time.

Alyson Hagy:
Hardware River: Stories

> If I could tell them the story of my growing up and turning away—the slow, frightened moment I set myself in retreat—I'd want it to sound as true and clear as the call of a cardinal on a lone cedar branch.
>
> —"Native Rest"

At first impression the chief characteristic of the seven first-rate stories that are gathered together in *Hardware River* is their variety. A couple ("The Grief Is Always Fresh" and "Kettle of Hawks") are novella length and as populated and eventful as many novels. "A Seeming Mermaid," on the other hand, is "sudden fiction," short, lyrical, tightly focused. No two are told from precisely the same point of view. And though most of the stories are set in Virginia, chiefly in a line running from the Shenandoah Valley into the mountains of the southwest, the settings go as far afield as Scotland and Nicaragua. Finally, there is a wide range of language, sometimes within the same story, from the bedrock of accurately rendered country talk to some breathtaking lyrical high-flying. The first impression of Alyson Hagy's work is of a wonderful virtuosity joined together with an unfailing accessibility. Sentence by sentence they are a pure pleasure to read.

Taken together, however, the stories add something more, build toward a unity and power beyond virtuosity and skilled writing. Each of these splendidly physical and sensuously realized stories, one way and another, has to do with love and with loss, often marked by an uncontrollable sexuality. Though she is graceful and never pornographic, Hagy writes about various kinds of sexual drives with the unflinching empathy of D. H. Lawrence at his finest. All of the stories, no matter where set in fact, center around rural life in Virginia; and Hagy can render setting—the New Market Battlefield in "The Field of Lost Shoes"—or a timeless, quotidian event—washing a horse in "Kettle of Hawks"—with easy authenticity. And, with the first and title story setting the tone, all of these stories refer directly to and echo the resonance of folk music.

A native of Rocky Mount, Virginia, Alyson Hagy is a young writer who taught at the University of Virginia and now teaches at Michigan. Her first collection, *Madonna on Her Back* (1986), received widespread and enviable reviews. *Hardware River,* coming from a major publisher, seems likely to earn her work even more attention and a host of new readers.

William Peden:
Fragments and Fictions: Workbooks of an Obscure Writer

It should be no surprise that William Peden's new book, a collection of related stories and his first book of stories since *Night in Funland* (1968), is a highly sophisticated, albeit adroitly accessible and highly individual, exploitation and transformation of some of the most immediate concerns and fashions of contemporary fiction. Critic, scholar, editor, longtime teacher of literature and writing, founder and, for a time, director of the distinguished University of Missouri Press, Peden has inevitably been not so much a close student of as an active participant in a half century of our literary life and history. For many years, together with the late Ray B. West, Peden served as the most prominent reviewer-critic of the short story, his reviews regularly a feature of the *New York Times Book Review* and the old *Herald Tribune*. Probably nobody alive knows as much about the directions and diverse possibilities of short fiction in our time. Married to translator Margaret Sayers Peden, who translates Carlos Fuentes and other outstanding Latin American writers, he has likewise been unavoidably exposed to the whole Latin American tradition, which, with its self-reflexive forms and the free-wheeling distortions of factual truth into the level of experience called "magic realism," has haunted the art of many contemporary American writers.

It is somewhat helpful (though not strictly necessary) to know who William Peden is and something about him and his life at the outset, a condition the publisher seeks to create with the efficient use of pertinent jacket copy. Partly autobiographical, *Fragments and Fictions* is mostly about the writing life and the making of fiction, a subject it shares with any number of recent collections by well-regarded writers. For example: Nicholas Delbanco's *The Writers' Trade* (1990) and Leonard Michaels's latest collection, *Shuffle* (1990). Peden's collection is constructed somewhat differently than either of these, though Michaels uses a "journal" also. It is, in fact and despite initial impression, a carefully structured and unified experience, all of it arising from the life and imagination of the same central character, the author. The curtain raiser, "Fragments from the Workbooks of an Obscure Writer," is precisely that, no more and no less, a sequence of more than three hundred notebook entries of varying length, subject, and purpose, authentic in format and without any explanation, exposition, or interruption. We are simply set to reading the private notes and, thus, in a sense the thoughts and notions, of the author. There are one-liners; lists, including titles and subjects for possible use; anecdotes; paradoxes and nuances both funny and sad; encounters with and judgments of a wide variety of people known and unknown. Many of these encounters and people are literary. Some of them are (in order of appearance): Fred Chappell, Andrew Lytle, Brendan Behan, Erskine Caldwell, Dylan Thomas, James Baldwin, Nelson Algren, Jorge Luis Borges and Carlos Fuentes, Mary McCarthy, Allen Sea-ger, Katherine Anne Porter, George P. Elliot, Vance Bourjailly, Ward Dorrance, Denis Devlin, Allen Tate, Tom McAfee, Don Drummond, Ben Belitt, Hardin Craig, Robert Penn Warren, Hortense Calisher, W. D. Snodgrass, Jean Stafford, John Cheever, etc. The rhetorical effect of all this is simple and natural. Not name dropping; these names coexist easily with others not known and not literary; rather they are the natural texture of a varied literary and academic life with conventional encounters over several generations. Here an explanation of the adjective *obscure* is in order. I take it as not disingenuous; that is, it is neither an expression of false nor well-deserved modesty. It is not so much that the writer-author is famous or not. That common definition ("of little or no prominence") is only one of many paradoxical implications of the word. I take it as having most to do with light and darkness, with a shadowy world. In and among the shadows we begin to discern some things about the character and consciousness of the author who will, in "Mini-Fictions," the second half of the book, present fifteen short-short stories, written by William Peden, and all but one, "Dead Bird in the Basement," published in twelve different literary magazines and two anthologies. In other words, the first part of the book introduces us to and gives us a complex first impression of the man who wrote the stories, but not in any other sense than as a writer talking to himself. From the apparently random sequence of notes and notions we quickly learn a number of crucial things about the inward and spiritual man: that he is sensitive to and struck by all kinds of deformity and ugliness and full of straightforward pity for human suffering; that he loves what is beautiful and of good report, though the former includes much more than obvious impression and the latter must always be tested for its quotient of hypocrisy; that the gratuitous cruelty of human beings and the random cruelty of events moves him to an almost ineffable sadness and compassion; that sex is much on his mind, both the force and the high and low comedy of it; that dreams and day dreams are an important part of his consciousness, and that his mind and spirit are open to mystery, to experience which, if not supernatural, is without easy rational explanation. By the end of the "Fragments" we have met and enjoyed the company of a decent, joyous, compassionate, vigorous, altogether likable man.

The fifteen short–short stories following are another step forward, by him as well as about him. There are interesting relationships, sometimes intricate ones, between the notes and the stories. Some of the notes are directly used to make fictions, and some of these are subtly or radically transformed. Others come from other sources and inspiration yet are closely, if obscurely, related to the essence of the "Fragments" and the man who made them. The stories, all more or less autobiographical, have no easily discerned sequence except that they seem to move more and more toward the supernatural, developing from more or less mundane texture to the final story, "The Polar Bear in the Ozarks," a superior example of down-home, homegrown "magic realism."

This is a wonderfully interesting and instructive little book, itself a kind of short course in the complex pleasures of the creative process as well as being a demonstration of the art and craft of fiction by an artist at the peak of his powers. Peden's mastery of the tropes of the very latest fashions is also, in and of itself and not surprisingly, a critical act, an invitation to new forms and directions in the art of fiction.

Wallace Stegner:
Collected Stories of Wallace Stegner

Here we have thirty-one short stories, gathered out of Wallace Stegner's two earlier collections, *The Women on the Wall* (1950) and *The City of the Living* (1956), together with some others that, in various forms, found a place in several of his novels, including, most recently, *Recapitulation* (1979). Stegner's first book, the novel *Remembering Laughter,* was published in 1937. Since then he has published fourteen other works of fiction, ten books of nonfiction, and has edited *The Letters of Bernard DeVoto* (1975). He was awarded the Pulitzer Prize for his novel *Angle of Repose* (1971) and the National Book Award for *The Spectator Bird* (1976). A long life, then (born 1909), and a long, productive, and distinguished literary career.

The stories in this large and various collection range across all the years of that lifetime and the places the author has known. The largest body, a dozen stories scattered throughout the collection, enough to make a fair-sized book in and of themselves, are the hard-edged and utterly unsentimental tales of the life Stegner knew (and knew of) as a farm boy in Saskatchewan, a life that demanded as much as a man had and more. Here, it is described by a young Englishman in 1906, in "Genesis," surely one of the finest stories of a cowboy's life ever written by anyone: "And he thought he knew the answer to the challenge Saskatchewan tossed him: to be invincibly strong, indefinitely enduring, uncompromisingly self-reliant, to depend on no one, to contain within himself every strength and every skill." The young Englishman learns that he underestimated the unimaginable challenge by a good deal.

Matching these Saskatchewan stories are several equally hard-nosed accounts of country life in upper Vermont, where Stegner has spent at least his summers for the past forty-five years or so. These stories—"Hostage," "The Sweetness of the Twisted Apples," "The Traveller," and, especially, "Saw Gang," a celebration of the tradition of work well done—honor the toughness, the rectitude, and the integrity of the people there. Some of Stegner's happiest evocations of the natural environment, always a powerful and energetic force in his work, are found in these stories.

But his fine-tuned sense of time and what he allows in the foreword to be a "tyrannous sense of place" are not at all restricted to rural settings or characters. He can easily create the World War II home front in California in "The Women on the Wall"; the same period in Mexico in "The Volcano"; Salt Lake City in the Jazz Age in "Maiden in a Tower"; in "Impasse" the Riviera in the 1950s. He can present, with equal success and emphasis, Luxor, Egypt ("The City of the Living"), Manila ("Something Spurious From the Mindanao Deep"), the Los Angeles barrio ("Pop Goes the Alley Cat"), and glittering Bay Area highlife ("Field Guide to the Western Birds").

Variety—of place and of time, of characters (men and women and children are all gracefully given their due), and of styles tailored to fit well and unostentatiously with the particular circumstances of a specific story—is the primary, perhaps surprising experience of the book. In recent years we have grown accustomed to the limited habits of one tone of voice and to the imposed unities of one theme or point of view. What holds Stegner's stories together is at once stronger and more subtle. In part it is the investment of himself, making these stories what he modestly calls "a sort of personal record" in the foreword, by becoming equally engaged in all of them, long or short, large or small, deep or slight. He serves his forms and never bullies them or the reader either. He has every technical skill and the craft and good manners to camouflage his sleights of hand.

But he has some other extraordinary gifts. One of these is an astonishing ability to present the sensuous affective surfaces of whatever world we are invited to share. His evocative use of all five senses is a stunning accomplishment. Nobody I know of, not even the master of it, Nabokov, wakens and incites the sense of smell like Stegner; and a younger virtuoso, say John Updike, could learn more than a trick or two. All of which is to say every story in Stegner's *Collected Stories* bears the indelible signature of an artist. More than that, there is something some of the writers of his generation possessed that seems rare enough these days, perhaps soon to be gone for good. This is a complex notion, but, identified in its simplest form, it is the unerring capacity of the artist to be unselfconsciously at ease with all the social kinds and classes of America. Thus a character may be mysterious at center but never simply exotic. It seems that the best writers of his generation, and Wallace Stegner ranks among them, were able to imagine themselves into any set of skin and bones they wanted to, without contempt or sentimentality and with a full awareness of the limits of our knowing and imagining, even of ourselves. Stegner is fair to his characters in ways we have almost forgotten.

This is an age for the short story and this year will see the publication of many new collections. Some will be very fine, indeed. None will be better or more worthy of admiration than Wallace Stegner's *Collected Stories*.

Marianne Wiggins:
Bet They'll Miss Us When We're Gone: Stories

The first impression of the stories gathered together in *Bet They'll Miss Us When We're Gone,* Marianne Wiggins's sixth work of fiction, second collection of short stories, and her first publication since the successful novel *John Dollar*, is of extraordinary variety and of an almost assertive virtuosity. There is some truth in this impression on both counts. Each of the thirteen stories is told in a different voice or, in the special case of the three more or less autobiographical stories—"Croeso I Gymru," "Zelf-Portret," and "Grocer's Daughter," where the central character and narrator is clearly Marianne Wiggins, American writer, they are told in different tones of voice. Truth is, the three more personal stories stress different aspects of the author-narrator's perceived and revealed self; and the language, though always appropriate, is different in each of these, also, just as style and tone seem to differ distinctly in all the other tales. Some are quite short; for example, "A Cup of Jo" (three pages), in which an old man writes an imaginary letter to a dead friend, or "Grocer's Daughter" (five pages), in which the author summons up and shares some memories of her father. Others are of conventional lengths. The stories are firmly set in a variety of places—Tidewater Virginia and elsewhere in the United States, but also in Amsterdam, Zaragoza, London, and Wales. And the author has differentiated them, each from the other, by indicating at the end of every story the place and the month (in the case of "Evolution," the season) of composition. This listing tells us that the earliest story was written in May of 1979, the most recent in November of 1990. Seven were created in London, beginning in 1985; the others were written in Wales, Williamsburg, Martha's Vineyard, and "Welsh Borders."

In another kind of writer and within another sort of context all this might seem an affectation at the least. Here it proposes not to be. The relationship of the writer to her materials becomes an important part of the experience, thus the structure of this book. One notices at once that, for the most part, the place of creation bears next to no relation to the place of the story. It may; there's nothing rigid about this: "Millions" is set in contemporary London and was written there; "Croeso I Gymru," which comes closest to the spontaneous recording of what will interest many readers, the recent hard times of Wiggins and her ex-husband, Salman Rushdie ("We were on the lam in Wales, running through the Black Mountains like unarmed smugglers from the righteous with their guns"), is set in Wales and written there. Most are written, it seems, where they occurred to her, when they came to her; and this is in keeping with her theory of inspiration, explicitly declared in "Zelf-Portret": "Stories come like storms, they come like weather or natural disasters." Of course, a little later in the same tale she says: "The list of possibilities is endless and the writer always lies."

Gradually, then, one discovers, among these very different stories, whose differences are so emphasized, there are other forms of unity fitting them all together, hand in glove. All the stories are, one way and another, about memory, its persistence and failure. All are about language, the magic and the mystery of words, of real and imaginary names. All, even the most sophisticated, set out to prove the pathetic limits of thinking, of the human mind and the kinds of confused knowledge that thinking depends on. Here is the not uneducated Vy, the narrator of "Evolution," explaining something to herself and the reader: "Mutagens you will remember are those little chemical whatsos that cause changes in genetic throne rooms of our cells by mechanisms still unknown. This was in the *New York Times* last week dateline MADISON WISCONSIN so you know it's not elitist Northeast crap." Plagued by ignorance and superstition, often aliens even in their own homeland, mostly loveless and even without much desire unless it is an urge toward cruelty and a longing for death, the characters are from all walks of life and are oddly equal and are presented with an equalizing and hard-edged and pitiless irony.

Yet even this, as all things under the sun, changes. The final story, the first-written "Grocer's Daughter," in which Marianne Wiggins celebrates her father and her "shameless" love for him, is tender, loving, vulnerable, wounded. Suddenly all the wounds she has created for her characters, including herself, in the twelve preceding stories, can be seen in a new light, shadowy with sorrow and pity. These thirteen stories, brilliantly executed, end with a small, earned sense of unquenchable affirmation. This book should justly earn its author both attention and appreciation.

Mary Johnston

The Long Roll

I.

When the life and work of Mary Johnston (1870–1936) are discussed at all, there are several things that are usually said. About her life it is usually noted that she was a wonderfully well-read writer, though except for the briefest of periods (three months) never formally in school. She was privately tutored and self-educated. It is remarked that by the age of nineteen, following the death of her mother, she assumed the parental responsibility for her younger brothers and sisters and likewise served her father, John William Johnston, as companion, hostess, and housekeeper, until his death in 1905. After which she looked after herself and the others in the family, earning her living chiefly as a novelist.

Born in Buchanan in the Shenandoah Valley, close by the James River and at the edge of the Blue Ridge Mountains, she lived in Birmingham, Alabama, New York City, and Richmond, Virginia, and traveled with her father to England, Scotland, Ireland, France, and Italy. Later travels took her all over Europe and to Egypt, an amazing itinerary for a young woman of that age and of her background. A few years after her father's death, she bought, built, and lived in a large house, "Three Hills," beautifully situated on a high hilltop in Bath County near Warm Springs, Virginia. With her advances and earnings as a novelist she held on to this mansion for the rest of her life, though, in order to save it, she felt forced to change publishers (from Houghton Mifflin to Little, Brown, both Boston firms) and, as well, to take in boarders from time to time to make ends meet. "Three Hills" is still there, privately owned and serving as an inn and a restaurant.

The intellectual life and development of Mary Johnston is interesting enough to divert attention from her art. She was a leader in the Equal Suffrage movement and was instrumental in the formation of the Equal Suffrage League of Virginia. She was more than casually interested in socialism and studied its literature and attended some socialist party meetings. During World War I she was at least allied with those who were part of the pacifist movement. She studied science and was fascinated by many aspects and applications of evolutionary theory. In her mature years she became deeply interested in psychic phenomena and mysticism.

Her literary life and career are interesting and even unusual in a number of ways. Beginning in 1898 with *Prisoners of Hope* she was the author of some twenty-two works of fiction, one nonfiction book, and a published drama written in blank verse (*The Goddess of Reason*, 1907). A number of her works were successfully translated into film; several, early and late, proved to be best sellers; and one, her second novel, published in her thirtieth year, *To Have and To Hold* (1900), a novel concerned with the Jamestown settlement, was an enormous popular and commercial success, a true "blockbuster" before that term was invented, reportedly selling something in the neighborhood of 500,000 copies in hardcover. She was certainly, from that moment on, a "known" writer, for better and worse. Well and widely read in her own American literature—she was moved and influenced, one way and another, by James, Cooper, Hawthorne, Emerson, and Whitman—she also knew Thomas Hardy and J. M. Barrie of the British older generation; was both friend and correspondent to her colleagues Ellen Glasgow and Evelyn Thomson; and, by attending a number of conferences, she at least met some of the younger generation of moderns. For example, in the fall of 1931 she was one of the thirty-three Southern writers who assembled, at the invitation of Ellen Glasgow and Professor James Southall Wilson, at the University of Virginia for a conference of several days. Among those who were also present were DuBose Heyward, Paul Green, Allen Tate, Caroline Gordon, Donald Davidson, Laurence Stallings, James Boyd, Struthers Burt, Josephine Pinckney, and others, including Alice Hegan Rice, author of the highly popular *Mrs. Wiggs of the Cabbage Patch*. Another writer who was visibly and actively present both at the formal and purely social sessions (his first recorded words on arriving in Charlottesville were, "Know where I can get a drink?") was William Faulkner.

It is hard to believe, harder to understand, how someone as much a part of the American literary scene, certainly from her first book to her last, *Drury Randall* (1934), could have been so quickly forgotten, so largely ignored ever since, especially in view of the recent rediscoveries and acts of rehabilitation performed by feminist critics and scholars. This is also something that is usually said; though, reflexive or not, it still needs to be said.

Finally, and most pertinently, another notion about Mary Johnston needs to be reiterated. If she had done nothing else whatsoever except for her two Civil War novels—*The Long Roll* (1911) and *Cease Firing* (1912), she has earned honor and recognition for some of the most ambitious and successful writing about that terrible period in our national history. That a large and crucial part of both books consists of extraordinarily vivid and authentic (almost cinematic in a documentary sense) writing about combat is nothing less than remarkable. True, she had had the stories of her father, a Major of Artillery of the Confederate States of America, and her kinsman, the distinguished General Joseph E. Johnston (it is to the memory of the two of them that the two books are dedicated), to listen to; and we know from her papers that she mastered and made full use of all the primary and secondary sources available at the time; and that she went beyond that, walking the roads and exploring the terrain of the battlefields, seeking to make her story as factually accurate as it could possibly be. But none of this prepares the reader for the overwhelming impact of some of the finest writing about combat by any American before or since. That it should have been the work of a woman novelist in an age marked by habits of literary gentility and by the fashions of historical romance, fashions that she, herself, had earlier mastered and exploited to the fullest extent and success, is a stunning tribute to the power of focused imagination. This latter point, how she turned away about as far as she possibly could have from the acceptable literary tropes that had helped, thus far, to make her career and her living, is no indifferent matter. Literary habits and mind-set, both for writers and readers, are extremely difficult to shed or to transcend even when they are fully known and recognized. And beyond the difficulty lies great risk. The writing of *The Long Roll* and its companion, *Cease Firing*, demanded an act of great artistic daring, faith really, from Mary Johnston. On the strength of her ambition and daring alone she fully deserves to be remembered with honor. It is hard to make simple claims for the influence of these works. Who knows which, if any, of the writers of the wars that have been the continuing affliction and subject of the twentieth century, may or may not have opened either of her Civil War books or have ever even heard of Mary Johnston? But there are certain works that serve to change things, to alter our ways of seeing and being and thinking about things, including our past, ever after.

It is easier to make this point by analogy, easier to see in social and political thought than in literary art. But the matter is analogous. In 1638 a very young Englishman, fighting for his life alone in the Court of Star Chamber, said something passionate about how things relate to one another, about how things are linked for good and for ill:

> For what is done to any one may be done to every one: besides, being all members of one body, that is, of the English Commonwealth, one man should not suffer wrongfully, but all should be sensible, and endeavor his preservation; otherwise they give way to an inlet of the sea of will and power, upon their laws and liberties, which are boundaries to keep out tyranny and oppression; and who assists not in such cases, betrays his own rights, and is overrun, and of a free man made a slave when he thinks not of it, or regards it not, and so shunning the censure of turbulency, incurs the guilt of treachery to the present and future generations.

The young man was Freeborn Jack Lilburne, and the words he spoke to the judges at Star Chamber have been taken over to form the motto of the American Civil Liberties Union. And at his death, on one finger, Thomas Jefferson wore a ring with "Lilburne" on it, in honor of the ideas and ideals of Freeborn Jack.

I do not propose that we should wear rings in honor of the words of Mary Johnston. But I do suggest that among those of us American writers who have come along after her, we owe her something, a large debt, in whatever we may choose to write (or film) about the Civil War in particular and all war, combat, in general. I doubt if Shelby Foote owes her much of anything directly; yet her

two novels helped to form the climate that allowed him to conceive of and to achieve his masterpiece—*The Civil War: A Narrative.*
And without Shelby Foote there would have been no TV program—
"The Civil War." I seriously doubt if Norman Mailer, for example,
or, to be more recent, Tim O'Brien, have ever glanced at or even
heard of Mary Johnston's Civil War books. But they owe her something whether they know it or not, as do we all. She prepared the
way. And there are moments, passages and sequences in both *The
Long Roll* and *Cease Firing,* which are better writing about men at
war than anything in *The Naked and the Dead* (or anything in James
Jones for that matter) or the work of Tim O'Brien.

There. Some things that are *not* usually said about the work of
Mary Johnston.

II.

Like a lot of books of the early years of this century, *The Long Roll*
has illustrations. (It also has advertisements, but that convention
surprises only contemporary readers who, though bombarded
from all sides by advertisements, are somewhat disconcerted by
this lapsed convention.) The endpapers are maps of "The Valley
and Piedmont Virginia" and, on a large scale, the "Region of the
Seven Days' Fighting." Nothing could be more appropriate for a
book about a war than the empty and innocent and abstract maps
soon to be filled with soldiers of both sides, soon to become places
of human suffering, wounds and death. The book begins before
the war and then divides itself between the early Valley campaigns
and the larger battles fought in the east around the Richmond
area, ending with Chancellorsville. Each book has four color illustrations by N. C. Wyeth, a frontispiece and three others, scattered through the text and, yes, *illustrating* its line and development. The sequence of the internal illustrations in *The Long Roll*
follows the direction and sequence of the story, then, and offers
direct support to the narrative. The first, "The Lovers," might well
be a jacket cover for a historical romance, two beautiful young
people, a well-dressed young lady and a splendidly uniformed
Confederate officer standing in a gentle embrace, perhaps at the

moment of parting, in an attractive sylvan scene. The second, a couple of hundred pages later, "The Battle," is a swirl of smoke and fog and confusion. In the background, only partly visible, a torn and tattered Confederate Stars and Bars battle flag. In the foreground, several hatless, deadly serious men armed with muskets, one firing at close range, another evidently hit and falling down. The last, near the end of the book, a fully dressed horseman—high boots, overcoat and cape, visored cap, with a drawn revolver, alone and alert among leafless trees in a snow-dusted, wintry setting. "The Vedette" (*Vedette* was the term for a mounted sentinel out in front of the pickets) is a cold and menacing vision of a veteran soldier, a survivor. He is nothing else, neither more nor less, than a soldier. The frontispiece of *The Long Roll* is a picture of Stonewall Jackson, with his horse, Little Sorrel, Jackson standing on a high place, very stern and somehow ungainly, looking down, brooding about something. Brooding over all that follows. This is singularly apt, for *The Long Roll* soon enough becomes (among a good number of other things) the unfolding of the brief and brilliant story of Stonewall Jackson, that awkward and enigmatic man, who was, in the view of many and of this book, the South's great warrior. Its last pages give us his now famous last words—"Let us cross over the river, and rest under the shade of the trees." And the book ends with the historical scene of Jackson lying in state in the Virginia Hall of Delegates in the Capitol of the Confederacy.

Although Jackson is talked about by some of the fictional characters in the early stages of the narrative, the days leading up to the actual outbreak of the war, he does not appear in person until the sixth chapter of the book, "By Ashby's Gap," some 60 pages into the 683 page story. He is viewed and judged, in first and untested impression, by the narrator, a collective speaker and general point of view for all the characters we have come to know so far:

An awkward, inarticulate, and peculiar man, with strange notions about his health and other matters, there was about him no breath of grace, romance, or pomp of war. He was ungenial, ungainly, with large hands and feet, with poor eyesight and a stiff address. There did not lack spruce and handsome youths in his command who were vexed to the soul by the idea of being led to battle by such a figure. The facts that he had fought very bravely in Mexico, and that he had for the enemy a cold and formidable hatred were for him; most other things against him. He drilled his troops seven hours a day. His discipline was of the sternest, his censure a thing to make the boldest officer blench. A blunder, a slight negligence, any disobedience of orders—down came reprimand, suspension, arrest, with an iron certitude, a relentlessness quite like Nature's. Apparently he was without imagination. He had but little sense of humour, and no understanding of a joke. He drank water and sucked lemons for dyspepsia, and fancied that the use of pepper had caused a weakness in his left leg. He rode a rawboned nag named Little Sorrel, he carried his sabre in the oddest fashion, and said "oblike" instead of "oblique."

This is all in the public, historical narrative voice, one of a wide variety of voices Johnston uses to create a chorus for her story. But two things are worthy of noting. First, that everything in that straightforward block of information pays off later in action, in plot, in the story. Nothing, not a word or a thing mentioned, proves to be idle or irrelevant. The only other writer I've encountered who can do the same thing so effectively—the throwaway passage of detailed description or exposition that proves to be in each detail of the utmost importance, one way and another—is Nabokov. Secondly, this was and is a daring bit of narrative strategy. It challenges the reader with a strong first impression to *unlearn* acquired responses. Truth is, we learn that Jackson's widow, and others among his coterie of dedicated admirers who were still alive to read this far (evidently they read not much farther than his earliest appearances in the narrative) were very angry and upset. No matter. Johnston knows where she is going with his character and her story. She plunges us into the time and its quick, easy, ignorant, finally innocent judgments, making us contemporaries. A little later, after Jackson has begun to prove himself as a leader of men in combat, a leader capable of bringing courage and endurance, the best, out of them, that same collective narrator's voice offers another evolving judgment:

In peace, to the outward eye, he was a commonplace man; in war he changed. The authority with which he was clothed went, no doubt, for much, but it was rather, perhaps, that a door had been opened for him. His inner self became visible, and that imposingly. The man was there; a firm man, indomitable, a thunderbolt of war, a close-mouthed, farseeing, praying and worshipping, more or less ambitious, not always just, patriotically devoted fatalist and enthusiast, a mysterious and commanding genius of an iron sort.

Then we are allowed to see the great man earn his greatness, become a myth and at the last a monument. Something not lost on an educated private soldier ("a young man like a beautiful athlete from a frieze, an athlete who was also a philosopher") who speaks out loud to the corpse in the bier: "Hail, great man of the past!" he said. "If today you consort with Caesar, tell him we still make war."

This speaker speaks also for us. And, in the story and in his own time, he speaks more presciently than he can possibly know. For with Jackson's death, in Mary Johnston's version of the war, the South has already reached its high tide and that tide has now turned against the South. *Cease Firing* will follow, devoted to defeat, the unravelling, the ebb tide.

Between the beginning and the ending of *The Long Roll* there is a blended mixture of real and fictional characters. Among the historical characters who appear with more dimension than mere expository mention are Robert E. Lee and Jeb Stuart, Jefferson Davis, Fighting Joe Hooker, A. P. Hill, and many others with what we have come to call cameo roles.

Meanwhile the fictional characters are entrapped in plots and subplots that could, in another context, turn this story into a more conventional historical romance. Part of the suspense of the narrative, for the reader who was familiar with the literary fashions of the age and, perhaps as well, with Johnston's earlier work, was just how seriously to take and to respond to these elements. There could be little or no suspense, finally, about the outcome of battles and the end of things. But the shape of the story, itself, could be used to surprise the reader even as the characters are surprised. Moreover the narrative is an implicit critique of the truth of the world of historical romance, a world that is broken to pieces against the edges of hard facts. Among the fictional characters, each with a personal story and with personal problems and difficulties to be resolved, is a romantic triangle: Richard Cleave, Judith Cary, and

Maury Stafford. These are upper-class people. They have the usual Southern extended network of family, kinfolk, friends, etc. There are other central characters—for example, Billy Maydew, the mountain man, and Allan Gold, the schoolmaster. And there is a wonderfully realized cowardly lowlife, a character who fits into a more contemporary literary fashion, Steve Dagg, a miles gloriosus right out of Shakespeare, only with a Southern accent and dialect. He goes to great trouble to try to keep skin and bones intact in all situations. There are also the women and there are the slaves. All have different points of view and each has a slightly different language. The slaves alone always speak in phonetic dialect, something now routinely acceptable only from African-American writers. In Johnston's favor it should be said that in her use of this convention, widely popular at the time, she is very seldom condescending to the speakers or simply cute. There are the languages of the various classes, high and low, expressed in narration as well as in dialogue; and for the most part Mary Johnston's dialogue is excellent and authoritative. There are various levels of narrative rhetoric as well, ranging from an occasional voice close to that of straightforward textbook history (and, from time to time, of real and imaginary documents) to song lyrics (and in one case, page 275, the musical notation for a bugle call). Above all she is superbly the master of a remarkable range of points of view, shifting back and forth from the limited visions of individuals to complex expressions of collective points of view of collective actions. It is not done in a crudely schematic way, but gradually the collective vision and its point of view overwhelm and finally replace the individual points of view and, to a large extent, the individual problems, which come out of the individual particularities and peculiarities of character and out of the complexities of what was once plot, an expendable pattern of desires and events no longer of much importance measured against the huge and simple course of the war.

The war itself becomes something like an inhuman character with a life and a death of its own. One is reminded of an image near the end of Mary Lee Settle's memoir of her own service in World War II, *All the Brave Promises*, where, finally discharged from the British WAAF, late in the war, she goes to London to work for the Americans. She writes, "I was on the way to the American

Office of War Information in London, the cocktail parties, the conferences, the PX cigarettes, the frenetic turmoil of people who had names and thought they were running the juggernaut of war, which was only spending itself toward its own death like a great tiring unled beast." Never completely—it will be more complete in *Cease Firing*, where the war takes over from its managers, the generals on both sides, and from its performing victims in *The Long Roll*. Here, for example, is the collective viewpoint and language, developed out of a passage that began with a badly wounded soldier desperately searching for a drink of water, in which the suffering perceiver is no longer that single soldier but everyman, then and now, including the reader. The situation is an artillery "exchange" between Federal and Confederate batteries:

> The sound was enormous, a complex tumult that crashed and echoed in the head. The whole of the field existed in the throbbing, expanded brain—all battlefields, all life, all the world and other worlds, all problems solved and insoluble. The wide-flung grey battlefront was now sickle-shaped, convex to the foe. The rolling dense smoke flushed momently with a lurid glare. In places the forest was afire, in others the stubble of the field. From horn to horn of the sickle galloped the riderless horses. Now and again a wounded one among them screamed fearfully.

The movement of the whole passage is from small to large, from particular to general, from concrete to abstract (geometry). Then, at the end, that rush of riderless horses, some of them screaming fearfully, lights it all to the level of myth, alludes to the great myths, is somehow related to that great beast in the vision of Mary Lee Settle in *All the Brave Promises*.

What is generalized, however, is most often a pattern of particulars. Here, following the first day of the Seven Days, chapter 31, is a hospital for the wounded in Richmond, collective and general in impression, yet composed of highly sensuous, almost cinematic affective details. In sequence and context this chapter follows the account of a party at President Davis's house and precedes a vivid recounting of the combat around Gaines's Mill.

> The ward was long, low ceiled, with brown walls and rafters. Between the patches of lamplight the shadows lay wide and heavy. The

cots, the pallets, the pew cushions sewed together, were placed each close by each. A narrow aisle ran between the rows; by each low bed there was just standing room. The beds were all filled, and the wagons bringing more rumbled on the cobblestones without. All the long place was reekingly hot, with a strong smell of human effluvia, of sweat-dampened clothing, of blood and powder grime. There was not much crying aloud; only when a man was brought in raving, or when there came a sharp scream from some form under the surgeon's knife. But the place seemed one groan, a sound that swelled or sank, but never ceased. The shadows on the wall, fantastically dancing, mocked this with nods and becks and waving arms,— mocked the groaning, mocked the heat, mocked the smell, mocked the thirst, mocked nausea, agony, delirium, and the rattle in the throat, mocked the helpers and the helped, mocked the night and the world and the dying and the dead. At dawn the cannon began again.

In both the individual and collective sequences Mary Johnston sticks closely to the things that have mattered to soldiers for all of history—the weather, food and drink, and especially the latter. Thirst in battle is a continuing motif. "*Oh, water, water, water, water! . . . ,*" she writes.

We are so close and yet it all seems so far behind us. It is difficult to unlearn our own century, both the hard lessons and the misinformation, almost impossible to discard our own set of facts and fashions and to appreciate fully the stunning achievement of Mary Johnston's story of the Civil War. Some of the language, both literary and vernacular, is inevitably dated. It is still too near in time to have faded into the generalized past where the language is no longer a problem. It seems, for the time being, more like a slightly awkward version of our own; whereas, in fact, it is an earlier version of our own. In the language and telling of *The Long Roll* we witness the end of the earlier literary language of the late nineteenth century and the beginning of our own.

Then there are the problems of what reader expectations and experience demanded of fiction, this pressure being all the more powerful, if not imperative, when affecting a very successful writer. We should remember that a full decade later the young American moderns—like Hemingway and Faulkner and Fitzgerald—though they were in part inspired by the example of the new poets, were already finding and developing a language and a style to carry the burden of their visions, still had not found the larger secret—how to structure the new novel. I am reliably told that Hemingway's earliest drafts for *The Sun Also Rises,* though splendidly executed in the already established Hemingway *style,* were for a novel structured very differently from the final version he and Maxwell Perkins put together. I am reliably told that his early drafts were arranged in the classic, chronological structure of the late Victorian novel (what novels had he *read,* after all?) replete with many pages of exposition and narration that were eventually cut to pieces. Point is that we have great difficulty escaping our own models and the critical mind-set of our times. The problem was all the more acute for Mary Johnston since she herself helped to shape and form the model of the popular novel.

I believe it was the truth—the facts of life, the facts of war—that set her free. We tend to forget the simplest fact of all, that she grew up, among old soldiers, in a defeated society that had lost, killed or permanently disabled, one out of four of its males between the ages of eighteen and sixty-five. A society with one-armed and one-legged men everywhere. Shelby Foote mentions at the end of volume 3 of *The Civil War* that his home state of Mississippi budgeted twenty percent of its expenses for artificial limbs.

Mary Johnston knew the history of it at first hand. Knew also that to tell the truth of it she could not discard the ways and means of factual, historical narrative; but that she must awaken and engage the imagination of the reader and that the ways of fiction could serve this purpose. For all practical purposes she invented a form for our time, the novel that blends fact and fiction in subtle proportions and whose aim is to share the truth of an experience. John Dos Passos would later build an aesthetic and a reputation around just such a blending of real and imaginary history. And Mary Johnston, having finished with that great subject and going off in other directions and in her own way, would live to see that happen. She did not live to see the application of her methods in our own times—by Norman Mailer, in both fiction and nonfiction; by Truman Capote in his celebrated "nonfiction novel"; by E. L. Doctorow with his characteristic use of fictional and "real" historical figures in the same scene, on the same stage; and not least by

Shelby Foote, whose magnificent achievement works the other way, telling only a factual history without a fictional character or event, but telling it in the narrative manner and with the narrative selectivity of a novelist.

Our whole idea of what constitutes fiction, the full range of its possibilities, has changed steadily in response to the events and complexities we have faced in this century. Near the beginning of it Mary Johnston, seeking to honor her father's memory and to do justice to the most overwhelming and traumatic experience in American history, was forced to redefine the novel. In so doing, creating first *The Long Roll*, then *Cease Firing*, she served every writer who came after her. We are all deeply beholden to her.

Shelby Foote

The Civil War: A Narrative

One of the pleasures coming with the appearance of each of the three volumes of Shelby Foote's *The Civil War: A Narrative—Fort Sumter to Perryville* (1958), *Fredericksburg to Meridian* (1964), and *Red River to Appomattox* (1974)—has been the "Bibliographical Note" published at the end of each book. These notes can be read independently, of course, for they dutifully acknowledge each time the essentially unchanging primary sources, where, as Foote says, "you hear the live men speak." But they can also be examined in sequence, representing the changing and cumulative library of secondary sources, including what might be termed the "competition," the work of Bruce Catton and Allan Nevins, all the sources, which have expanded in wild growth, in startling quantity, over the years. (Perhaps not so startling; for both scholars and publishers aimed to make the most of the centennial years.) In any case, Foote's bibliographical notes offer a careful accounting of the historical research that has been going on during the twenty years or so that went into the making of *The Civil War.* Equally important, and perhaps more interesting, has been the stance of the author, his attitude and his tone of voice, as he has explained his aims, his ways and means, and his models of excellence, in the process of creating this work. The note to the first volume is thorough, solid, inclusive, and appropriately humble without false modesty. The anticipated problem is that of the novelist who invades the territory of the specialist. He does not retreat from his badge and chevrons as novelist, nor does he shy away from his commitment to that art: "Well, I am a novelist, and what is more I agree with D. H. Lawrence's estimate of the novel as 'the one bright book of life.'" But Foote is at pains to make clear the integrity of his method, if not to defend it:

> Accepting the historian's standards without his paraphernalia, I
> have employed the novelist's methods without his license. Instead of

inventing characters and incidents, I searched them out—and having found them, I took them as they were. Nothing is included here, either within or outside quotation marks, without the authority of documentary evidence which I consider sound. . . . In all respects, the book is as accurate as care and hard work could make it.

By the time Foote had finished the second volume he had passed through, unscathed, his baptism of fire from the historians. His work had been praised and appreciated by honorable and demanding critics. And he was now past the halfway mark in his own enormous task. The bibliographical note to the second volume is a virtuoso piece, threaded with some brilliant sentences of silver and gold. There is the veteran's earned swagger and no longer any necessity for self-defense. In fact, the mood expressed is expansive in its confidence. Concluding his particular list of debts to scholars, he writes:

Other, less specific obligations were as heavy. The photographs of Mathew Brady, affording as they do a gritty sense of participation— of being in the presence of the uniformed and frock-coated men who fought the battles and did the thinking, such as it was—gave me as much to go on, for example, as anything mentioned above. Further afield, but not less applicable, Richmond Lattimore's translation of the *Iliad* put a Greekless author in close touch with his model. Indeed, to be complete, the list of my debts would have to be practically endless. Proust I believe has taught me more about the organization of material than even Gibbon has done, and Gibbon taught me much. Mark Twain and Faulkner would also have to be included, for they left their sign on all they touched, and in the course of this exploration of the American scene I often found that they had been there before me.

For historical method Foote very gracefully invites comparison of his work with that of Tacitus and Thucydides. In context, then and now, none of this seems self-serving or outrageously illusionary. His pride is just.

The tone of the bibliographical note to the final volume is more relaxed, more casual, and more confident in a different way—the confidence of a survivor. The final paragraph says and shows it all:

So, anyhow, "Farwel my book and my devotion," my rock and my companion through two decades. At the outset of this Gibbon span, plunk in what I hope will be the middle of my writing life, I was two years younger than Grant at Belmont, while at the end I was four months older than Lincoln at his assassination. By way of possible extenuation, in response to complaints that it took me five times longer to write the war than the participants took to fight it, I would point out that there were a good many more of them than there was of me. However that may be, the conflict is behind me now, as it is for you and it was a hundred-odd years ago for them.

That is how it ends, not the story, but the task, the largest and most ambitious single piece of work attempted and completed by any American novelist in this century. In total, something over a million and a half words, it is longer than all of Proust and, give or take, just about the size of Gibbon's masterpiece. Begun in 1954 and worked at steadily, full-time, since then, it is a remarkable achievement, one which would be remarkable at any time, but is all the more so in our own time when our artists, like everyone else, have shunned the high risks of real adventure, hoping and settling for the hoarded privileges of easy recognition and, sometimes, a fast buck. Foote's choice and his commitment to it are simply unique. He could easily have taken the more popular, easier way. For by 1954 he had established himself as a serious, very productive, and, in the best sense, successful young novelist. If art were a horse race (as so many seem to think it is), Shelby Foote had already gained a good lead, a couple of lengths at least, on the rest of the pack, including some of the novelists who have since come to be regarded as our contemporary masters. He had already moved beyond the merely promising. Which is to say a number of things. The conception and execution of *The Civil War* was not a case of a writer "finding himself" or finding his proper form; not, then, a turning away from one form to another; rather it is the rarer example of a mature artist adapting and assimilating all his skills and applying these to a different sort of problem. It is not a question of loss, but of gain and change. The chances for loss, the risks involved, were staggering. For example, even assuming the good fortune of living to complete his marathon enterprise and doing it tolerably well, the odds were strong, if not overwhelming, that in a time of instant attention and instant oblivion, he would find himself and his work cheerfully forgotten. And to a degree that has happened, though there have been a few critics through the years who have preserved the memory of his reputation and accomplishments. (A notable example was the *Mississippi Quarterly's* fall 1971 "Special Issue on Shelby Foote.") But indicative of the risks and temporary losses is the fact that the announcement of the publication of the final volume of *The Civil War* was not "newsworthy" enough to place the book among the lists of promising and "significant" titles that were due to appear in the fall of 1974. (At the time of this writing there were good signs that the newspaper and magazine reviews might make up for that oversight.) Most important, Foote was freely willing to take all those risks in order to give himself to his great subject. The word for that is dedication.

It is probable that he will return to the novel now, according to the most recent interviews; but even if he does not, it is more than likely that his earlier novels will have a kind of second life, if only to be reexamined in the light of what he has done since then. With the advantage of time between, we can see some general things more clearly. For one thing, Foote's novels hold up very well. They have not "dated" much; they are, therefore, not to be taken as exemplary of any particular school or movement or, for that matter, any single *period.* They are highly individual, independent works. It used to be said by some that he was deeply under the influence of William Faulkner. Well, it is impossible for any Southern writer aware of his place and people and aware of his own literary tradition *not* to be influenced by the towering energy and example of Faulkner. Those who pretend otherwise (and there are a number) are either trying to fool themselves or us or both at once. It might be expected that Foote would be singularly susceptible as a Mississippi writer who knew William Faulkner as well and as closely as any other writer could. Yet, with the passage of time, it is clear that Foote was not influenced in any of the obvious and negative ways. His style and language were, from the beginning, and remain, distinctly different. Rhetorical tropes and certain trademarks of the Faulkner manner, including specific forms of verbal texture, now widely used (and often misused) by American writers of all kinds, are chiefly absent from Foote's prose, which is characterized by a kind of classic clarity and condensation, often transparent, though the *materials* he deals with may be complex and dark. Foote's approach to the presentation of character is different in intent and may be described, with obvious oversimplification, as a method of continuing *development* rather than characterization by discovery. There is one major characteristic in common. In Foote's five novels, as in all of Faulkner's, the basic pattern, a combination of structure and point of view, is different for each story. But Foote is a conservative innovator, which is to say that he neither invents new forms for storytelling, nor in any of his work is the means or strategy anything more (or less) than a precision tool for his overall purpose. None of which makes him "better" or "worse" than William Faulkner, but all of which makes his work different in its qualities. And these qualities stand out now even more distinctly from the more recent habits of deliberate overt and self-conscious innovation which have been fashionable in serious American fiction for the past decade or so. Finally, and in this he perhaps inevitably comes close to much of Faulkner, all of Foote's stories have been, to one degree or another, rooted in history. No present action is presented without a real or an implied historical shadowing.

Together with a rigorous fidelity to fact and a mastery of the materials, all the qualities already evident in his fiction were perfectly transferable to the writing of narrative history. The clarity and the compression of style and language are great strengths in the history. He put it very accurately in a July 15, 1973, interview for the Memphis *Commercial Appeal:* "I'm working with a very large canvas, but at the same time I'm trying to do each paragraph the way you'd write a sonnet. I'm trying for precision on a large scale." Characterization presents another sort of challenge. Conventional history, even the best written, most often, for the sake of convenience and efficiency if nothing else, introduces each character in the prose equivalent to the unveiling of a statue. The figure is revealed, all at once, solidly and in three dimensions, and, in exposure, is judged. Then we are shown actions and events involving the character, and such suspense as there is, lies in the analytical game of determining to what extent the character conformed to or deviated from the initial judgment. Foote used the novelist's means, his own, allowing the individual characters to develop and change in and with action and events. We have first impressions, not judgments, and these impressions change continually as we go along. The consistency, the core of the character, is there by inference and implication. Which is to say characterization is dramatic and dynamic and becomes a source of narrative suspense, thus of forward motion in the whole narrative. There are a thousand ways to do this, and a cast of thousands to handle; but one way is in finding the exact and appropriate moment in the action, and usually only once in the entire narrative, to present certain relevant details. A superb example of this typical care comes in the opening pages of the final volume, when Foote describes General Grant and his son checking into Williard's Hotel prior to Grant's receiving his promotion to lieutenant general and assuming his final command. We see him as others—the desk clerk and observers in the lobby—in fact saw him, unimpressive, another major general in a town full of stars. When he signs the register and is known, there is a classic "double-take," and we are given, the only time in the book, the objective physical facts of Grant's appearance, ironically, just at the moment that, by virtue of his name and fame, he is magically transformed in the eyes of his beholders. "Here before them, in the person of this undistinguished-looking officer—forty-one years of age, five feet eight inches tall and weighing just under a hundred and forty pounds in his scuffed boots and shabby clothes—was the man who, in the course of the past twenty-five months of a war in which the news had been mostly unwelcome from the Federal point of view, had captured two rebel armies, entire, and chased a third clean out of sight beyond the roll of the southern horizon." It is a question of dealing out bits and pieces, shards, of information. The effect is that these figures are seemingly in constant motion. Combined with a similar arrangement of psychological details, this novelistic method results in a suspension of the habit of snap judgment until such time as judgment becomes both dramatic and requisite. To put it another way, in conventional historical prose judgments are regularly rendered (and, indeed, are required) by the author. In Foote's narrative history there is a narrator who must, from time to time, enter in, "intrude" directly; but when this happens in Foote's story it is direct and dramatized, usually in terms of one character's judgment or misapprehension of another's actions or motives and is justified by coming with a slight shift in point of view. An excellent, and typical, example of the careful entrance of the narrator into action comes in volume two. Forrest has just given his commander, Braxton Bragg, an outrageously insubordinate, personal denunciation, called him a coward and threatened his life. The scene ends with Forrest riding away with a companion whom he reassures that no real trouble will come from his outburst, that Bragg will not mention it or do anything about it. Since Forrest has long since been established as one of the narrative's genuine heroes, and since Bragg has revealed himself in many ways as a serious scoundrel, we are delighted. *Then,* and only then, we are given the benefit of intrusive judgment that, among other things, gives us a single fact about Bragg that subtly changes our view of him and Forrest as well. "Forrest was right in his prediction; Bragg neither took official notice of the incident nor disapproved the cavalryman's request for transfer, which was submitted within the week. He was wrong, though, in his interpretation of his superior's motives. Braxton Bragg was no coward; he was afraid of no man alive, not even Bedford Forrest." Foote then moves to explore the real, and on the whole laudatory, motives behind Bragg's willingness to shrug off Forrest's misconduct. We learn two things from the brief episode, some sense of the limits of Forrest's imagination, intelligence, and judgment, and some awareness of strengths in Bragg's flawed character. Both become more complex figures as a result. The same rigor is observed throughout the entire narrative. Which means that direct acts of judgment are few and far between, and when they occur they are functional. That in turn creates what critics used to call a "tension"; for, to a greater or lesser extent all readers of this story know much of the story in advance and come to it with preconceived notions and with a baggage of prejudicial judgments. The methods of characterization work actively to unsettle us from certainties; and, thus, by narrative devices and construction, old events are renewed and engage us with the demands of raw experience itself. Which means, further, that *Foote's* judgments of characters, of Lincoln

and Davis, of Lee and Grant, and of all the others, can be appre-
hended only in terms of the whole story, the accumulated revela-
tions of details in the presented sequence of the entire work. (This
is exactly the opposite of the mingling of fact and fiction that has
been named "The New Journalism.") With that roundness and
complexity of characterization and with strict adherence to the
angles of point of view within the omniscient scheme goes the
capacity to treat some of the less than worthy characters more
fairly, thus more accurately. And so Foote is able to do justice to
high-placed scoundrels like Bragg and Henry Halleck and Edwin
Stanton, men who have been scorned because they were scoundrels. In answer to a question about this, Foote has replied, succinctly enough: "Pricks too have their point of view, and sometimes it's an interesting one to investigate, especially if what you're
after is a sense of 'how it was.' "

His interests in innovation and his structural skills as novelist
have been applied to enable him to achieve what very few historians of any stripe have managed, a sense of the simultaneity of
diverse actions. And it is this feeling of simultaneous actions that
gives us, in my opinion, for the first time in accounts of the Civil
War, a real and continuing awareness of the war in the west and,
as well, of the war at sea. All this adds up to a larger awareness of
the whole war, its size and scope; and, so, for example, in this
context, the war in the west assumes its proper weight of importance. Foote, in his final bibliographical note, states that he has no
"thesis" about this to maintain, but he is willing to claim "that
Vicksburg, for example, was as 'decisive' as Gettysburg, if not
more so, and that Donelson, with its introduction of Grant and
Forrest onto the national scene, may have had more to do with the
outcome than either of the others had, for all their greater panoply,
numbers and documentation."

Because *The Civil War* is primarily, though not entirely, a combat
history of the war, the other elements, political and social and eco-
nomic, are realized dramatically and in that context. They, too, are
shown and implied, or are to be inferred, in action and in character. It would be a serious misreading to conclude that any of
these elements are missing, but it would be a critical mistake to
look for their exploitation in conventionally analytic and expos-

itory terms. The richness of mid-nineteenth-century America in a multiplicity of forces and details, large and small, is there in the narrative; but these appear, occur to us, *happen* to us much as they happened to those who were too much involved in the experience of the war to be self-conscious or especially analytical about either the larger ghostly patterns within and behind events or the small, taken-for-granted things on the surface of daily life. Reading *The Civil War* is, then, an experience, one which is analogous to the experience of a novel with a richly sensuous affective surface rather than a recapitulation of events. It is superb history by any standards, but it is unique history as well.

It is far too early (and it would be purely presumptuous) to report anything more than these most general reactions. My judgment is that the work is, without question or qualification, a masterpiece, one of the very few genuinely great literary works of our time. Time will tell. And one can't say that much about many books in a lifetime. We shall be a long time coming to know *The Civil War* deeply and in detail. Perhaps our children and grandchildren will know it better, for it seems most probable to be the version of our most tragic time which will be passed on to them. It may well have been a knowledge of what he had achieved and of its likely continuity and posterity that led Foote to take his story on beyond the war's end, the series of surrenders, parade's end, and the Reconstruction, to the death of Jefferson Davis in 1889 for its curtain. For this allowed him to suggest—again, as in the unbroken line of the narrative, by inference and by dramatic perception—some of the things that all of it means, most especially in what it meant to those who fought the war and survived it. In terms of casualties we have never experienced anything like it. "Approximately one out of ten able-bodied Northerners was dead or incapacitated," Foote writes, "while for the South it was one out of four, including her non-combatant Negroes. Some notion of the drain this represented, as well as the poverty the surrendered men came home to, was shown by the fact that during the first year of peace the state of Mississippi allotted a solid fifth of its revenues for the purchase of artificial arms and legs for its returning veterans." But the last word of the veterans and survivors is chosen by Foote to be represented by twice-wounded, former

Captain Oliver Wendell Holmes, who came close to matching the eloquence of Lincoln's Gettysburg Address with a speech in Keene, New Hampshire, in 1884, in the midst of what Mark Twain called the Gilded Age, a time in which these soldiers, old from their youth, were out of place. What Holmes said for them becomes, in essence, the summing up of the whole experience of *The Civil War*:

> The generation that carried on the war has been set aside by its experience. Through our great good fortune, in our youth our hearts were touched with fire. It was given to us to learn at the outset that life is a profound and passionate thing. While we are permitted to scorn nothing but indifference, and do not pretend to undervalue the worldly rewards of ambition, we have seen with our own eyes, beyond and above the gold fields, the snowy heights of honor, and it is for us to bear the report to those who come after us.

James Jones

Viet Journal

I.

In mid-January of 1973, just as the formal cease-fire in Vietnam was being (finally) finalized, James Jones, age fifty-two and living in Paris, was asked by the *New York Times Magazine* to go to Vietnam and to write some pieces for them. As Robert Wool of the magazine put it to Jones, they were not interested in a political piece. What they wanted was "a novelist's viewpoint." They wanted "the sights, the sounds, the smells of Vietnam—after the end." Jones had been, inevitably, asked to do this kind of thing before and, for various reasons, had always refused the assignments. This time he agreed to go. *Viet Journal* is a personal account of his journey to Vietnam and back, returning by way of Hawaii so that he could briefly pay a visit, his first since 1942, to the place he served as a young soldier in the regular army and the setting of his famous first novel—*From Here To Eternity.* The whole trip had to be hurried, for the cease-fire was to begin January 28, 1973, and all American forces were to be withdrawn by March 28, 1973. Jones managed to get there, to visit places and to accomplish goals he set for himself, to experience real danger, and, indeed, to come under fire (cease-fire or no, the North Vietnamese kept up the killing as much as they were able to). From his journey and experience came first the assigned articles for the *New York Times Magazine,* as well as other pieces in *Harper's* and *Oui.* In 1974 there was the book, which included versions of these magazine pieces, revised and fit together with other materials and in a different structure. Not a strong commercial success, as various other books by Jones had been, *Viet Journal* earned mixed reviews. Biographer Frank MacShane (*Into Eternity: The Life of James Jones, American Writer,* 1985) is wrong when he describes *Viet Journal* as receiving "universally favorable reviews." It was not reviewed nearly as widely as all of Jones's other books had been. Some of the key early reviews were strongly supportive. *Publishers Weekly* praised "writing that is gripping, human and far superior to much of the copy that emerged from Indochina during the peak of the war—and a book full of poignant echoes." *Library Journal* (not always friendly to Jones) strongly recommended it: "An interesting, readable, and highly personal account, recommended for public and academic libraries." But John Reed, writing for the *New York Times Book Review,* called the book "a disappointment," adding: "Much of it seems to have been written hastily and without passionate conviction, pro or con, about Vietnam." P. J. Ognibene, in the *New Republic,* complained that "he never penetrates deeply into Vietnam or the Vietnamese." The *New Yorker* gave him a solidly negative thumping, called *Viet Journal* "a hackwork book," arguing that "he writes in haste with rancor for opposing views and shoddily." A tip of the head (if not the hat) for a prodigal son, the kindest sentence in the *New Yorker* review did not write him off as forever beyond salvation: "His heart may be in his subject, but not his craftsman's hand." It is entirely pertinent that one of the few writers about Vietnam whom Jones singles out for criticism is *New Yorker* writer Frances Fitzgerald. He sarcastically notes: "In her book *Fire in the Lake,* Frances Fitzgerald presents a marvelous apologia for Viet Cong and North Viet political assassination and terrorism." He concludes: "The whole thing smacks of a schoolteacher's dissertation on the moral superiority of marital sex over unmarried sex."

And it may not have helped Jones, who more than once had claimed to be a liberal, with fellow liberals to be not so much praised as accurately described by the conservative *National Review:* "Leaving philosophy for the armchair analyst, he combines the style of an artist with the toughness of a realist who is finely attuned to the foibles and fiber of the U. S. Army."

Beyond the simple record of mixed reviews there are more subtle signs that, in spite of its subject matter, which still occupies the attention of writers and reporters and historians, *Viet Journal* has failed to earn the kind of attention that has been given to Jones's other work. Anecdotally, I found that a number of major university libraries, libraries which have all of his other books, do not have *Viet Journal* in their catalogs and stacks. And at this writing (summer 1991), the book is out of print. The American intellectual establishment does not directly suppress or censor books and ideas, perhaps because it does not need to. Aleksandr Solzhenitsyn noticed this and commented on it in his speech, "The Exhausted West," at Harvard's Commencement, 1978: "Without any censorship, in the West, fashionable trends of thought are carefully separated from those that are not fashionable. Nothing is forbidden, but what is not fashionable will hardly ever find its way into periodicals or books or be heard in colleges."

II.

I am prepared to argue that *Viet Journal* is one of James Jones's best and best-written books; that tightly focused and deliberately limited as it is, *Viet Journal* is also one of the most important books, then or since, about the Vietnam War; that the experience of Vietnam and the creation of the book out of that experience was a liberating experience for Jones, a significant breakthrough that, as these things often do, at once made sense out of his past as it freed him to face the future.

III.

Dedicated to Fred and Arline Weyand (Fred Weyand was, at the time, a four-star general and commander of Military Assistance Command Vietnam) and to "The United States Army To Which My First Novel Was Also Dedicated," *Viet Journal* is composed of a sequence of roughly eighty subtitled units, some very short, less than a page, and some as long as a conventional short story. The longest unit, or chapter, is the "Epilogue: Hawaiian Recall," where Jones, headed home from 'Nam, stops off to visit some of his old haunts, including Schofield Barracks and remote, almost unchanged, Makapuu Head, a defensive beach position of five pillboxes cut out of virgin rock and occupied by his infantry company from December 7, 1941, until they shipped out for Guadalcanal on December 6, 1942. Makapuu Head served as the setting for his early short story, "The Way It Is," and for his short novel—*The Pistol* (1959).

You can look at the structure of *Viet Journal* as being analogous to a movie, a sequence of scenes, continuous forward motion first to last. Or you can take it, at one and the same time, as an assemblage of fragments, made after the facts, its forward momentum gained by the stance of one voice/first-person narrator (Jones) and a primarily chronological development—before, during, and after Jones's trip to Vietnam.

Basic narrative suspense is generated in several ways. The first twenty or so pages are devoted to the *Times* invitation, his doubts and acceptance, his difficulties in getting the necessary visas (at first he was to go to North Vietnam also) despite promises by the *Times* to take care of it and despite his personal friendship with people like Mary McCarthy, who had visited Hanoi and written favorably about North Vietnam. Jones takes his shots, including one for bubonic plague, buys the things he needs, packs his bags and, thanks to a phone call to Arline Weyand in Bangkok, gets his visa to South Vietnam and is on his way. Once he has landed at Tan Son Nhut airport and settled into room sixty-two at the Continental Palace Hotel in Saigon, he discovers that, like the other reporters in town, including the not especially helpful *Times* crowd, he is unlikely to get to any of the places he had heard about and hoped to visit. He turns to General Weyand, who once upon a time had commanded Jones's old outfit, the Twenty-fifth "Tropic Lightning" Infantry Division, and things begin to happen. In addition to some of the usual places, Jones wants to visit Pleiku ("an armed camp"), Kontum ("a town under seige"), and Dak Pek, a remote and dangerous Border Ranger Post, held by South Vietnamese and montagnards and located far north, surrounded by the North Vietnamese. Will he get to go to Dak Pek? This remains a question and a problem until almost the end of his visit to Vietnam. Weyand is very helpful to Jones, putting him into the capable and sympathetic hands of Brigadier General Mike Healy, a Special Forces officer who came up through the ranks (Healy wears a third dog tag on the chain around his neck which reads: "IF YOU ARE RECOVERING MY BODY, FUCK YOU") and is the most fully developed figure in the book. Healy and Jones have to collude, if not conspire, for Weyand has given orders that Jones is not to be put into danger. They get around this. Jones manages to get to Pleiku, Kontum, and (finally) Dak Pek, as well as Hue, Quang Tri (where he witnesses a prisoner exchange), Da Nang, Can Tho, Tay Ninh. He flies over and has a good look at My Lai. Visits the central highlands, the coast, the Mekong Delta. And in every case gives the reader a strong personal sense of the place through the perceptions and judgment calls of the narrator—himself.

We believe Jones. And that credibility, overwhelming in its integrity by the end of things, is masterfully created (by the author) by the steady accumulation of information, of details, of self-revelation. In the beginning he is bravely open with his readers, at least as to what his assumptions are and where he stands. Liberal by inclination, he is politically "neutral," doesn't like *any* politicians very much and admits to being "cynical about both sides, including U.S. involvement." Nothing there to alienate him from his imaginary reader. His troubles with bureaucrats of all sides and kinds, including the *Times*, and his justly earned contempt for paper pushers, are not likely to lose him the sympathy and attention of readers, either. Nor are his amusing accounts of his vulnerability while taking the necessary shots for the trip. Not counting junkies, who enjoys getting stuck with needles?

The idea of sympathy and engagement, of *trust*, then, suddenly reminds us that in the second paragraph of the book, almost as an aside, Jones tells us something about the suicide of his father in 1942. He ends this brief moment of confession with judgment: "I loved my father, and I hated to see it end like that. He deserved a better fate."

This wounded and whole man is hard to dislike and easy to believe. Next and early on we are given a sequence of sensory details which, as in a novel, serve to make the place and the experience "real" even as they establish the physical dimensions and sensitivity of the witness-narrator. Here Jones arrives: "Bangkok prepared me, in a way. Partially. From the air, the flat winding river. The flat sheen of flooded rice fields. Off the plane, the soft 7 am tropic air, full of tropic smells. Stagnant river, burning charcoal, heaped-up garbage. Heaped-up trash, a different, wet-paper odor. Weaving through these like bright threads the scents of the flowers: jasmine, frangipani, bougainvillea, gardenia."

Coupled with this high degree of sensory alertness, which is more or less maintained throughout, there is an equally important presentation of his inner feelings and reactions, including both fear and panic, not usually admitted. He has a kind of symbol for these feelings and others which follow him—a vaguely simian shape, "my chittering toothsome apelike friend," first noticed on the way to Orly airport in Paris and a recurring vision in the story. At last, near the end of things in "The Simian Figure," he admits that he is uncertain whether he really saw this being or not. "Whether I actually saw him as a hallucination with my real eye, or imagined him at the time of the experience, or whether I invented him later when writing about the experience, he was just as authentic." The figure is, then, "authentic," a real part of the experience. It is also a symbol, but one Jones is not willing to nail down: "Could he be a symbol of the race, and our needs for fury and danger and fear and their excitements? Maybe he was a mirror image of myself?"

". . . *whether I invented him later when writing about the experience* . . ."

Without being tediously self-reflexive, Jones does, also, invite the reader from time to time to remember both aspects of his experience—the events, themselves, and then his writing about them. This gesture likewise serves to make the narrator a reliable and honest witness.

The next element in this process is the presentation of characters, the *other people* in the story. For such a fast-moving, lean story, depending much on evocation and illusion, there are a lot of well-realized characters: M. Franchini, owner of the Continental Palace Hotel; Monsignor Seitz, the only white bishop left in Vietnam; Hilary Smith, a nurse for the Montagnards, an archetypal sixties liberal who has changed her tune by a note or two; General Hiestand, General Ngo Quand Truong, General Frank Blazey, and a whole host of army officers and enlisted men; among the women, also, are the Vietnamese, Miss Minh (who speaks Black English) and Co Van, and, at the end of the story, "The Beggar Woman," with her baby—"She was all of Vietnam to me."

The style works for him as well. Close to colloquial, clean, accessible, transparent. The narrator is not showing off or trying to dazzle or confuse us with sleights of hand, tricks of the trade. Moreover the easy use of acronyms and place names and Vietnamese words, all of which make good sense in context and do not need any more explanation and exposition than they receive, helps keep the reader closer to the experience, *sharing* it, as it happens with the narrator.

The people he selects from the crowd of faces to tell us most about are interesting and worth knowing. In a kind of refracted light their vivid presences tend to give more life and credibility to the central character, Jones himself. Therefore we tend, also, to take his judgment calls, his opinions and conclusions more seriously. He has earned our attention by the time he begins to pass judgment on his experience. For example, this comment arising from his observation of the extraordinary physical courage of Mike Healy: "But to a good professional soldier physical courage is like physical fitness, it is not a fetish but a foregone conclusion of the line of work, an accepted fact, a necessary tool of their trade, and they don't think about it much." Or Jones's view on why the full, true story of the horrible killings at Hue in 1968 did not get told then or later (even now): "Anti-U.S. feeling was popular at home. Why buck it in the cause of unpopular truths. . . . They had not really happened as far as liberal America was concerned."

(The most recent study of the times, *The Vietnam Wars, 1945–1990*, by Marlyn B. Young, minimizes the casualty figures of the Hue Massacres and, a little like Frances Fitzgerald's complicated defense of murderous terrorism, tries to make a best-case retroactive scenario for the North Vietnamese and the VC: "Most of the victims seem to have had some connection with the government of South Vietnam or the Americans." Of one batch of four hundred bodies Jones had seen unearthed, all of them clubbed to death, he remarked: "It is no easy thing to club down 400 people.")

Consider this observation from the flight over dangerous country to Dak Pe: "At home it was easy to talk about the basic kindliness and good intentions of the VC and North Viets. Out here (I realized suddenly, perhaps more than I ever had) in Vietnam, they were the enemy. They would kill you if they could."

Opinions like that made new enemies for Jones, to be sure, among the politicized intellectuals of America, to whom and for whom most of the Vietnam books have been and are written. In context, a context that includes the absence of cosmic and geo-political generalizations, Jones's opinions are earned and persua-sive to the open-minded reader. That same reader will find a good deal to honor and very little to hate in the military men Jones has chosen to introduce in *Viet Journal*. Indeed, it is difficult for the reader not to sympathize with Colonel Jack Whitted, who told Jones this: "My old daddy told me not to stay in back in 1950. In 1950 soldiers were still heroes. But in twenty years, my daddy said, they'll be shit again. Every twenty years. He said, in 1912 every store in Brownsville, Texas carried a sign: Soldiers and dogs not allowed. But me, I wouldn't listen to him. But you tell them, Sir. Tell them Jack Whitted said for them to remember we're not all Draculas."

IV.

But there is a subtext to *Viet Journal*, plainly indicated by the per-sonal beginning with the death of his father and the end, the last line in fact, where Jones admits he has finally lost the memory, the image of himself—"I had come back hoping to meet a certain twenty-year-old boy, walking along Kalakaua Avenue in a 'gook' shirt, perhaps, but I had not seen him."

But that loss may have been a necessary precondition for Jones's future development. In Paris since August of 1958, Jones had fin-ished and published *The Thin Red Line* (1962), but he had not been able to make much progress on the third novel of his World War II trilogy, the story that would be published posthumously as *Whis-tle* (1978). But he had been learning things without really being aware of the process. In *The Ice-Cream Headache and Other Stories* (1968), through the characters of John Slade and Tom Dylan, in a series of related stories, he had learned to write directly about his painful childhood. In *The Merry Month of May* (1971), he discov-ered he could write about contemporary political events (the Paris student riots of 1968) with authority. His thriller, *A Touch of Danger* (1972), taught him to cover more story with less heft. All the nov-els, except for *The Pistol*, which is basically a long short story, had been large, prolix if not sprawling. With *Danger* he learned how to handle complicated events and a fairly large cast of characters efficiently, without wasted space or motion. All these qualities come together in *Viet Journal*, which, in turn, changed things for him. He moved back to America for keeps. Wrote the admirable text for a wonderful picture book—*WWII*. And then, and only then, he was able to put together, all but a few pages, *Whistle* before he died. *Whistle* caps the trilogy that, taken together, is his major accomplishment. But in a sense *Viet Journal*, which he did live to finish in the terms he elected and which liberated him even as it brought together everything he had learned so far, is his finest hour. Certainly it is a brilliant example of reportage and narrative and, as well, is a primary document in the history of a dark time.

Reynolds Price

The Tongues of Angels and *The Foreseeable Future*

These two recent reviews of Reynolds Price were written for that remarkable monthly magazine the *World & I*, which, among many other surprising things, allows about 150 pages in each issue for book reviews, all of them almost full-scale essay reviews. Other reviews in this book also appeared first in the *World & I*—the reviews of Bobbie Ann Mason's *Love Life*, Paul Fussell's *Wartime*, Madison Smartt Bell's *The Year of Silence*, and Hilary Masters's *Cooper*.

The Tongues of Angels

As Bridge Boatner of Winston-Salem, North Carolina, tells it, and us—for, like *Kate Vaiden* (1986), Reynolds Price's successful and highly regarded novel that won the National Book Critics Award for fiction in that year, *The Tongues of Angels* is a consistent first-person narration—this story is mainly an accounting of the summer of 1954, when Boatner was twenty-one, now being recalled in his fifty-fourth year. Any first-person story, from whatever angle and distance in space and time from the events depicted, is, in fact, a tale of here and now and essentially amounts to the time of its telling, just as the essential primary and dramatic action of a first-person story is not to be found in the events themselves but in the telling of the tale. That is to say, in any first-person story the telling is the main thing that happens. Past and present are always here and now and are equal for as long as the telling may last. In such a context there is an almost absolute freedom in time and space, to be exercised or inhibited as the teller (and, behind the teller, the artist) wills. There is freedom to react to events, to comment on events even as they are presented, and, when it pleases, to digress from the mainstream of action. In fact there can be no such thing as a digression in a well-executed first-person story.

Nevertheless, creating a special tension within this chosen form,

The Tongues of Angels is a novel of precisely split time, of a then and a now, of highly significant past events being reviewed by a man mature and experienced enough to be skeptical of his own earned wisdom and more than a little surprised at his earlier state of innocence. In our time—as distinct from the convention of the old-fashioned, first-person story, the framework of the "discovered" manuscript (*The Turn of the Screw*) or the spoken voice, listened to at a specific time and place and later recalled (*The Heart of Darkness*)—first-person stories are usually assumed to be told somehow out of thin air, tilting between the extremes of the simply spoken and the purely written. In this slender book, we learn fairly late that the narrative of Bridge Boatner is, in fact, a written one (which we are reading over his shoulder, as it were), being addressed to a specific person, his younger son Rustum Boatner. And, a little later, we learn that Bridge now intends to share it all with some of his friends. "Maybe these words will also last," he writes, "not till the sun burns out of fuel, begins to swell and then ends Earthly life. . . . I mean also to give this to friends. More than most people I've watched through the years, I've had miraculous luck with friends, more friends in fact than I can maintain." In a sense, this late revelation of the actual frame of the narrative is wonderfully apt, for it appropriately explains and justifies not only the range of prose styles, which includes elements of high style as well as the adroit recapitulation of the living vernacular, but also makes clear and meaningful the use of occasional self-reflexive elements in a context which is firmly opposed to the familiar tropes of fashionable metafiction. As, for example, when Bridge pauses briefly to explain his difficulty in describing the process of creating a painting: "Again I'm up against a serious problem here. The thing is, I need to describe my difficulties in painting a particular canvas without a boring amount of technical discussion or art-critic hot air and without reproductions of the picture in its various stages. The only writer I can think of who comes even close to managing the task is Virginia Woolf."

The Bridge Boatner who tells this tale is a gifted and quite successful painter, a *representational* painter, as it happens, who (rather like his own creator) has managed at once to be faithful to his own gifts and ideals and yet to survive the prevailing and antithetical fashions in the art world. The summer of 1954 was the time when Bridge managed to create his first important painting, "the first really decent accomplishment in all my work"—*The Smoky Mountains as the Meaning of Things*. As Bridge writes, "Whatever else I did wrong that summer—and it was plenty—I managed to paint one sizeable picture, thirty-six by twenty." He did this while working as a counselor at a classic boys' camp of the period, Camp Juniper, where he also began to grow beyond the grief of his father's death the winter before and where he was wakened to much in himself and in the world as a result of an intense relationship with a young camper, Raphael Patrick Noren, a gifted dancer and a beautiful young man whose Indian name, *Kinvan*, aptly means "Airborne." (During the summer Bridge himself formally earned the name *Wachinton*, or "Wise." Like so many things in *The Tongues of Angels* this is more double-edged in implication than it is merely ironic or ambiguous.) Raphael, called Rafe, named for the great artist, but functioning in this story like his angelic original, is possessed of a secret and tragic past and comes to a sad end, an ending for which Bridge is at least vaguely responsible. There is guilt involved (nobody is blameless or guiltless in a Price novel; we are all sinners in need of grace, healing, and salvation), but not quite in the conventional and secular sense of it.

"Rafe Noren marked me," Bridge writes. "Not a wound or a scar but a deep live line, like the velvet burr in the darkest shadows of Rembrandt etchings, the ones I've mentioned where demons lurk. Let this be clear—never have I let myself for one instant think that Rafe died so that I might work with his rich fertilizing life behind me." A little later he allows, "All I meant was, Rafe Noren's life enabled me. And now I've lived to say so."

This complex story stands at the center of the novel, forming an elegy for all lost innocence and youth. "No young person known to me, now or past, has thrown a stronger light than Rafe Noren or farmed more corners of the world he touched with serious laughter. Young as he was, it was laughter launched with open eyes in full sight and knowledge of the final jaws."

Anyone familiar with the fiction of Reynolds Price knows that there is always a serpent in the garden. In the fable of *A Generous Man* (1966) there was a "real" one, a python named "Death." But there is also always light in abundance; and the garden, the *place* where his people live their lives, is richly evoked and realized. So are the Smoky Mountains here. And there is always an irrepressible, essential sense of humor, partly a matter of sly and sometimes elegant wit, a turn of phrase that comes out gentle smiling, but there is also the belly cheer of deep rural American laughter, unabashedly vulgar and funny: "I silently reminded my upstaged self that body wind in its two main forms, belches and farts, is half the foundation of boyish humor. I rightly suspected I'd hardly begun to experience their virtuosity in ways to smuggle farts like anarchist bombs into the highest and most sacred scenes of camp life." Just so, narrator Bridges can smuggle bombs of laughter into the most sacred scenes.

Nostalgia—if there is a better book about "camp life," in general and in detail, I don't know of it—reigns supreme. Here Price makes as much of time, those much misunderstood 1950s, as he does of place. And the power of first-person storytelling to digress without loss of purpose allows Bridge Boatner to comment on the times. Here, for instance, moving from a picture, half amused and half in awe, of Albert "Chief" Jenkins, "youth leader and founder-owner of old Camp Juniper," Bridge says something, with a typically witty turn at the end of it, about the true history of those times:

> The time of my boyhood was a far more fervent time than many now believe. Today anybody whose eyes glint fire, and who sees himself as a gift to the world, is likely to be a flimflam man or an out-of-state strangler, maybe both. But don't forget, we boys born in the early 1930's had watched our parents body-surf the Depression and in some cases wipe out. We'd been too young to fight in the Second World War but just old enough to hear the news and understand what an all-time evil genius had brought on the conflict. And we got a thrilling dose of patriotism and high moral expectation from our participation in scrap metal drives, old bacon grease drives (to grease shell casings), paper drives, war bonds.

An important historical observation, that the generation of the 1950s was, likewise, children of Depression and the Second World War. Bridge has also been "as an artist-journalist" to the later war in Vietnam.

The particular triumph of *The Tongues of Angels* is that so much is accomplished, and so gracefully, no sweat and no strain showing, in such a brief, lean novel. A lesser artist than Price would sink under the weight of events and the undeniable, if well-disguised, complexity of the story. A lesser artist than Price could not have introduced and kept alive such an extensive crew of distinctive characters: Sam Baker, former Marine and now head counselor; Kevin Hawser, a Yale boy, "the Robert Redford among us"; Mrs. Chief, "a flawless Victorian matron with remorselessly even porcelain teeth and breastworks that might have saved Richmond from Grant"; Possum Walters, "a would-be lawyer from Wake Forest" (Bridge goes to Chapel Hill); a nameless young country girl who shows Bridge and Kevin around the old Thomas Wolfe house in Asheville; Bridge's girlfriend, Viemme, off "waiting table at a hotel on Mount Desert Island, Maine"; Mike Dorfman, anthropologist among the Sioux and "one of that summer's really good influences on my life"; a real Sioux, Bright Day; Clara Jenins, "Chief's sweet-natured old-maid niece, maybe forty"; and not least, the seven campers, adding up to fourteen in the two sessions, in Bridge's cabin 16.

Price is at a peak of artistic skill and maturity, able to challenge some strong literary fashions and daring enough to take great risks to achieve his goals. *The Tongues of Angels* proves that it is possible to be as witty as can be without being clever or smart-alecky. It also demonstrates that a complicated love story, homo-erotic but much more than that, can still be told and celebrated. Raphael Noren, angel/messenger/muse, is a richly dimensional ambiguous character. More to the point, in Price's novel he is, for as long as the telling lasts, entirely credible. Daring? Well, at a time when most American writers are cultivating the ways and means of cynicism, Price continues to write stories of great sweetness. He can do this—and never better than here—without being silly or sentimental. He plays at the edges of the sentimental like a child at the beach, running just ahead of the waves. Never gets wet. His stories, none more so than this one, are about forms of healing. He celebrates the possibilities of healing when easy nihilism is all the literary rage.

Are there no flaws, no reservations and qualifications? Well, a few. The choices a true artist makes are more or less political.

There are always trade-offs, losses and gains. The calm and serenity achieved by Price are sometimes at the expense of pure energy. This carries over to the characters. For example, compared to the great Gulley Jimson in Joyce Cary's *The Horse's Mouth*—and sooner or later every modern book about an artist has to come to terms with Gulley—Bridge Boatner is about half asleep. Cary's basic subject, the creator learning to live and work in a world characterized chiefly by injustice, does not enter into the professional life of Bridge Boatner. Price's portrait of the artist, an artist of his own age and sharing much with the novelist, does not seriously imagine possibilities of failure. Perhaps, who knows?, this is because Reynolds Price, though sometimes subjected to unfair and unjust criticism, has nevertheless never experienced artistic failure. His first book, *A Long and Happy Life* (1962), won the Faulkner Foundation Award for first novels, and he has, as writer, remained in the comfortable winner's circle ever since. Nothing wrong with that. He earned his way. But there is something missing, an edge of anxiety and simple suspense, in the story of any artist whose only serious artistic problem is being, from time to time, out of fashion.

No matter. *The Tongues of Angels* is a wise and wonderful novel, a gift from a major artist who understands as well as his central character "The Smoky Mountains as the Meaning of Things."

The Foreseeable Future

The Foreseeable Future, Reynolds Price's twenty-second book in a productive career that began with a bang in 1962 with the publication of *A Long and Happy Life,* consists of three long stories, one, the title story, almost of novel length, each related to the others by a network of thematic concerns, by place, Price's North Carolina, by a variety of technical devices, and by a series of subtle echoes, images, and shadows. The first in the sequence, "The Fare to the Moon," concerns one full day in the life of Kayes Paschal, the day he must report for his preinduction physical during World War II, and the lives of a group of kin and loved ones close to him—his wife, Daphne, and young son, Curt, whom he has more or less abandoned for the sake of his passionate love for Leah Birch, a black woman he has known all his life (she is the niece of his grandmother's servant and cook); and his brother, Riley, who is running the family farm and doing his level, decent best to hold things together. In this story, as in the other two, the narrator works and stays close to the protagonist. Yet, by means of a delightful sleight of hand, like a magician's, Price allows the omniscient narrator—so graceful are these segues that they are barely noticed except where the voice changes from third person to first, or vice versa—to enter and establish the points of view of each of the other central characters, adding kinds of complexity and ambiguity (not to mention verisimilitude) that give these stories deep roots. "The Face to the Moon" has an unusual closure, in a sense pushing the reader forward into the next story. Kayes Paschal passes his physical and is shipped off to Fort Jackson for his basic training. (In one of Price's very few errors he calls it "boot camp," a term which was, until very recently, reserved for the transformation of civilians into Marines or sailors in the U. S. Navy.) Riley has driven Leah off to the bus station. Price does not, and need not, note that an actual interracial marriage would have been unlawful at that time. The story ends with the son, Curt, half in a dream, forgiving his father and becoming a man, about to enjoy "the first whole day of his grown man's life."

"The Foreseeable Future" takes place during the week, specified and identified, chapter by chapter, of Sunday, May 6, 1945, through Friday, May 11. Whit Wade, a badly wounded veteran of the D-Day landing in Normandy less than a year before, now making his way as a troubled civilian and as an insurance claims adjustor, goes out on the road, Monday through Friday, doing his job (people *work* for a living in these Price stories), fighting despair and a deep death wish, a feeling, in fact, that he has already died once in France, and all the while stumbling into people—Juanita Branch, called "Mother Marie," a strange and strangely loving spiritual counselor; his uncle Tuck and Martha Burton, a black woman whom he had once loved, by whom he had a son, now dead, he never knew of, a woman he learns he still loves; a young fatherless country boy named Tray, who saves his life after an accident and makes Whit long for a son of his own; a beautiful woman on the Outer Banks, Rebecca Barksdale, who had long ago as a teenager secretly loved him; a dwarf named Sherf; an aged, reclusive aristocrat, Mr. Drake, who has memories of the Civil War; and a giant, Carle Towns, who, like himself, is a deeply wounded veteran of the ongoing war. V-E Day comes during this week, but nobody, not even the prescient visionary Whit, foresees the ending of things in the Pacific.

By Friday night, his journey and quest completed, Whit is home again and healing. He takes his wife, June, and his daughter, Elissa, called Liss, to a restaurant for a family feast. ("Fried onion-rings were new in the South like tossed salads.") The feast, a kind of communion, allows Whit to triumph over both his past and the immediate future, to begin to live again. As he puts it, speaking into a brand new machine, a Victrola Living Memories machine that will make a record of the speaker's voice, he suddenly says (among other things): "Pa hopes you know the part you played in haling him back from his long trip. You and your mother are where I've landed. For now at least, the foreseeable future, this May the 11th, 1945. I enjoy the view of both you ladies and the world behind you. May you bypass places that steal your soul. May you find your own home base like me."

By the conclusion of the second story we now have some complex relations and recurring motifs joining the separate parts of the book together and in a structure. Whit is not the same man as Kayes; yet they have much in common. Each has a single child he loves, and fears for, beyond measure. Each has loved, passionately, a black woman. Each man is depicted as *fully* conscious, more than mind alone, a creature of dreams and dream visions. Whit is more of a visionary and more of a deep dreamer. But for both men there is an intense spiritual world beyond the limits of ordinary thought. In a serious sense Whit might well be a version of Kayes. If Kayes dies in the war (as seems foreshadowed and likely), Whit rises from the dead and then at the end of his journey, no less a quest than Jason's or Gawain's, freely chooses life.

The third story, "Back Before Day," features Dean Walker, Vietnam veteran and now the football coach for Don Watson High, and his family, five-year-old Brady, called Brade, and Dean's wife, Flynn. It is the brief story of a marriage in trouble, mostly through misunderstanding, of a family about to break up. In the end, sorely tested, things hold together for Dean Walker and his wife and child, leaving him feeling "very little but thanks and a general peace in all his parts." He, too, is a dreamer and able to summon visions, from time to time, including what he names "the dream of perfect goodness." The dream, like inspiration, seems to be a gift; but there is a conscious creative process, not unlike the author's, that helps him to find solace and strength: "As his mind related the ancient hope, it added more details of peaceful deeds like beautiful girls in slow-motion dances outside each window and all of them singing songs from a world where fairness is all life asks or gives."

In each of these stories peace somehow replaces war, the family love of good, if not at all saintly, people overcomes a multitude of troubles and temptations, and dreams and visions enlarge consciousness and light a way forward into the foreseeable future.

Somehow Price manages to be compassionate with all his characters without lapsing into sentimentality for any of them. This just uniformity of attitude is another of the ties that bind these stories together. Narrative technique is another. In all these stories there are startling examples of the sudden switch of point of view that dramatizes at once the paradox of separation and communion among friends and enemies. The dialogue has a marvelous authenticity. It sparkles and crackles with life. And the language is layered in virtuosity. The neutral narration slips unobtrusively into the right, apt words and expressions for the character or situation in focus. There is a distinct language for action and event, for the mind thinking its way in a maze of troubles, for the spirit dreaming its way home. The range is from the bucolic and earthy to high eloquence, always surprising, like the best poetry, yet always precisely appropriate. And it is all rooted deep in a language of living folklore. Author-narrator and his characters share a common capacity to create and render again and again similes that restore the language to its full value even as they re-create a memorable image. A flock of starlings in "The Fare to the Moon": "They flung their bodies through the woods like handfuls of fat black seed; then walked around like important Negroes, casing the leaves." In "The Foreseeable Future" Whit Wade's mind "snagged on doubt like a dry wood splinter." And a moment later he speaks to himself: "But I feel like the worst old broken window the wind flows through." Or this narrator's moment, one among many, in "Back Before Day": "They were in deep country, a two-lane cement road with no center line; and on both sides, their lights brushed trees—black pines and cedars so old and knobby they could make you feel carefree and blessed, if you paid any notice and knew about trees."

It is a pleasure to watch an artist, Price, at work and at the peak of his powers, able to make magic by the simplest gesture, brave and whole enough to write a book that nobody else I can think of could accomplish.

Whether the writer chooses a subject or is in fact chosen by it (and no one, not even the writer, can ever be sure and certain about that) there remains an irreducible mystery, an almost ineffable enigma shadowing the relationship of a writer to a subject. Could Shakespeare have written *Volpone*? Why not? Could John Cheever have written classical westerns if he had wanted to? Could Elmore Leonard produce Kafkaesque metafiction? Of course they could have if they had wanted to and if the form and its appropriate subjects had seized them. It may seem to be a silly statement in the form of an irrelevant question. But it is not quite as simple as all that. What we look for in our best writers is the quality of living imagination. The power and the glory of our finest writers is to have found (by design or by stumbling upon it) the subject that fires and liberates the imagination. And there is no telling, at least from the sum of all the parts of our literary history, whether that subject will be close to the "real life," the outward and visible experience of the writer. Hemingway and Fitzgerald, richly imaginative writers, worked very close to the rough edges of the autobiographical. Others, Faulkner for example, seem to have needed to create fictive lives for themselves, not for the sake of writing false autobiography, but, most often, for liberating the empathetic capacity to identify with a wide range of credible characters the likes of which neither the writer nor the captured readers ever met.

All of this generalization is to point out and to celebrate the power of imagination in Reynolds Price. In what we know about the life and times of Reynolds Price—and he and his publishers, over the years and in a variety of public forms, have told us a good deal about him—he is quite different in interests and experience, if not entirely in background, from the people he usually writes about and the situations in which they are apt to find themselves. Although from the earliest days until now most Southern writers have been townspeople, it is hard for all but a very few Southern writers to be far removed from rural experience. Neither Theocritus nor (later) Virgil, both favorites of the Southern literary tradition, was ever a shepherd, but neither one had to look far to see a real one doing his work. The agrarians were not farmers, but, like most Southerners, they had farmers in the family and a family farm or two somewhere in the near background. So Reynolds Price's constant concern for rural folk is at once conventional and authentic; and, in truth, so is the cultural clash between the immemorial rigor and dignity of rural values and the gradual spreading (a stain, some would call it; others would call up the gradual, inexorable southward gnawing of the Sahara) of urban and modernist values into the world and scene of the South. It is not so much that Price defends the old against the new, the tried and true against the "new and improved," as it is that he honors the sometimes baffled points of view of many good country people, people of good will, whose beliefs, values, and, in time of war and tribulation, whose very lives and loves are threatened by events which, distant or not, impinge directly, not abstractly upon them. It is very hard for many Southern writers, at least of Price's generation and younger, to write about these people without condescension or cuteness or both. The problem is all the more exacerbated by the undeniable fact that from the days of the Civil War until now, condescension and cuteness have been praised and well rewarded by native as well as alien critics. There were indeed some bits and pieces, flashes of cuteness, in Price's early and highly successful work; but all that has been refined out of his work, as his style and use of fictional forms have grown ever more supple, fluent, and simplified.

But the point needs to be made that Price is an unlikely candidate for the role he has found himself playing. Price is, first of all, a legitimate intellectual, a certified academic, a graduate of Duke, a

Rhodes Scholar, a longtime member of the faculty of Duke, able, evidently, to hold his own in the glitzy era of Stanley Fish, functioning, alive and well and unbowed amid a feeding frenzy of politically correct colleagues. It has been said, by more than one wag, that with Albania now moving toward democracy, the Duke English Department may well be the world's last bastion of utterly unreconstructed Marxist theology. In any case, not a hint of this, or of other intellectual fashions and follies of our times, appears in Price's work. Price treats these people with respect. They are often fun, but he never makes fun of them. Their thoughts and ideas, dreams and visions, are as valid as anybody's, not a function of intellectual fashion. At four in the morning of Monday, May 7, 1945, when that fine, strong woman, June Wade, wakes up and can't get back to sleep, she turns to the precisely appropriate book for her time and place; but Price does not make fun of her because she isn't literary enough to please a big-time deconstructionist: "At four in the morning, June woke as she often did. She checked Whit's breathing—deep asleep still. Then she switched on her lamp to read a soothing few pages in her book, *The Robe.*" Not merely an intellectual in good standing, but a highly sophisticated and civilized man, the earliest accounts of whom describe him as something of a dandy and an aesthete even in his undergraduate days, Price makes only the slightest inferential judgment of June's taste. She finds *The Robe* soothing. Good. She has earned some soothing.

All three of the central male characters in these short novels are (or have been or soon will be) citizen soldiers in times of war and trouble. Price treats their thoughts and feelings about this condition with authoritative seriousness and, perhaps more surprising, with genuine authenticity. Reynolds Price is one of the very few American writers of his generation (John Updike is another) who did not log his years, few or long, in military service. It is a tribute to his honest imagination that he neither sentimentalizes nor overstates the case of his soldier boys. By the same token, except for a few evocative details, he does not deceive anyone by taking the reader where the author has never been in fact or flesh. He does not need to. In this bloody century millions of young Americans served their time at least up until the deferments and evasions possible during the Vietnam War. Wisely Price has elected to engage the imaginations of his readers, a large number of whom can add memory and experience to these imagined events.

All the above is courageous behavior. Equally so, and a triumph, is the celebration of marriage and family love, in large and small, by a lifelong bachelor with no children of his own. His depiction of the erotic pleasures (and pitfalls, too) of husbands and wives is beautifully realized, unfailing in its decency, unflinching in its authentic re-creation. Writing honorably about sexual experience, neither scanting the erotic nor nudging toward the prurient, requires a kind of magical artistry—something like a musician's perfect pitch. Clearly one of the things which Reynolds Price has done to earn our praise and admiration, above and beyond the creation of these lives of these characters in this book, and many others, is to celebrate and liberate the imagination. As noted, his characters have vivid, active imaginations, which sometimes rise to the level of the visionary. In these things, and in his authorial relation to them, Price is telling us something about himself, ourselves, and, as well, the richly complex, deeply dimensional lives of ordinary people whose humanity is anything but commonplace.

Madison Smartt Bell

The Year of Silence

I.

It seems that we have now arrived—and perhaps our ground time here will be blessedly brief—at a time and a place where youth, in and of itself, or, in the case of some of our very prominent "young" writers, apparent or self-proclaimed youth, is widely considered to be not merely a fragile fact of life, bound to be changed soon enough come what may by the implacable and grinding attrition of spent time, but rather as a kind of providential virtue that, like the purely and simply genetic accident of outward and visible beauty or, maybe the fortunate, blind chance of inherited wealth, is worthy of reflexive awe and admiration and of more than ample rewards. So be it. And how else could it be in this, our age, in which we have been urged, at times *required* to know and to honor the everlasting *image,* not the reality? The image which, unlike the truth it spurns and distorts, will never set us free; but which is intended to keep us a whole lot happier—if, as Dean Swift asserted, happiness is the state of being well deceived.

In any case, youth is being well served in this late literary season. Attention is being paid. From the Establishment and its glossy trade journals one hears more and more about what are being called the Baby Novelists, and the Baby Editors who have risen to eminence on the youthful shoulders of their writers.

Take the case of Bret Easton Ellis, whose new and second novel, *The Rules of Attraction,* has recently appeared to considerable critical attention, even the well-earned and predictably negative reviews acting, as if in a kind of cuckoo affirmation of Gresham's law, to take away space and attention from more worthwhile books. What can be said? Ellis is young, that's what. He was, after all, only twenty, or thereabouts, when *Less Than Zero* came along. (Amid the reams and webs of publicity it was never clear whether he *wrote* the book at twenty or was twenty when it abruptly surfaced.) But he gives signs already of maturing. Maybe too much for his own good. At writers' conferences last summer, agents and editors were overheard announcing a concerted search (and destroy?) mission. "We're looking for a young Bret Ellis," they said. And we should not forget or ignore his Bennington classmate, Jill Eisenstadt, whose *From Rockaway* is out there brightly in the bookstores, another youthful jape which (as the jacket copy cheerfully announces) "takes us into the closed, tribal world of a group of young lifeguards (and their friends) from Rockaway, New York." (*Beach Blanket Bingo*, anyone? Would you believe *The Horror At Party Beach*?) There's the whole celebrated motley crew from 1986's *20 Under 30*, some (to use old army terminology) overage in grade well before the book came out.

And still uncertainly young, still a vaguely new voice, there is the inimitable Tama Janowitz, already better known for her amaretto and lime juice advertisements (and for the company she keeps in the latter) than she is for her well-publicized though somewhat less-than-best-selling books, including the tacky *Cannibal in New York*. Finally, towering above all, there is that role model for all restless scribbling youth, Jay McInerney, who may yet live to bring back that old TV advertisement line (was it for Geritol?): "You're as young as you feel!" It may or may not be ironic, but is unquestionably coincidental, that one of the most publicized of the Baby Editors, Morgan Entrekin, was Madison Bell's classmate in high school. Somehow they missed each other. That was, apparently, their last contact.

Enough. The point—that literary silliness is spreading faster than AIDS or herpes II—has been made.

II.

For those who, surveying the official literary scene, may have come to feel that Oscar Wilde's famous observation was more likely British understatement than cynical wit, let me cheerfully assure you that youth was not wasted on Madison Smartt Bell. He spent a lot of it working hard, writing; and, as a result of his labors, prior to his thirtieth birthday this past August, he had three novels—*The Washington Square Ensemble* (1983), *Waiting for the End of the World* (1985), and *Straight Cut* (1986)—plus a collection of short fiction, *Zero dB and Other Stories* (1987), in print, not counting this, his latest, *The Year of Silence,* which was already circulating in bound galleys. Nobody, not even his publisher, has noticed much or made a lot out of Bell's youth; maybe because, from his first published works (stories) until now, he has written like a grown-up about serious grown-up situations, events, and problems, always involving fully realized, solidly presented, three-dimensional characters. Male and female characters, as it happens, of all kinds of backgrounds, of all ages, and, indeed, of every kind of race, creed, color, national origin, and sexual preference. For example, the central crew of characters in *The Washington Square Ensemble,* a team of five drug dealers, includes thoroughly credible presentations of Santa Barbara, a Puerto Rican deeply engaged in voodoo; Yusuf Ali, a seven-foot black Muslim and a serious student of the Koran; Porco Miserio, drifter and musician; as well as Holy Mother and Johnny B. Goode, whose backgrounds are more conventional, Mafia-bred.

The characters in *Waiting for the End of the World* are equally well rendered and even more widely various, including intellectuals and winos and terrorists, Russian émigrés, and even a ghost or two. All this rich gallery of people is treated with humor and compassion, never sentimentality; and the best and sanest of them demonstrate the same kind of humor and compassion, never self-pity, also.

III.

From his first novel on, this born-and-bred Southerner, who grew up on an old farm in Tennessee (and who has written first-rate "Southern" fiction in some of his stories while living in New York), has kept to an established turf, aptly described on the jacket of *Waiting for the End of the World* as "the underbelly of Brooklyn and Manhattan." *Straight Cut,* primarily a thriller, and a very smoothly, skillfully executed variation on that genre, not unlike the best of the "entertainments" by Graham Greene, is international in scope;

but its homing point is always New York. *The Year of Silence* all takes place in a gritty and authentic re-creation of contemporary Manhattan, except for a final, rural scene.

It is an interesting, perhaps surprising, fact that the most detailed and authoritative contemporary literary treatments of New York City, as a singular and troubled region in this nation, should have come from Southern writers, most recently from Tom Wolfe and Madison Smartt Bell. Both have New York novels out this year. Wolfe's *The Bonfire of the Vanities* has already generated a firestorm of advance publicity. We witness a kind of high/low approach, for Wolfe, primarily interested in social status, has always dealt with New York highlife; and even here he treats the lowlife as an exotic phenomenon, if not alien. Bell, who has lived deep in black and Hispanic Brooklyn and worked as a security guard and a TV sound man in Manhattan, knows the scene from the street up. A generation, of course, separates the two writers; but there are also significant differences in the Southern background. In an extensive profile in the October 1986 issue of *Vanity Fair,* Wolfe is described as "profoundly affected" by his family's awkward status as country gentry who moved to Richmond and had to contend with "one of the haughtiest and most closed societies of the South."

Bell is a direct lineal descendant of several of the most deeply rooted, aristocratic families of Tennessee. His people took the opposite track, moving out from Nashville to the country by choice. Other likenesses and subtle differences are interesting. Wolfe is Presbyterian, attended Washington and Lee, and played baseball. Bell is Episcopalian, graduated from Princeton, and is (like a couple of characters in *The Year of Silence*) a master of and a professional instructor of violent Oriental martial arts. Wolfe is, as the world knows, a well-tailored dandy. The *Vanity Fair* piece is titled "The Evolution of Dandy Tom." Prior to his recent marriage to poet Elizabeth Spires, Bell cultivated an appearance that might have been politely called The Writer as Young Wino or Future Bag Persons of America costume. For a while at Princeton he was something of a cult figure, on account of his karate, his banjo playing, and his writing; and other students dressed like him for good luck. Goodwill stores, for miles around Princeton, were picked clean.

Bell treats the region of New York as if, somehow, it were Southern. That is, he treats it with the same kind of close observation and deep respect you find in Faulkner's Yoknapatawpha, or Flannery O'Connor's south Georgia. He does not settle for clichés and stereotypes of either people or places, seeking and succeeding, instead, in seeing this familiar milieu freshly. There is great love of the place even though he is, if anything, more unblinking and disillusioned than Tom Wolfe was in his early essays. It is a real world, and you quickly see that the same world, as found in the work of McInerney, Janowitz, and the Baby Novelists, is shabby and more than a bit phony in comparison to Bell's re-creation.

Add to strong, diverse people and vividly evoked settings the fact that all of Bell's novels, so far, have at least an element of the thriller in that they are strongly suspenseful, built around a solid core of what Aristotle called *fable*, moving with an inexorable energy toward a powerful climax. They are all page turners. These qualities would be rare enough at any age and stage of artistic development; and so it is that from the beginning, only a few short years ago, his youth has been a factor only in a positive sense, in the qualities where it legitimately matters and ought to be present.

That is, Bell is demonstrably a young writer in his enormous energy, his blithe daring, his dazzling verbal brilliance, and his surprising angles of vision. Otherwise he writes like his seniors of all ages. He belongs, at the very least, in the hierarchy of prominent serious writers a good ten years and more older, people like Richard Ford and T. Coraghessan Boyle, both of whom have been recently favored with front-page reviews in the *New York Times Book Review*. Truth is that he has written and published a good deal more than either one of them. In a slightly different case, one might strongly argue that he certainly deserves similar notice and honor here and now. In Bell's case it isn't absolutely necessary. Because even if the Literary Establishment were to join in some jolly collusion to keep him safely in obscurity, if not oblivion, the work is already there.

Meanwhile, there are still plenty of people who can read and write, weigh and judge. He already holds the winning hand. It is only a matter of time, then; and given time, he can only enhance his reputation as he grows in wisdom and stature and increases his mastery of the art. The masters of our times are clearly his role models and, appropriately, his real competition. It seems equally clear that he aims to be counted honorably among them—a master of the art of fiction.

IV.

The Year of Silence is his finest work so far, taut and slender, swiftly paced, profoundly evocative, and an architectural concept of storytelling that is unusual, may well be unique. (I know of no example of anything exactly like it.) It is told in eleven titled and independent sections, some as outwardly separate as short stories, others linked together by ongoing events and characters, all united by being concerned, one way or another, with the central character, a gifted young woman, Marian, who died a year before the story begins, maybe as a suicide, maybe by accident. It is a book about what she and her death come to mean to others, some, like her lover, Webber, and her cousin, Gwen, terribly close to her; others, two policemen on patrol, an old woman in a wheelchair, a man who saw her once in a bar, a dwarf who loved and admired her from a distance, friends and enemies alike, who have an empty place in their lives now because of her absence, whether they fully know it or not.

We, the readers, know more than any characters, by the end, learning something new and significant from each section; but, finally, for us there are mysteries, boundaries beyond which we are unable to pass also. In that curious sense the omniscient reader is not godlike, after all, but *shares* the experience of the story. Like all the others, the reader is then left with an empty place, created by a vanished life.

Does it seem complicated? It is not. It is refined to great simplicity, readily accessible. Even the extraordinary virtuosity—each section has, for example, a different style and voice—is so highly refined as to seem entirely decorous and appropriate. It is uniformly brilliant without ever being self-serving or clever. It is intricate and elaborate without once being self-conscious or smart-assed. It has all of Bell's characteristic humor and compassion and, at several times, will touch you to tears. Even truncated and lifted completely out of a close context, the final sentences of the middle chapter describing Marian's death, from her own point of view, are astonishing and moving:

> Rising, she felt no contact with the floor; she seemed to hover in the midst of the space of the room, but although the walls were pulsing a little it was easy to move forward. . . . She floated forward, in the direction of the door. Then gravity reasserted itself and she was falling, seeing the hall table flipping over under an unfelt pressure of her outflung hand and the telephone sailing away from the table top and settling in a corner by the door. The pile of clothing on which she lay was airy as a cloud. She began to giggle and for some time could not stop. The spilled telephone chirped and whirred like an insect and Marian was lying in a round field bound at its edges by a cottony substance. Just at the edge of her vision a balloon came wandering across the sky trailing a long, long string through the crisp stalks of dry grass in the field. The string ran undulant like a snake's tail through the grass, lifting as the balloon lifted, so that gradually less and less of it touched the field. The tail end of the string dripped and bobbed, grazing the points of the winter grass, contact attenuating, until it touched the earth nowhere at all. The balloon was higher and smaller and rising more swiftly away and the sky had become less blue, more silver, and the balloon was the same color as the sky.

Somehow or other, in this brief, yet weighty novel, this unflinching, unsparing, and yet graceful story, Bell magically manages to arrive at an upbeat ending. It is not happy, by any definition, but it is life-affirming and all the more powerful for being so. There is every conceivable chance for him to exploit the prevailing contemporary fashion of glittery nihilism, but he chooses something deeper and more daring. It's a truly remarkable book by a remarkable, very likely a major writer. But it is already behind him. Reached at the Iowa Writers Workshop, where he is teaching and writing this year, Bell cautiously allowed that he is already deep into the process of writing "a long book about the South," something that ought to be worth waiting for. Meantime you will wait a long time before you find anything to read as exciting and satisfying as *The Year of Silence*.

Bobbie Ann Mason

Love Life

I.

She smiled with her gums showing, like Lily Tomlin.

—"Private Lies"

A lot of things have happened since Bobbie Ann Mason's first book of fiction, *Shiloh and Other Stories* (1982), arrived on the literary scene, winning for itself and its author the PEN/Hemingway Award and earning nominations for the National Book Critics Circle Award, American Book Award, and PEN/Faulkner Award. (In a prize-happy age, one notes that publishers have recently taken to listing near-misses in a kind of honors-by-association ploy. From time to time these days you will see books of poetry listed as "Runner-Up for the Pulitzer Prize," an odd claim to fame since every other book considered that did not receive that particular award is a "runner-up.")

Since the undeniable literary splash made by the appearance and reception of *Shiloh*, Bobbie Ann Mason has brought out two well-received novels, *In Country* (1985), which is being translated into film, and *Spence + Lisa* (1988); and she has reclaimed public credit for her earlier scholarly/critical titles—*Nabokov's Garden: A Nature Guide to Ada* (1974) and *The Girl Sleuth: A Feminist Guide to the Bobbsey Twins, Nancy Drew, and Their Sisters* (1975). Her work has received serious critical attention manifested not only in prompt and widespread reviews of her books as they appear but also in an impressive list of critical pieces about her work and interviews with her. Mason has been honored with a Guggenheim Fellowship, a National Endowment for the Arts grant, and another one from the Pennsylvania (where she lives now) Council on the Arts. Perhaps most important for a good and serious writer seeking to build an audience for her work, she has witnessed the reprinting of her first three works of fiction in Harper & Row's handsome Perennial Library trade paperback editions. Here are all the signs and symbols of a literary overnight success. It is always a cause for wonder and admiration in America when a new writer has apparently earned attention and audience on the strength of a (first!) collection of short stories.

Evidently, the truth is that it wasn't all that easy. Writing about Mason in "Writing in the Cold: The First Ten Years," Harper & Row editor Ted Solotaroff makes that point: "Mason spent some seven years writing an unpublished novel, and then story after story, sending each one to Roger Angell at the *New Yorker*, getting it back, writing another, until finally the twentieth one was accepted." In another place in the same essay he expands on this story:

> She began writing fiction in 1971, after she got out of graduate school, and for the next five years or so wrote in a desultory way, finding it hard to get focused. In 1976 she finished a novel about a twelve-year-old girl growing up in western Kentucky who was addicted to Nancy Drew novels. "It took another two years before I began to find my true subject, which was to write about my roots and the kinds of people I'd known, but from a contemporary perspective. It mainly took a lot of living to get to that point. I'd come from such a sheltered and isolated background that I had to go through culture shock by living for years in the North to see the world of Mayfield, Kentucky, in a way I could write about as I was now—in a kind of exile. Also it took me until I was in my thirties to get enough detachment and objectivity to see that many of those people back home were going through culture shock too."

II.

> He laughs, imagining George Washington coming back in the twentieth century and trying to make sense out of laundromats, Midnight Magic, and crazy women.
>
> —"Midnight Magic"

From the beginning, with the sixteen stories of *Shiloh*, these elements, the exile's vision of and nostalgia for home and the impact of the culture shock created as old ways collide with the latest contemporary trends, have been the basis for the primary conflicts in Mason's fiction. The contemporary reader is not so much invited as impelled to share an experience of culture shock as well; for it is unlikely, except by extraordinary accident, that the typical reader of contemporary fiction can or will know much, beyond certain comforting social and literary stereotypes, about the raw places and the plain people whose lives, both joys and sorrows, are the source of Mason's art.

The majority of Mason's stories are presented in third-person omniscient narration (only two stories in *Shiloh* and two in *Love Life*—"Marita" and "State Champions"—are essentially first-person stories), offering the reader the benefits of the guidance of a complex narrator, someone who shares a good deal of the distance and the sophistication of the author (and her imaginary reader), yet also, simultaneously, someone who, like Mason, comes straight out of the same place and from the same general background as most of her characters and thus maintains a steady, ambivalent sympathy for them. Mason's language, clear and concise and often no more than a breath and a step away from direct first-person narration, preserves this perilously delicate balance of empathy.

The narrator knows a whole lot more about things than most of her characters (and she lets you, the reader, know that she knows more, too); but most of the time she talks very much like them. Mason demonstrates a fine ear for the nuances and rhythms of American speech, and many critics have praised her for the authority and authenticity of her dialogue, somehow missing the more important ways, easy and graceful, she handles the spoken vernacular in her narration. In *Shiloh* that narration was most often in the (briefly) trendy present tense. There were twelve present-tense stories and four in the narrative past. This time, in *Love Life,* the majority of the stories—"Hunktown," "State Champions," "Private Lies," "Coyotes," "Wish," "Memphis," "Sorghum," and "Airwaves"—are told in the traditional past. One, "Marita," integrates past and present as it neatly mixes first- and third-person narration.

Much, probably too much, has been made of the trend and convention of the present-tense narrative. It has always been around, but for a time, about the time of the making of *Shiloh*, it was a real literary fashion. Now it is more a matter of choice than convention. Besides proving that an author knows the latest literary/editorial fashion, the present tense offers an initial immediacy and intensity. But, ironically, once a story is under way, the tense is more or less irrelevant and usually unmemorable. Novelty and surprise are worn off after a page or so, all the more so if that same novelty is simply the fashion; and what remains is purely and simply narrative, no matter what tense it affects.

III.

Now they were called hair-dressers, or better still, cosmetologists, which sounded like a group Carl Sagan would be president of.
—"Private Lies"

Writing twenty stories under the editorial tutelage of the *New Yorker*'s Roger Angell (and it is to him that both *Shiloh* and *Love Life* are dedicated) surely constitutes, by any kind of measurement, an intensive and practical course in creative writing; and it is no surprise that Bobbie Ann Mason has acquired a repertoire of formidable and efficient, if conventional, skills. She knows what she is about, both in her art and her literary career. Inevitably she has acquired habits, also, learning, as all artists do, what works best for her and what doesn't and what editors and readers have come to expect from her and how she can, in Keats's terms, surprise them "with a fine excess."

Her development, itself, has been somewhat surprising. Most successful writers in our shabby age tend to become more and more conservative (in art, not politics), devoting themselves to tried-and-true ways and means, spending more time and effort in consolidation than exploration. They tend rather quickly, even the young, to settle down to cultivate their own little garden of inhibitions and obsessions. Mason has not been able to escape this fate completely; substantially, to the limited extent that *content* is a substance of a story, the stories in *Love Life* are also more adventurous technically—she is trying some new and different things.

And they are more varied. The result is a strong sense of artistic growth.

The most interesting and adventurous of the stories in *Love Life* are not the stories editor Angell took for the *New Yorker.* Four of the stories in *Shiloh,* including the title story, appeared in the *New Yorker.* The title story and five others in *Love Life* were first published in the *New Yorker* and are elegantly executed versions of their kind. But the best of the stories, those with a significant difference in both form and content, were published elsewhere: in *Mother Jones,* in *Southern Magazine,* in the *Boston Globe Sunday Magazine,* in *Harper's,* and in the *Paris Review.* The *Atlantic Monthly,* a foster home for many of our best story writers, is also acknowledged in both *Shiloh* and *Love Life,* but the stories that appeared there first are virtually indistinguishable from the *New Yorker* stories.

What is characteristic about Mason's *New Yorker* (and *Atlantic Monthly*) stories is their amazing doubleness. You might describe them as two-faced if it were possible to eliminate the pejorative connotations of that term. Since her chief fictional subject is the survival (or failure) of ordinary people in the New South, she has to present a double view of both the Old and the New.

In an often-quoted paragraph from "Shiloh," Mason sets her stage deftly and precisely: "The farmers who used to gather around the Courthouse square on Saturday afternoons to play checkers and spit tobacco juice have gone. It has been years since Leroy has thought about the farmers, and they have disappeared without his noticing." To which the author adds, in "Love Life," the attitude of another native son: "Randy Newcomb told her she had just been away too long. 'We're not as countrified down here now as people think,' he said." The mixture of old and new is exemplified by Cletus Summer in "Sorghum," an old man who makes traditional sorghum molasses with antique equipment but who lives "in a new brick ranch house, with a shiny white dish antenna squatting possessively in the backyard."

IV.

> Around here, if you don't wear coordinated pastel polyester, people look at you funny.
>
> —"Marita"

Looked at through the famous lorgnette of Eustace Tilley, these people and their problems are undeniably pretty "countrified." Pretty funny, too. They tend to have odd names—Opal and Randy, Lynette and Cobb, Jolene and Nova, and Shayla and Lexie. (A writer giving blacks the burden of these names might be deemed a racist.) Even their dogs end up freighted with names like Buford and Obadiah. They drive around, usually with muffler problems, in their Camaros, Lynxes, Thunderbirds, and Chevettes. (An exception is the psychic, Sardo, in "Midnight Magic." Sardo is a "thousand-year-old American Indian inhabiting the body of a teenage girl in Paducah." Sardo drives a Porsche.)

More people have jobs and work for a living in Mason's stories than in most contemporary American fiction. But mostly they labor at entry-level, dead-end jobs in places like Wal-Mart and Paycheck Discount, or the mattress factory, the tire plant, the post office, the Pepsi bottling plant, or the Holiday Clothing Company. Some of the women work as waitresses at the Cracker Barrel, Villa Romano, or the Bluebird Lounge. One of the few characters to get ahead a little says it all: "When I was little I wanted to be a cowboy, or a policeman, or a sailor," he said. "It never would have occurred to me to run a shoe store."

For recreation these folks tend to drink a good deal of stuff like 7-Up and Jim Beam, to smoke a little dope, and to watch a lot of TV: *Dynasty, Miami Vice, The Equalizer, M*A*S*H, Moonlighting, 20/20, Nightline, David Letterman,* the *PTL Club,* and *Phil Donahue* (among others, including a lot of reruns). They quote and cite Donahue the way their parents quoted Scripture.

Their private lives are often bleak and deeply troubled and haunted by random violence (most often auto wrecks) all around them. They spend a lot of time, most of their time in fact, thinking, feeling, remembering. Very few of them ever do any reading. A few paperback romances. A college girl reads *Zen and the Art of*

Motorcycle Maintenance ("It isn't just about motorcycles, she has told them." Get it?) Another young woman "reads a book called *Working*, about people's jobs. 'It takes all kinds,' she tells her father when he asks about the book."

You can see how all of the above would be very reassuring to those in the world of Eustace Tilley. Those of us out in the deep boonies—which, of course, is anywhere else but New York City— have funny names and funny habits. Except for country music, our aesthetic taste is simply execrable. As critic Maureen Ryan has noticed (in "Stopping Places: Bobbie Ann Mason's Short Stories"), we live out our lives in "a plastic, superficial world of television, Sara Lee cheesecake, and Star Wars toys." All this allows Eustace to have a few chuckles and to pity us as well, even as it confirms his most profound suspicions concerning mainstream, Middle America. It also confirms his good sense (and good luck) in choosing to live out his life at the bright, hot, ruthless center of things. Where last laughs can be manufactured, come what may. Where Robert Gotlieb's purse collection can be taken with high seriousness in spite of the irrelevant horse-laughs of middle America.

V.

It wasn't just men Faye was after. She had an interest in the peculiar.
—"Sorghum"

That Bobbie Ann Mason has rhetorically captured and displayed this contemporary conflict between different kinds of haves and have-nots is no small accomplishment. But she has done more than that. There is a strong sense that she loves these people, her people, even as she condescends to them and makes sport of their lives. There is a lot of truth, not merely a matter of surfaces, in the world she left behind and came to make her own. There are also important parts of their (our) lives she has left out. For one thing, mainstream America is much more political than people seem to realize. Politics remains a genuine American passion even in the age of Donahue. In *Love Life* only a couple of characters—Vernon in "Airwaves" and Donald, the Vietnam veteran in "Big Bertha Stories" (neither of these, by the way, published in the *New Yorker*), have any political interest or concerns of any kind.

Another thing missing is the deep feeling of resentment on the part of these people (ourselves, most of us) at being constantly manipulated and deceived, used for fun and profit, used for their own purposes and pleasures by alien others. That resentment is real and pervasive, but mostly absent from her stories. There is a good reason for this. Resentment might easily be misinterpreted as self-pity, and few of her people indulge in that unacceptable and undesirable emotion. Most often they face the hardest of times with a certain tacky, unquenchable, and altogether admirable courage: in "Marita," "A fat woman emerged from the interior of the clinic and announced, 'Thank God it was an 'east infection! I thought it might be the herpes or the AIDS.'"

For whatever reason (perhaps her *New Yorker* audience?), Mason does not allow that religion plays the important part it still does in the lives of these people. In these stories religion is mostly used for comedy, not for consolation. And, finally, Mason is often overly sentimental about the old days. But, then, who isn't?

These are minor flaws and foibles in the work of an artist who is beginning to show a potential for major accomplishment. In the meantime, *Love Life*, a first-rate collection of stories by any and all standards, preserves her place among the better writers working today.

John Barth

Giles Goat-Boy and *The Tidewater Tales*

Giles Goat-Boy

Since both the form and content, the subject and its treatment, are riddled with ambiguity, doubt, and contradiction—deliberately so, for that is the essential burden of this remarkable novel—it is extremely difficult to write about *Giles Goat-Boy*. Difficult to write about, yet ironically the book requires, and has been demanding, critical attention as one of the most significant works of the art of fiction in recent years. Perhaps the author anticipated this. It is certainly fitting, for it is precisely the kind of ambiguous contradiction he is concerned to exploit and to satirize.

Certain general things can profitably be said, however, at the outset. There are things that the artistic achievement and relative popular success of this book make clear. The publication and the success in the marketplace of *Giles Goat-Boy* represent proof of a turn in the direction of American fiction—the emergence and the triumph of the novel of deliberate (even outrageous) artifice. It is not so much a triumph *over* the more conventional modes of dramatic "realism" as it is a powerful challenge to the single dominance of any one method of storytelling at the expense of other possibilities. Of course John Barth is no outright pioneer. There are examples and ample precedents, both in theory and practice and in our own time, for the novel that makes no pretense of following the rules of "realism," makes no effort whatsoever to disguise the fact of its art and form. And this has been true in other and more popular forms of literature such as the drama, where the fiction of the proscenium stage and the imaginary fourth wall has been all but abandoned, and in the film, where the camera (therefore the *director*) has become an overt, active, open participant in the aesthetic experience. John Barth's particular triumph is to have done what he has done as boldly and openly as possible and to have succeeded. What might, even a few short years ago,

223

have seemed oddly avant-garde is now perfectly acceptable, indeed almost *respectable.*

In form the author makes no bones at all about removing his fable as far as possible from all the assumptions of "realism." In fact, by a kind of extreme exaggeration, he manages not only to satirize the usual tricks of establishing some "credibility" but also to make some good sport of his own method as well. The book opens with a "Publisher's Disclaimer" by "The Editor-In-Chief," a statement that includes within it the statements of four other editors concerning the book that is to follow. Two of them favor publication; two are dead set against. The Editor-In-Chief settles the impasse by casting his vote for publication. While cheerfully, and quite accurately, satirizing the style and manners of modern publishers, Barth also in the context of this total comedy creates some strong and contradictory views of his own work. Each of these, as it develops, turns out to be at least partially justified. This opening section is followed by a "Cover-Letter to the Editors and Publisher," in which Barth as the author appears to explain how it was that he happened to come into possession of the manuscript of the work that follows, now revealed on a new title page as R.N.S.: *The Revised New Syllabus of George Giles Our Grand Tutor.* The manuscript came to him, he asserts, from one Giles Stoker (or Stoker Giles) who purported to be the son of the George Giles of the narrative. The narrative, however, is *directly* the work of no one. It has been "written" by a "remarkable computer . . . (a gadget called WESCAC)" from bits and pieces and fragments of tape kept in storage after being "read in fragmentarily by George Giles himself in the years of his flourishing: taped lecture notes, recorded conferences with proteges, and the like." The central narrative structure, then, consists of two "volumes," arbitrarily organized by WESCAC, each composed of three reels of tape which have been *transcribed.* This is followed by a short "Postape," which is a final but quite separate commentary on the central narrative, possibly by George Giles himself. The "Postape" is in turn commented upon by the author, it would seem, in a "Postscript To The Postape." This "Postscript" evokes a final brief word from the editors in "Footnote To The Postscript To The Postape." All of which adds up to an elaborate use of the ancient and honorable fictional device of "the discovered manuscript" carried to the nth degree. The more conventional and familiar use of that device in our literature, as for example in *The Scarlet Letter* or *The Turn of the Screw,* is intended first of all to place the real author at a certain aesthetic distance from the narrative and at one and the same time to heighten the immediacy and the apparent "reality" of a first-person narrative text. In Barth's hands the device, of course, does this, reflexively as it were, but it also becomes something else entirely. Again, and again all the various "authors," even WESCAC itself, argue therefore that, since this is a sort of fable or parable with "reality," and the trappings of verisimilitude are so far removed as to be irrelevant, the true "reality," the truth of this fable, is in its language, in the rhetoric and in the text. Not *texture,* but *text,* all seem to argue, thus reversing Nabokov's famous line from *Pale Fire.* But then in high bold comedy and virtuosity (wheels within wheels within wheels) the reader is, by seeming inadvertence, given every reason in the world to doubt the validity of the text at any stage or level. There is the very basic—and unanswerable—question as to the integrity of the computer. Beyond that, Giles Stoker (or Stoker Giles) openly admits to having "silently edited" the text. Next, John Barth says he has exercised the power and the duties of an editor. The Editor-In-Chief states that he and his (nameless and faceless) staff have edited the whole. The "Postape" appears to be of doubtful authenticity, and Barth argues against accepting it in "Postscript To The Postape." Then in the final "Footnote," an editor (which? who?) points out that the "Postscript" may or may not be from John Barth, but in any event is in a different typescript from the "Cover-Letter." And thus either or neither or both may or may not be the work of "J. B.," who is presumably John Barth, the author, or may be one or two characters in the whole complex narrative.

Textually, the result is enough to make a mock of the life work of all the great bibliographers.

The basic form, then, the *envelope* of the novel, is the ultimate degree of ambiguity and self-contradiction, asserting nothing definite enough to be named as "real." This is perfectly in keeping with the whole content of the parable, which may be taken, as demonstrated by the "editors," at least five different ways to start with and no two much alike. The strength and decorum of this zany form shows itself as it allows Barth to deal with some of the most profound and troubling questions of philosophy, history, theology, and science, than which nothing could be more *real*. It also allows him to touch upon the untouchable, to mention the unmentionable, and to be desperately serious within a context of the absurdly comic. This, in itself, may be a kind of working definition of what recent critics have chosen to label "black comedy."

The "plot" of the narrative history of Giles, the Goat-Boy, is so richly complex and intricately involved that it cannot be adequately synopsized, summarized, or abstracted without doing grave injustice to the book. All of the great narrative forms and devices are employed, but at the same time all are subjected to bald parody. Allegory, fable, constant allusion, puns brilliant and puns cheerfully crude and bawdy, open parody, including a fifty-page *complete* parody of the tragedy of another famous Goat-Boy, *Oedipus Rex*, satire, poetry, advertising copy—name it and it is there. The traditional bildungsroman takes a beating. Yet that is what the story is. Turns and counterturns of plot, shifts and mistakes of identity in the gusty spirit of Henry Fielding, whom Barth has elsewhere acknowledged as a master and favorite, jostle with the Kafkaesque and the magic of *The Arabian Nights*. In its own way the novel is as deeply impenetrable as *Finnegans Wake,* and in the same sense almost everything that has ever happened is there; certainly no stone is left unturned (and no turn unstoned) from what we take to be the whole of the Western Greco–Judeo-Christian tradition. It is a social, political, and spiritual history of the world we know (or think we do) seen as a Campus, and the Universe (here the University); an allegory adhered to with the exact and methodical precision of *The Pilgrim's Progress*, becoming, even as it works comically and aptly, the self-destructive, self-consuming end of all allegory. In this sense the whole weighty novel vanishes in a sudden puff of smoke, not at all unlike those self-destructing reels of tape in spy films.

Giles, reared as a goat, then educated as a man, uncertain ever as to whether or not he is a true or false Messiah (Grand Tutor), never sure whether his destiny is his own or has been programmed by the computer, is the by-now conventional "Christ figure" of modern literature. He either succeeds or he fails, or both, in all his quests and in his great aim to teach all Studenthood how to Pass, to Graduate, and, at last, to go through Commencement Gate. His life and story on the West Campus of New Tammany College become for him, as well as the reader, either an example of "tragic affirmation" or "absurd nihilism" or both. By the end of the experience there are no clear answers to anything, large or small; and one is left to wonder (i.e., *to question*) if there were many questions to be answered in the first place. The book, if "unreal," then becomes a superlative example in a larger sense of what modern theologians call "a description of reality." Satirizing scripture, it is almost scriptural. Making fun of exegesis, it is an exegetical delight.

Giles Goat-Boy, in both form and content, has been, as might be expected, taken by some critics as a dark document, profoundly and supremely nihilistic, a revised new version of the Apocalypse, in which all human history, affairs, concerns, and aspirations are shown to be not so much vanity as beneath contempt. Possibly so. . . . It is certain, however, that the author has succeeded in satirizing the clichés and conventions of practically everything under the sun, including art and himself as maker. But in the end, when all the apparatus has vanished like Prospero's pageant, what is left is something, enormous *energy.* Bawdy, scatological, grotesque, the lush of language, the pure and unflagging demonstration of the power of invention, become something at once wholly extraordinary and beautiful. It is energy pure and simple. The author, spending his own energy with a reckless virtuosity, succeeds in creating a magnificent celebration of energy—which is life itself. One thinks of Emerson's oddly prophetic comment in the essay "Experience": "Then the new molecular philosophy shows astronomical interspaces betwixt atom and atom, shows that the world is all outside; it has no inside."

The *letter* of this comic gospel may be glossed in many ways. The spirit, always festive, remains ceaselessly affirmative. While critics may and must wrestle with one another and tangle with the text, John Barth's huge achievement, ironically, is manifest on campuses all across this country, where students armed with paint brushes have lifted both the rebellious letter and spirit of the book to paint "FLUNK YOU!" proudly on the cold stones of public places. Thus, in a final lovely turn of things, it is John Barth who asserts *his* claim to be a Grand Tutor of a generation eager above all else to . . . *Graduate.*

Consider one further irony, one oddly in keeping with the spirit of this book: the fact that this wild and woolly work is exemplary, almost an archetype, of the American success story. Barth's first two novels, *The Floating Opera* and *The End of the Road,* passed virtually unnoticed by all the critics and reviewers, and found very few readers. The "turning point" in his career came with the recognition of his talent as demonstrated in *The Sot-Weed Factor,* not at once, but gradually, well after that book had played out a brief hardcover life. The eventual result of this belated recognition was the *possibility* of publishing a book like *Giles Goat-Boy;* a chance, as it were, to "cash in" on years of lost and lonely labor. He proceeded to bring forth the most ambitious, outrageous, and daring work of his career, as if thumbing his nose at the whole tedious process by which we first ignore our artists, then try to kill them off with "kindness." The result of that gesture? Success; and a success above and beyond even the particular success of this particular book. After it came, success and, as well, a kind of justice so rare that almost none of our great writers has ever lived to experience it. For in Barth's case all his earlier work has been reissued, brought out again to enjoy a miraculous second chance and a new life, risen from the dead. These works are now read and glossed by the critics in terms of the new dispensation of *Giles Goat-Boy,* and they can now safely be forgiven their earlier sins of omission, even though, true to form, they will be the last to confess and repent and ask forgiveness.

Some, mildly cynical from experience, may see in this happy turn of events the seeds of destruction, the very mantle of success becoming as it has for many other fine writers, a constricting straitjacket of silence. But Barth wrote the book, after all. Like the things of and in the book, this is possible, but doubtful. More to the point is all that energy. So long as the energy remains he can clearly write anything he wants to. And whatever it is will be worth waiting and hoping for.

The Tidewater Tales

In this season of great-big, huge novels, books large enough to be classified as deadly weapons, breakthrough volumes requiring both hands on the beach and somebody else to open the umbrella and spread the blanket—Gore Vidal's *Empire,* James Dickey's *Alnilam,* Marge Piercy's *Gone To Soldiers,* Larry McMurtry's *Texasville,* and Joseph McElroy's *Women and Men,* for example—John Barth's latest, *The Tidewater Tales: A Novel,* looks to me to be, surely must be, the best of the whole lot. Certainly it is Barth's best work so far in what has proved to be a long, productive, and distinguished career. More to the immediate point of this summer of 1987, it is great good fun, all on its own, an exemplary and energetic adventure, an affirmative action coming just at the time when we could all sure enough use a break, not only from the incredible absurdity of our world of hard facts, the droll and deadly surround, but also (maybe even more so) from the habitual and fashionable gestures of unearned, glitzy nihilism, which we have been forced to associate with the most successful and honored of our serious fiction. Of course, Barth has done his share of shrugging and yawning, too; and his die-hard, hard-core fans, a small but noisy group of groupies who have written (it seems) more words about him and his work than are in his work, whole pyramids and sphinxes of (fortunately) virtually unintelligible books and articles. A regular Maginot Line, apparently designed to defend him personally from any widespread contact with what used to be called, in happier times, the reading public. Of course Barth is a bona fide intellectual himself and, sometimes at least, a thinker of the heavy-footed Teutonic persuasion (the Günter Grass of American Lit?). He can and does actually communicate with these people. Well, no denying, Barth is something of a hard case; but he shouldn't be blamed, any more than, say, Freud or Marx or Lenin, for the words and deeds of self-selected disciples. Nor should he be subjected to the always arguable ordeal of guilt by association.

The writers he is most often linked and lumped with are really very different. Hawkes has once and for all established himself as the Prince of Tedium, the Michael Jackson of Literary Melancholy; Gass, like Harold Brodkey, is coasting along on fumes and promissory notes; Gaddis has gone off rafting the white water of the Mainstream; Barthelme is very quietly, perhaps even heroically, bearing up under the burden of chronic, could be terminal, cuteness; Coover, always a little anorexic, has by now become so minimal that there appears to be nothing left for us to applaud but a gritted grin in the empty air rather like that of the celebrated Cheshire Cat. Like the ladies of Boston who (already) have their hats, these guys already have their full share of medals and prizes, honors and awards. They are a little like the generals of the old Austro-Hungarian Empire—the last thing they want at this stage is any dangerous and risky active duty. It is a distinct pleasure to be able to report here that even though the ranks of the Fabulous Fabulators are beginning to thin out (like those of the Twenty-fourth Regiment of Foot at Isandhlwana, January 22, 1879?), John Barth, a born survivor, has been steadily working, changing, and growing in wisdom and stature. True, he hasn't always helped his case along in the past, in an impressive number of interviews and some important, self-supporting critical pieces, by his reflexive loyalty to his own club and by his demonstrable indifference to any number of other perfectly reasonable and valid approaches to the art of fiction. But, after all, the primary obligation of any serious writer in these bleak times is simply survival; and nobody dares blame the man for wanting attention to be paid to his work. Sometimes you have to shoot yourself in the foot and do a kind of dance to win that attention.

In one way, and among many other better things, *The Tidewater Tales* is exactly about a writer growing and changing. Peter Sagamore is a writer, a minimalist, now pared down to pure titles, who, together with his wife, Katherine, consultant in folklore and oral history to the Enoch Pratt Free Library, and something of a poet as well, goes sailing in the Chesapeake Bay, between June 15 and June 29, 1980. Katherine is eight and a half months pregnant. (There are, by the way, Barth fans, any number of neat little connections with *Fellini 8½*, beginning with the same sorts of images of likeness and difference between Barth and Sagamore as between Fellini and Marcello.) As in the case of Barth's previous novel, *Sabbatical*, the story is narrated by both husband and wife, though here the chief burden falls on Peter, who is challenged to tell stories as they go along. Which he does and which all add up to be a huge novel by him called *The Tidewater Tales*. The last page is the title page of *that* novel, which differs from the title page of *this* novel by omitting two words, *John Barth*, from it. It is full to the brim with stories, anecdotes, tales, jokes, both old and new, subtle and heavy-footed. It is full of doubling and twins, also. Indeed Katherine gives birth to twins at the end, and they are addressed directly in a number of forward-flashing places. Barth, himself, is a twin. The fictional Sagamore becomes something of a twin to the real Barth. *The Tidewater Tales*, in general and in many details, is a twin to *Sabbatical*. And so on. The relationship of the many twin and/or mirror images here seems as much a matter of what Benoit Mandelbrot, father of fractal geometry (nonlinear dynamics), calls self-similarity as of the older literary concept of *doubling*. Barth scholars will tell us all about that soon enough, I am sure. Meantime, however, the reader has some marvelous good times and treats in store. Some of the best writing about sailing I have encountered in a long, long time. Lots of good food, good fun, good sex. Solidly realized and completely credible central characters, people with lives and histories, living in a world as full of wonder and great danger (and suspense) as our own. If the reality evoked here is gritty and edged, the fabulous is a match for it. We have dreams and psychic adventures. We meet up (maybe so, maybe not) with Odysseus and Nausicca, Scheherazade, Don Quicksoat, and a whole gang of others, including Mark Twain, who does not appear so much as a character in as the conscience of this narrative. How do all these fit in? We are told clearly enough near the end: "Do Homer, Scheherazade, Cervantes, and Mark Twain then and there embrace our P as their peer? Not yet, and no matter: They're stars he steers by, not his destination. Anyhow, he has work to do: Once upon a time is only the beginning." On top of everything else there is a comically complex and deadly serious C.I.A. genre story, alas self-similar to a good deal of recent factual history. This is a book with all the narrative, every kind and shape of story, you could possibly imagine. All that anybody could ask for. Some early reviews have noticed that it seems more *relaxed* than Barth usually is. True, but only because he makes it all look so easy. Behind the virtuosity this is in many ways his most complex construction. Readers who have not yet found him will have no trouble here discerning the joyous and celebratory heart of the matter. Readers of his recently published essay, "Teacher," in *An Apple for My Teacher,* will know why he's feeling good, feeling fine these days, almost in spite of himself. Aren't there any flaws, flies in the ointment? Nothing serious. So it's a little trendy in its topics and attitudes. Well, that is appropriate for the people in the story; and, besides, it is the very tic and shtick of genuine intellectuals, as is the curious inability to recognize that there are far greater dangers to the good, creative life than our own C.I.A. and the Military-Industrial Complex. Peter Sagamore and John Barth have been spared a lot and more than somewhat sheltered. But that, after all, is part of their charm. Meanwhile this reader is charmed and takes *The Tidewater Tales* to be a blooming masterpiece. I commend it to you, eagerly, sincerely.

Hilary Masters

Cooper

I.

Hilary Masters's latest novel, and his fifth so far among seven books, is first-rate fiction. Lean and economical in both style and structure, it moves urgently forward without any wasted motion—especially the familiar wasted motions of self-conscious and showboat virtuosity or of trendy minimalism. It is, however, more evocative than exhaustive, thus allowing you, the reader, to bring yourself and your sum of experience to the story, inviting you to think and feel and judge as things go along. As intelligent as it is gracefully stylish, *Cooper* is concerned with problems that matter from the first time you meet them until the last time you see them. It is, then, that rare thing in our time, a novel whose appeal is more than merely aesthetic, a story that moves you as a complete experience. Thus it becomes a part of memory. Something to think about afterward.

Does all this sound like a book-jacket blurb? Good. In a real sense I mean it to. Hilary Masters, here and in his other books, is just too good to be missed. And chances are that you might miss him; for, with the exception of *Last Stands: Notes from Memory* (1982), his highly original autobiographical essay, his work has been missed by too many. How has that happened? It is a story in and of itself, and we shall have to deal with it (later) here. Writers, certainly publishers, and probably most readers really don't like to hear about those good writers who, for one reason or another or for many reasons, have not been as well known and as well honored as they ought to be. In this sense, the writers who have been over-looked tend to be like "the undeserving poor." It is almost a matter, a danger, of bad luck to bring them up. Even those who admire and support a really good writer like Hilary Masters continue to do so in the hope that this book or the next will surely be the "breakthrough" that will, at the least, confirm and validate their own good taste. There are very few people, in the literary world anyway, who are so unsophisticated as to hope that a change for the better will serve to bring a just, retroactive redefinition of the past. Like it or not, then, we are going to have to consider the hard case of Hilary Masters. But first it is more pertinent and cheerful to talk about *Cooper.*

Cooper is set partly in New York City and mostly in the quiet and dying (except for its summerhouse potential) little upstate village of Hammertown, a place not unlike Ancramdale, where Masters lived for years. Hammertown, past and present, and many of its people, was the unifying subject of Masters's 1986 book, *Hammertown Tales,* a gathering of thirteen short stories. *Cooper* is, of course, entirely self-contained, but the reader who has read and enjoyed *Cooper* is well advised to seek out *Hammertown Tales,* whose stories will add to the experience with a wider and deeper "surround." *Hammertown Tales,* in the tradition of its small publisher (Stuart Wright), also happens to be as handsomely made a trade book as you are likely to find anywhere.

To Hammertown from the city have come Jack Cooper, who is a back-issue magazine dealer, and his wife, Ruth, a poet, and their son, Hal, a retarded young man. Probably the main reason they have moved into the country is so that Hal can at once have a chance for a life of his own and the kind of privacy (and safety) city life could not offer him or them. There are other significant characters—Clay Peck, a local carpenter and craftsman, whose wife has just left him; Ron and Ethel Knox, an older couple who befriend the Coopers; Kelly Novak, a New York editor with a summerhouse in Hammertown; and, unseen but enormously influential, Roy E. Armstrong, a retired captain from the old Army Air Corps, who writes to Jack about old flying magazines and his own experiences. Roy inadvertently electrifies Jack Cooper with a simple P.S. to his first letter: "A postscript in a large, shaggy hand boasted, 'I'm an old cloudbuster and flew Nieuports, SE-5s and Pups in the First War and then flew for the Loyalists in Spain.' That single line had switched on Cooper's imagination. Armstrong must have some real stories to tell."

II.

Flying, imaginary flying, is at the very heart and center of Cooper's inner life. He is an inward and spiritual air ace. As child and man, he has made many beautiful model airplanes. The passages dealing with this art and craft, how to make model airplanes and to make them right, are some of the finest writing in the book. To entertain Hal and himself, Cooper has made up a whole series of flying tales. By letters and later, following his death, with his journals, the fabulous Roy Armstrong fuels Cooper's imagination with first-hand stories out of the First War and the revolution in Spain. We are given chunks of these things, both Armstrong's prose and Cooper's, and it is a tribute to Masters's skills that these passages, while clearly not the work of clever wordsmiths—for both Cooper and Armstrong are influenced to saturation by the flying magazines they love—are entirely credible without being, for one instant, condescending. That is to say, the author is so committed to his characters in this matter that the reader not only feels but shares their excitement and at no point is invited or allowed to feel superior to it. At the same time, no other claims are made for what is, after all, a hobby, albeit at times a passionate one. And if you don't think that kind of fine-tuning and control is rare, you have been spared the greatest part of our serious contemporary literature, where, by and large, everyone who appears is treated with classic condescension. There is another, more subtle point—*demonstration*, rather—for Masters is always presentational and dramatic, never didactic—made by these shared tales and myths of Cooper and Armstrong. They may be equally unliterary, in a purely verbal sense, but they are equal in their interest, appreciation, and understanding of the flying stories. Armstrong speaks out of actual experience. For Cooper it is all imaginary, though deeply imagined. Yet their visions, while not identical, fit together hand-in-glove. And by the end of the experience of this novel, we, the engaged readers, are able to see palpable evidence that at the cortex or kernel of their cockamamy tales of adventurous flying there are some great and real and immutable truths, that there is a place where inner life and outer life, spirit and flesh, join together, however briefly, in a dance that is transcendently wonderful. This subtle parable, working always and only by inference and implication, is, in passing, as elegant a defense of imaginative literature as any I have seen.

But *Cooper* is about a good deal more than that. It is about what happens to good people in a very hard world. You will seldom encounter in a contemporary novel so many good and well-mannered people. There are some "heavies," to be sure, but it isn't a book about human villainy. The things that happen are not by any means earthshaking even though, for a time, they shake the lives of all the characters. Ethel Knox kills herself. Kelly Novak tries to get Jack Cooper to write a best-seller, a commercial book based on his otherwise innocent flying stories. Cooper gives it a shot, seriously but half-heartedly, and nothing much comes of it in any case. Ruth teaches in a community college, works at her poems, and pines for the mild glitter of the New York City poetry scene. She is deeply disturbed by the death of Ethel Knox. Hal finds some solace and learns a good deal by working with the lonely, inarticulate, and gifted carpenter, Clay Peck. And at its hard center, *Cooper* is about how Cooper and his wife, much in love, sustain their lives and love in spite of the constant attrition, the abrasive effect of Hal's disability on both of them. This, as everybody knows, is the great untold story of the disabled in our society, the secret universal truth that is only alluded to, hinted at, lightly touched on in the literature, including film and television, dealing with the subject. Hal, without meaning to, indeed meaning nothing, it seems, beyond his own pure and simple being, nearly wears these good and loving people down to naked bone and nerve. His presence and suffering nearly tear them apart. And yet . . . and yet they somehow hold together and are still together at the end of things. The end of things! I cannot, without spoiling at least one great pleasure of this book, reveal the ending, the final soaring and ecstatic scene. Except to say that it comes implausibly (though perfectly plotted) out of nowhere and proceeds with complete authority and credibility to bring together all the central concerns and images of the story in a joyously ambiguous sequence that Fellini, that magician of amazing endings, would surely envy. The book jacket does not lie when it promises "a passage as moving and memorable as any in contemporary literature." It is not hard to get there. The novel may be quiet, but the events are hard-edged with reality. And the characters, each and all, are fully dimensional. They cast shadows and are mysterious enough to keep some secrets no matter how well we get to know them, and they know each other and themselves. It needs to be said that, without ostentation or self-congratulation, Masters's imagination is "gender free." Ruth, a major character, and Ethel, a minor one, are as well realized as all of the male characters and are as solid, as contradictory, and as essentially mysterious as any characters, male or female, you will find in your bookstore and most of your local library. Character is really Masters's strong suit, though the writing itself is unfailingly exact, lucid, and engaging. The place, the weather and seasons of it, are deftly, beautifully evoked and presented by the accretion of many small touches and observations. Created also in a few bold, large gestures, of which one especially deserves mention here. It is the account of the adventures of Clay Peck's Doberman bitch, the hottest bitch for miles and miles around, who runs away almost simultaneously with the departure of Peck's wife ("Had Grace Peck left before the dog escaped, or had the dog fled the coop first?") to become, in a few short pages, a mythical, legendary beast worthy of Faulkner or Melville, and a lot funnier:

> She was reported everywhere at once, an ebony dart that streaked across the countryside. She was seen in Irondale, on remote hilltop farms, at the crossroads in Copake and even on the outskirts of Green River. Sometimes a movement would catch the eye, a speck that moved across a far hillside, from dark to light to dark, and it would be the sleek Doberman, racing like a greyhound, accompanied by several male dogs who galloped after her like grenadiers escorting a monarch hellbent on some emergency of state. She was making the rounds.

And that is only the beginning of one of the truly splendid set pieces in the literature of our times, the best of its kind (for my money) since a couple or three in Faulkner's Snopes trilogy.

What Masters has done in *Cooper* is to take a very difficult subject, though a deeply relevant one involving millions of American families, and with the strengths and skills, the art and craft of a writer who has been practicing his vocation for a long time (it's been twenty years since his first novel, *The Common Pasture*, was published, and he was writing well before then; and, of course, he grew up literary, for his father was poet Edgar Lee Masters), treat that subject, and several complex themes, directly and simply, to create a quiet and powerful work of great depth and compassion and, finally, as indicated, of almost ecstatic affirmation. Sex and violence and craziness and all of our trendy "problems" are so much easier to write about. Isn't that why we are getting so many novels by senators and ball players, newsmen and rock musicians, and call girls and others of the celebrity ilk? You don't have to be able to write to write your average late twentieth-century "popular" novel. It probably doesn't help a bit. And, anyway, publishers always have people who can make your subjects agree with your predicates. In which case, won't we soon have thrilling novels by Donna Rice and Fawn Hall, maybe a roman à clef by Tammy Faye? Sad to say, judging by the results, you don't have to write very well, either, to be successful in the "serious" writer circuit. I shall name no names, but mostly they are much better known, and more often featured on book pages, than Hilary Masters. And they are still working at mastering the sentence and building a paragraph that will stand on its own for fifteen full minutes. Character and storytelling are well beyond their means and so have been dispensed with as reactionary and irrelevant. Well, you can read your Krantz or King at the beach and not miss out on the sun and surf and scenery. You can read (why *not* name a few?) your Hawkes or Coover or William Gass and watch MTV at the same time, and both experiences will gain from the juxtaposition. For Masters in *Cooper* you really need some light, some quiet, and an open mind and spirit.

Another problem Masters has suffered from is that his stories, both book length and individual short stories, are very difficult to *talk about*. They are experiences. They have to be shared to be decently discussed. This is a quality that Masters shares with a number of first-rate twentieth-century writers including, for example, Joyce Cary and Masters's friend Wright Morris. These people are difficult to *teach* by conventional ways and means, and they do not require a critic to tell us what they are really trying to say but are unable to. Morris and Masters have something else in common.

Both happen to be outstanding photographers. In addition to a good deal of commercial photographic work, Masters has had well-received, one-man gallery shows of his work in New York, Boston, Pittsburgh, and elsewhere. Morris, of course, has been an acknowledged photographic master since the 1930s. Though their prose styles are distinctly different, alike only in the refinement of their clarity, both are expert in their use of visual frames and in choosing what *not* to present visually. In both cases, photography seems to have taught them much.

Here is Hilary Masters, then, a productive professional writer since the early 1960s, at the peak of his considerable powers, who has created a major novel, worth a grownup's time and worthy of our best attention. *Cooper* should easily have gained that attention. After all, *Last Stands* was widely reviewed and praised nationally. This story of his grandfather, the Indian fighter, and his father, the poet, and of himself, has been routinely called "an American classic." What critics and reviewers don't choose to know or remember is that *Last Stands* was around and available for years in manuscript before it found a publisher. To their shame, but not to their embarrassment (how can you embarrass a *publisher*?), every major commercial publisher in America rejected *Last Stands*. Most didn't even think it was publishable at all, by any kind of publisher or press. It was finally published by a small press, David Godine, and was very successful. Godine also published his next novel, *Clemmons*, to good reviews and moderate success. But even Godine was not interested in publishing a collection of Masters's best short stories. That privilege remained for the young publisher Stuart Wright of Winston-Salem. *Hammertown Tales* is an impressive collection and was well received wherever it was reviewed. The basic problem of all small-press books is that no matter what their quality, they are a low priority item for reviewers. Came then *Cooper*. It, too, was widely and thoroughly rejected by many commercial publishers before it finally found a home at St. Martin's Press. One prominent and highly regarded editor allowed that if Masters were only younger (he's over fifty) he would have accepted *Cooper*.

III.

What I am trying to say, as simply and calmly as I can, is that Masters is every bit as good as any of the best American writers of his generation. I will stand by that; the work is proof of it. I mean, then, Masters is every bit as good, by any standard, as Updike or Oates or Roth or as anybody. But unlike any of those and many more, he has had enormous difficulty getting his goods to market, earning his moment in the light. Unlike the others mentioned, Masters not only had to create the works but to waste precious time and energy trying to find a publisher for them. A deeply discouraging situation. The same thing was true, in a slightly different way, for his father, who was, in a sense, one of the most influential American poets and writers of this century, but who, despite his accomplishment, was so ignored and ill-treated by the literati that at the end his simple survival was in hazard. Read *Last Stands*.

There is one way in which Masters has (briefly) achieved a high visibility and has done good, indeed major, service to the literary community as a whole. Masters is a free-lance journalist, and a good one. In 1979 he was commissioned by *New York* magazine to do an investigative piece on possible problems concerning the National Endowment of the Arts writing fellowships. He did the piece assigned, but the magazine changed hands, and the new regime wasn't interested in the subject. Paid off and free to publish it elsewhere, he tried any number of likely places, both commercial and literary. Several times the article was accepted, then "killed" by magazines that came under pressure not to print it. Finally (if somewhat timidly) it was published by the *Georgia Review* in the summer of 1981 as "Go Down Dignified: The NEA Writing Fellowships." It was a bombshell, a strong, well-researched piece of investigation showing clearly a pattern of cronyism and corruption in the literature program at the NEA. After much sound and fury, the NEA cleaned house thoroughly, and the methods of evaluation and judging and awarding by the literature program are now strictly organized to prevent all kinds of cronyism and conflict of interest. The radical changes in methodology (additional proof of the accuracy of his critique) have made the literature program at the NEA far more fair and open to American writers of all factions and persuasions.

The case of Hilary Masters tells us a lot about the present state of letters. Probably the most important single thing his own story tells us is that, all protestations to the contrary, things have not changed very much at all in this enlightened age of ours, that in spite of all the elaborate programs, grants, fellowships, awards, medals, and the expensive search for talent and the honor accorded it when it is found and recognized, significant numbers of gifted American writers regularly "fall through the cracks," are virtually unknown, even—perhaps especially—among their more fortunate peers. Some of these, like Masters, are artists of the first rank by all standards, and their obscurity is as great a waste as it is a shame. Look, it happened to William Faulkner for most of his life. It has been happening to Wright Morris for most of his. Morris did once win a National Book Award years and years ago, but it was only very recently that he was recognized again. And there are many others, some evidently condemned to oblivion from the outset, others who have experienced some ups and downs in the turning of Fortune's wheel. Of course, it wasn't and isn't fair to the artists in question, but I am not here addressing such an obvious and immutable truth. More important by far is the effect of the waste of gifted lives upon us. We who read and care about reading are constantly looking for those precious few things that are worth our time and energy. We are missing so much. The System—greedy publishers, lazy book reviewers, arrogant critics, and the terrified and threatened lucky few writers who have somehow been recognized and fear most, not without reason, that a mistake has been made—is cheating us. We are lied to and cheated as much in the world of the lively arts as we are in any other areas of American life, even politics and television news. What can we do about it? Not much. We can at least tell each other what we know. I am telling you it would be a shame to miss the work of Hilary Masters and his latest and finest novel—*Cooper.*

Paul Fussell

Wartime: Understanding and Behavior in the Second World War

I.

I think I know a new myth and this is it:
The strength having gone out of certain old men, Formerly
terrible, they are changed to gulls
And follow over endless ocean hulls
Of their rejecting states, wishing for them
Catastrophe. But we shall prosper yet.

—William Meredith, "Transport"

Paul Fussell is completely and characteristically explicit in announcing, and then honorably following, the outlines of the text and the subtext of *Wartime*. The opening paragraph of the preface succinctly says it all and deserves to be quoted in its entirety; for Fussell fully adheres to his intentions even as he is strictly conditioned by them. Those who share the identified values and virtues he celebrates are here reassured. Those who view the history of the times somewhat differently—and there will be plenty of these, some parting company from the author on account of personal history and experience, others out of more abstract, intellectual quibbles or quarrels—are adequately warned:

> This book is about the psychological and emotional culture of Americans and Britons during Second World War. It is about the rationalizations and euphemisms people needed to deal with an unacceptable actuality from 1939 to 1945. And it is about the abnormally intense frustration of desire in wartime and some of the means by which desire was satisfied. The damage the war visited upon bodies and buildings, planes and tanks and ships, is obvious. Less obvious is the damage it did to intellect, discrimination, honesty, individuality, complexity, ambiguity, and irony, not to mention privacy and wit.

For the past fifty years the Allied war has been sanitized and roman-
ticized almost beyond recognition by the sentimental, the loony
patriotic, the ignorant, and the bloodthirsty. I have tried to balance
the scales.

The reader needs to keep in mind that the aim of *Wartime* is corrective (in that sense close to satirical), to overcome the dangerous
imbalance of fifty years, by whatever means necessary, within the
self-established guidelines he announces. That is, he will try not
to be anything but discriminating, honest, and sometimes witty
even as he explores the complexities, ambiguities, and ironies of
those times, times that have been, in his best judgment, distorted
"beyond recognition."
    That he largely succeeds in accomplishing his assigned mission
is an extraordinary achievement and must be announced at the
outset.
    Fussell's purpose is to treat the experience of the Second World
War in much the same way as he dealt with the life and times of
the First World War in his triumphant and prize-winning success,
The Great War and Modern Memory (1975), linking the two works
and experiences even as he allows for important differences. *The
Great War and Modern Memory*, already distant enough in time to
have been easily kept at arm's length by abstraction, was firmly
affixed to the author's personal experience, his *own* memory, by
the dedication, which broods over the whole text to follow before
a word of it, other than title and subtitle, has been uttered:

To the Memory of
Technical Sergeant Edward Keith Hudson, ASN36548772
Co. F 410th Infantry
Killed beside me in France
March 15, 1945

This dedication, set and shaped like a tombstone (and bearing
every American soldier's uniquely private/public identity, his one
and only serial number), says any number of things simultaneously, efficiently, and with a deeply moving (troubling) resonance.
It announces that this old war, the subject of Fussell's study, which

took place and ended close to forty years earlier, matters *personally* to the author. It asserts, before one word of argument or explication has been advanced, that there is a felt connection not only between the living writer and the dead sergeant to whom he has come to dedicate the book, but also between the events of the two wars. It establishes as an assumption a requirement, prior to any discussion of the matter, that there is a continuity between then (1914–1918) and then (1939–1945) and finally the here and now of writing and reading and remembering. This assertion, maintained throughout the text, becomes the principal subject of the final chapter—"Persistence and Memory"—wherein Fussell indicates the multitude of large and small ways in which, in fact and fancy, life and art, the haunting memory of that war remains fixed in our minds and spirits and continues to fix and set both. He cites H. M. Tomlinson: " 'The parapet, the wire, and the mud,' Tomlinson posited in 1935, are now 'permanent features of human existence.' Which is to say that anxiety without end, without purpose, without reward, and without meaning is woven into the fabric of contemporary life." Fussell makes another kind of connection in that final chapter, noting how time and sundry changes have at last made it possible to remember a war and to write about it:

> As we perceive in the work of Mailer and Pynchon and James Jones, it is the virtual disappearance during the sixties and seventies of the concept of prohibitive obscenity, a concept which has acted as a censor on earlier memories of "war," that has given the ritual of military memory a new dimension. And that new dimension is capable of revealing for the first time the full obscenity of the Great War. The greatest irony is that it is only now, when those who remember the events are almost all dead, that the literary means for adequate remembering and interpreting are finally publicly accessible.

It was almost certain, from then on, that Paul Fussell would be working toward the goal of "adequate remembering and interpreting" of the Second World War.

Moving swiftly, deftly, through a structure of eighteen titled chapters in *Wartime*, Fussell tries to tell us all about it, gracefully managing to waken and to reconfirm the memories of those who, one way and another, were there and lived through the experience; likewise teaching, with accuracy and fidelity, the ignorant, if not especially innocent young, whose knowledge of those times and that war, where it exists at all, is essentially abstract, a schoolroom matter, riddled with stereotypical errors and twisted and distorted not only beyond recognition, but also almost beyond recovery. The intense difficulty of this double standard, the unavoidable prerequisite of a kind of rhetorical split personality is daunting, to say the very least. And that Fussell comes about as close as anyone has or could possibly do so is a cause for praise and celebration. It also demands of the critic something of his same clear-eyed, hard-nosed integrity. Anything less would be unworthy. The demands Fussell imposes upon himself would be severe enough even if the people, places, and things he summoned up were part of some coherent pattern of events. But he is unflinching in his earned belief that this "good" war was, at its center, "so serious it was ridiculous." It is all just beyond imagining: "It was a savage, insensate affair, barely conceivable to the well-conducted imagination (the main reason there's so little good writing about it) and hardly approachable without some currently unfashionable theory of human mass insanity and inbuilt, inherited corruption."

Fussell turns directly to the concrete, to the details of the wartime culture, at home and in the hellholes of combat, high and low and official. He treats the posters and slogans and advertisements, the cartoons, the popular songs and movies and radio shows. He recalls the uniforms and rations, the candy bars and cigarettes. In a wonderfully instructive chapter, "Drinking Far Too Much, Copulating Too Little," he re-creates that long-gone time when booze was consumed (whenever possible) in staggering quantity, and sexual satisfaction was limited by ignorance, availability, and the impact of long-standing, deep-rooted moral code: "Sex before marriage was regarded as either entirely taboo or gravely reprehensible." Fussell has found a good deal of material concerning what the British like to call *wanking*, but argues that even that kind of relief was basically irrelevant to the lives of the real fighting men. "Interesting as this is," he writes, "it is notably what frontline troops would stigmatize as a rear-echelon problem. Sexual deprivation and inordinate desire generally did not trouble men on the front line. They were too scared, busy, hungry, tired, and demoralized to think about sex at all. Indeed, the front was the one wartime place that was sexless."

He discusses some of the basic weapons and equipment on both sides, mostly obsolete and often murderously inadequate. He writes of the jokes and rumors, myths and prophecies and superstitions, the protean shapes of propaganda and official and unofficial censorship and press coverage. He writes about the books they read and liked, especially the Nonesuch editions for the British and the special and quite wonderful Armed Services editions for American GI's. He patiently, with ironic pedantry, redefines the differences and nuances of chickenshit and bullshit, proving, even as he does so, that he himself is fully capable of exercising the good soldier's absolutely essential ability to know the difference between shit, in all its forms, and Shinola. He is at some pains to expose fully and to ridicule the crude stereotypes that were imposed upon friend and foe alike to deny any sense of honor or virtue to the foe and to justify any cruelty and brutality on our side. And also to conceal some common sins so successfully that even now they seem to have the weight and shock of news: "If it is a jolt to realize that blitzed London generated a whole class of skillful corpse robbers, it is because, within the moral assumptions of the Allied side, that fact would be inexplicable."

He also deals with the language of the war, the wicked and false language of gassy public oratory (even Churchill's famous speeches do not escape the common condemnation) and the official cultivation of euphemisms that served not only to camouflage and conceal unpleasant truths, but also to create "sanguine misapprehensions" that could then only be dispelled, as they most certainly were, through inescapable, incredible trauma. Here it is a pleasure to report that as a servant of the truth Fussell is fearless, bringing his irony and contempt to bear in hard, bright focus upon all sorts of cultured heroes (icons), unforgiving to this day toward all those who, for whatever reasons, sound or selfish, sold their souls to the company store. Among the Americans who are skewered and spitted for their crimes are the pompous likes of Archibald MacLeish, Carl Sandburg, John Steinbeck, E. B. White, Thornton Wilder, and (would you believe?) Arthur Miller. Strangely, unless I somehow and somewhere missed it, the late Lillian Hellman lucks out and escapes the satirical notice her treatment of the war, during and after, so richly deserves. Oh well, he can't whip them all; and he manages to do some very good, if selective, service.

As anyone who has read Fussell's *Class* (1983) could easily guess, from the literature—poetry, fiction, memoirs—of and about the wartime period, Fussell strongly favors the language and literature of high culture and the language and literature that seemed to grow up naturally and extravagantly, like kudzu, out of the unembarrassed, unapologetic, and undisguised demotic, the slang and lingo of the fighting soldiers (Fussell appropriately hates ferocious desk-jockeys, sock-counters and staff officers even more than Bill Mauldin did) of all sides. *All* sides? "The soldiers on one side know what the soldiers on the other side understand about dismemberment and evisceration," he writes, "even if that knowledge is hardly shared by the civilians behind them." His best examples of the literature of high culture are, unexceptionally, British. Evelyn Waugh, Osbert Sitwell, and, above all, Cyril Connolly and his magazine *Horizon* are honored and celebrated. Allowing that "*Horizon* might convey the impression that the European war was being fought about literature and art history . . . rather than about Poland's territorial sovereignty or the right of the European Jews to survive," Fussell nevertheless, in what amounts to a genuinely passionate set piece in the chapter "Compensation," argues that *Horizon* was an absolutely vital force in the war (against friend as well as foe) "against artistic and intellectual barbarism." He praises *Horizon* as constituting "one of the high moments in the long history of British eccentricity. As a cultural act, it was as stubborn as Churchill's political behavior." "Addressed with such steady intellectual respect," Fussell maintains, "an audience fit though few, intensely loyal, was accumulated, and very many readers were servicemen sick of the stupidity and chickenshit who regarded their monthly *Horizon* as their only handhold on the civilized world." Among those working out of what Fussell calls "the demonic-ironic idiom," he cites any number of poets, including the Americans Randall Jarrell, Louis Simpson, Richard Eberhart, and he at least briefly mentions Karl Shapiro and John Ciardi. But his chief examples are the Englishman Gavin Ewart and the American Lincoln Kirstein, whose *Rhymes of a PFC* and later poems have not until now been properly noticed for their accomplishment and influence.

Fussell has not much use for the safe middle ground in fiction occupied by Leon Uris, Herman Wouk, and James Gould Cozzens, and no use at all for the morally pompous, high-minded stuff ("Wartime was a moment when everyone felt obliged to instruct others in ethics") by the likes of Stephen Vincent Benét, Robert Nathan, MacKinlay Kantor, Louis Untermeyer, and a long roll call of others, most of whom, Fussell is pleased to report, are "names remembered today largely by the literary historian alone." For the whole truth in fiction Fussell sticks with his trinity of heroic works from *The Great War and Modern Memory*—Joseph Heller's *Catch-22*, Thomas Pynchon's *Gravity's Rainbow*, and Kurt Vonnegut's *Slaughterhouse Five*. But there are the pleasures of some significant discoveries and rediscoveries. Among them: Robert Lowry's *Casualty* (1946), Tristan Jones's *Heart of Oak* (1984), Brian Aldiss's *Horatio Stubbs* trilogy, and Kingsley Amis's long story, "I Spy Strangers," which appeared in the collection *My Enemy's Enemy* (1962) and is examined at length and in depth in Fussell's key chapter, "Chickenshit, An Anatomy." And Fussell pays considerable and respectful attention to E. B. Sledge's eloquent memoir "of Marine horrors," *With the Old Breed: At Peleliu and Okinawa* (1981). Most of the other significant American and British texts of all kinds are at least mentioned, cited, or referred to, proving, once again, as if that were necessary, that Fussell has done his homework.

II.

God help the ones who opened
the coffins.
            He didn't help us,
lugging those lumps of dead flesh
down the hill to the six-bys
waiting to move them out
to the airstrip and long flight
to the warehouses in Bombay
or Calcutta or somewhere.

—Paxton Davis, "1945"

But there is more than all this to *Wartime*. There are other important points that Fussell wants to make, some of them bound to shock the innocent and the un- and ill-informed. Fussell insists that both the tactics and strategy of the war, all around, were a series of blunders and disasters. He calls attention to some that are known, but probably not well enough known—the Dieppe Raid of 1942, the Sicilian and Salerno landings of 1943, the perilous potential for disaster at D-Day in 1944, the *probable* catastrophe of the planned invasions of Japan and the Malay Peninsula in 1945. And he flashes a bright light on somewhat less-known blunders, like the Great Slapton Sands Disaster of April 1944 and the Great Dakar Fuck-Up of August 1940. What is central to Fussell's argument is that these moments were/are not exceptional, but inevitable. And, by inference, it is clear Fussell would feel cheerfully free to rename the war of 1939–1945, calling it the Second World Fuck-Up. In any case, the sense of the whole war as something completely out of control, directed by no one, something *wholly other* with a life and momentum of its own, is not unique, by any means, to Fussell's point of view. In her brilliant memoir of war service, *All the Brave Promises* (1966), Mary Lee Settle describes herself, finally discharged (with "signals shock") from the WAAF and "on the way to the American Office of War Information in London, the cocktail parties, the conferences, the PX cigarettes, the frenetic turmoil of people who had names and thought they were running the juggernaut of war, which was only spending itself toward its own death like a great tiring unled beast."

Other points made in *Wartime*, disabusing many readers of cherished clichés if not finally disillusioning them, are closely related. That the war was fought in an "ideological vacuum" and that nobody, at least no one among the *fighting* forces on either side, was silly enough to *believe* in any of the things they were supposed to; and that their main and dedicated enterprise was desperately trying, without any good reason or much hope, to save their own sweet asses, to keep themselves from being killed, dismembered, eviscerated for as long as possible. That the war was fought on both sides, by a surprisingly small number of fighting men (the crowds were always in the rear, "in support") who were scared witless most of the time. ("The relative few who actually fought know that the war was not a matter of rational calculation. They know madness when they see it.") That the fighting men on both sides were about equally cruel and vile and brutal and greedy for whatever kinds of crude, small pleasures and comforts they could find and take and, while they were lucky enough to be alive and ambulatory, were toughly indifferent to any other human suffering except their own. And that, therefore, the war didn't add up to, didn't *mean anything* except itself. Better at the time, anyway, to have been among the winners than the losers. Better, perhaps, all things considered, to be alive and old now than to have died suddenly, however badly in whatever bloody bits and pieces, in the pride of youth. ("But what time seems to have shown our later selves is that perhaps there is less coherent meaning in the events of wartime than we had hoped.") That any accounts, then or now or later, of the war, which do not take all of the above into account, are therefore to that extent untrue and do not amount to anything much.

Depending, of course, on the extent and limits of their own real and imaginary experience, veterans of that war (or of any of the others that have come along since), may quibble with one or another of the general implications of *Wartime*. Some will think he overstates his case to make some valid points. Plenty, though perhaps not as many, will think that he has *understated* it and that it took a long time, more than forty years, for him to come to terms with it and himself and to discover the obvious and undeniable truth about this war and all our wars, large and small, fore and aft. But Fussell was (as we know from other works) an officer. Wars are more likely to be a "learning experience" for the young officers than for those who finally earned their proper name in Vietnam— the *grunts*.

And some veterans of wars who have pondered these things in their hearts will think that there is one great flaw in his vision. That he has failed to point out the ecstatic joy and exaltation, the incredible "high" that accompanies all the other feelings. That joy that led Robert E. Lee to remark (in the middle of a worse war, the worst war, in fact, in modern history, for any country) that it is well, a good thing, that war is so terrible else we should love it too much.

I have no good idea, cannot imagine how others may react to the truths and hard sayings of *Wartime*. Those Americans who have somehow or other avoided all forms of contact with this century's principal activity, the bloodsport of warfare—and this group consists nowadays of many of the "best and brightest" of their generation, intellectuals, "opinion shapers," who have been allowed to take their own thoughts and feelings seriously for most of their lives; perhaps because their parents' generation was deprived of that privilege—may find Fussell's book offensive. They have managed to politicize practically everything in American life, past and present; and the official position is that the Second World War was "good" and "just" because of the results. Because of what Fussell, with irony on full throttle, calls "the Allied victory and the resounding Allied extirpation of flagrant evil." The last good and just war. Of course they, our best and brightest, might have done it better, better tactics and strategy and clearer and more moral goals and guidelines, if they had been around to manage things better.

That kind of criticism, should it come along, will only serve to confirm the wisdom and importance of Fussell's book.

III.

It's hard to realize that the war began over forty years ago. I mean the war that matters, the one that divided Europe down the middle, shrank Germany, transformed China, begot the Third World, conferred Southeast Asia on the luckless Americans for a generation, and reduced Britain to the status of the Netherlands.

—Paul Fussell, "The War in Black and White"

There are a few more things that must be said.

One is that *Wartime*, though it is a very good book, indeed, and probably better than we deserve, also an *important* book, if only to challenge conventional mind-set and stir up fading memory, is not the success, in realization of its own terms, that *The Great War and Modern Memory* was. In part the reason for this is that *Wartime* is at once a more difficult book and, in spite of kinship, a different kind of book. But there are other reasons, too.

It is in the accumulation of little things, the concrete details, that Fussell's writing in both books derives its energy, authority, and cohesion. But the details of the Second World War are better known and far more plentifully accessible to the memory of many. To keep his book within reasonable length and to avoid the model of the encyclopedia, he must judiciously select one detail from among many. The authority of choice must be self-evident. Nobody is likely to be happy with all of his choices. If he mentions the Tin Pan Alley war song "The Japs Don't Have a Chinaman's Chance," then why not also "You're a Sap, Mr. Jap"? And if this novel, that poem, those stories, then why not others? If you have Jarrell and Eberhart and Simpson, then why not do more than mention John Ciardi, some of whose poems of combat in the Second World War have been published posthumously within the last couple of years? Why not Richard Wilbur and William Meredith and Louis Coxe, for instance? Fussell's problem is that everybody (secretly or not so secretly) wants to write this, his book. And it becomes more complicated wherever fact and opinion meet. There develops another kind of debate with the reader. For instance, very few veterans will question his claims for the German 88, a downright deadly flat trajectory gun if there ever was one. But I can conceive of many veterans of several wars who will not share his easy dismissal of the Browning Automatic Rifle, the BAR, which, if old, remained as late as the Korean War a first-class weapon in the right hands. And so it goes.

It needs also to be noted, as it will be, that there were moments on all sides when individuals and whole outfits were possessed by something that can only be called honor, in the old-fashioned sense, and acted upon it. Aleksandr Solzhenitsyn, who was in some of the worst combat on the Eastern Front, describes such a moment in the First World War in his newly revised novel *August 1914.* Here the Dorogobuzh Regiment, out of ammo and everything else, does its duty:

> Here was a miracle greater than the fortitude of the officers: soldiers, half of them reservists, peasants who had reported for duty only a month ago in birchbark clogs, their minds still on the sights and sounds of home, their fields, their prospects, their families, to-

tally ignorant of European politics, the war, the East Prussian campaign, the objectives of their corps or even its number, did not flee, or slink into the bushes, or hang back, but, possessed by some unknown force, passed the dividing line beyond which love of self and of family and even the instinct of self-preservation cease to exist, and, belonging now not to themselves but to their cruel duty, rose up three times and advanced into gunfire with their noiseless bayonets.

In his need to dispense with all the other false illusions, Fussell is forced to overlook this one, which sometimes gave a sense of meaning to the soldiers' meaningless deaths. He has forgotten to say how much pure courage, false or true, displayed by friend and foe, means to the fighting man.

Another thing, a small thing but a defect, he has forgotten is how to apply the same rigorous truth searching and telling to the wars that came after his. Dealing with Vietnam, in passing, he does not apply the same rigorous demands and standards he exercises in re-creating the Second World War. He buys the stereotypes—that the South Vietnamese military were uniformly cowardly and that this cowardice had some political meaning and ethical import—promulgated by the media. He likewise seems to feel that the TV was more "honest" in its depiction of the war in Vietnam than the governments had been in earlier wars. To which it needs to be said that this cliché is at least debatable and one day will have to be examined by someone who was a witness in the same way Fussell has looked at his war. Meantime, it does begin to seem that the overwhelming problem in conveying from one generation to the next the truth of war in general is that though it is possible to learn to read and comprehend the wars of the past, the wars of the next generation are incomprehensible to us and we slide, perhaps mercifully, into the vague shade of stereotype and cliché. We can only tell them truly about our times. We lack the knowledge or language to speak to and of theirs.

There is no easy escaping this whole problem except by unflagging accuracy and concentration and, I think, by intensity and force of personality. Fussell has an intense and personal war story to tell, as we who have followed him and read his essays in *The Boy Scout Handbook and Other Observations* (1982) and *Thank God for the Atom Bomb and Other Essays* (1988) know well. Both of these books have any number of splendid essays, powerful and moving, about aspects of the Second World War. Including Paul Fussell's bloody personal share of it. *The Boy Scout Handbook* has an entire final section, "Versions of the Second World War," covering much of the same material as we are given in *Wartime*. It is odd. Some items, even sentences, overlap, appear in that book and this one. Some things are improved and, strangely, some are not. Other things are simply lost between the volumes. One of these is the moving authority of Fussell as a Lieutenant of Infantry, of the man who won a medal and was twice wounded and wept in the hospital for his dead friends and, yes, sir, for himself and the world, too. This Fussell, alive and kicking in *The Boy Scout Handbook* and *Thank God for the Atom Bomb* is more urgently needed in *Wartime*. If only to help offset the witty, elitist, opinionated, curmudgeonly, apparently self-assured narrator whom we also have come to know through the star turns of *Abroad* (1980) and the "Introduction" and copious editorial notes of *The Norton Book of Travel* (1987), not to mention the half-breed, half Kafka and half Stephen Potter, and master of high jinks who created *Class: A Painfully Accurate Guide through the American Status System* (1983), whose cocksure arrogance is sometimes a little tough to take. It seems a little ungraceful, something on the order of asking Coriolanus to bare his wounds for plebeian votes; but Fussell, as narrator in this book, needs the extra weight of the authority he has, in fact, earned. He is easier to believe that way. Fussell is a very sophisticated writer; true sophistication is his civilized ideal. And one thing sophisticates fear and shun, almost as much as the old ennui, is repetition and redundancy. He has already said these things, shown and told, once. Why again? Because of the urgently important context of this book—a culmination of at least one large part of his life's work. In the full context, Fussell's (the narrator's) frequent arrogance of manner is offset by a gentle vulnerability. At the risk of redundancy, he has, in a number of times and places, identified himself as the literary child of two godfathers—George Orwell and Cyril Connolly; and somewhere in the portrait gallery, Swift and Dr. Johnson look down, shining on his efforts. The trick is to keep these things in balance. Most of the time, as, mostly, here in *Wartime*, he manages it like a magician.

David Slavitt
The Tristia Of Ovid

The coming together of the contemporary poet
and translator David Slavitt and the often ignored *Tristia of Ovid* is
an example of the happiest kind of literary coincidence. Once accomplished, it presents such a likely and fortunate conjunction of
gifts and subject matter as this late day (century of bloodletting,
age of rusty iron) would require an amazing accident to happen.
That there are only a handful of American poets adequately trained
in the classics—of which Slavitt is surely to be numbered, for he
began his classical studies as a teenager, working with Dudley
Fitts at Andover—is a given condition and shouldn't raise an eye-
brow anywhere. But that the best-known and most celebrated of
our contemporary poets (names? please pick up any recent anthology, especially those graced with glossy photographs) are, at
best, only faintly informed concerning matters of form and most
lightly dusted, as with some sort of glitter dust, with bits and
pieces of the received knowledge of our long literary past and are
not in the least seriously interested in laboring to correct deficiencies and to overcome an almost invincible ignorance, is always
surprising, no matter how familiar. Ovid, of course, is more or
less unavoidable. No Roman poet (repeat: none) so greatly and
deeply influenced Western culture for so long. He has almost always seemed more contemporary than so many others. There
have been splendid translations by fine poets over several centuries; although many parts of Ovid, including the poems now
named as his Book of Exile—*Tristia* and *Epistulae Ex Ponto*—were
seldom translated into English for a number of reasons. One was
simply the accessibility of Ovid's poetry in Latin while Latin was
still the intense center of the liberal arts. Everybody who received
as much as a grammar-school education (and, until the eighteenth
century, that was the overwhelming majority among the English)
had a considerable acquaintance with the chief works of Ovid in
the original. Witness William Shakespeare, whose reflexive allu-

sions to Ovid's poems are easy and altogether comfortable. Later, late nineteenth and for all of our century, the need for translation became real enough, but energy and interest were spent more on the earlier, better-known works—the *Amores* and *Heroides, The Art of Love* and *The Pure of Love,* and, of course and above all, the *Metamorphoses.* The later works became the private property of specialists. But beyond all that there was another factor that rendered the *Tristia* a low priority item for translation into our vernacular, beginning sometime in the eighteenth century and continuing until very recent times. This problem was more substantial. Slavitt deals directly with the matter in his "Prefatory Note":

> But let's be honest and admit that the *Tristia* haven't fared well. My not altogether original explanation for the inattention—and sometimes actual disesteem—this work usually gets is that the classics curriculum was set in the nineteenth century, by British and German educators who were interested in molding character. Horatian stoicism is good for that. These poems of Ovid's are complaining and even whining, so they weren't included among the usual offerings and if anyone took notice of them at all, it was to apologize for them one way or another or to condescend.

Slavitt adds that it was precisely "the self-pity of these neglected works of Ovid's exile that drew me to them, or, put it another way, the bold and imaginative use to which the poet put his own biography for rhetorical and practical ends." Always subtle and elegant in debate, Slavitt manages to modify our acceptance of Ovid's sad personal story with a qualification as accurate as it is uncomfortable, noting that "it is rather to our shame that we are better prepared now to understand Ovid's miserable predicament than the scholars and readers of the nineteenth century could have been." With a certain delicacy Slavitt does not choose to mention in his "Prefatory Note" another kind of problem that has plagued Ovid's reputation in our own times—his freely acknowledged, unembarrassed facility as a maker of verses. And, with that facility, an honest and irrepressible taste for frivolity. He translates it in a number of places, especially in IV:10 of the *Tristia*:

> I used to waste my time trying to write verses—
> our father called it a waste: he disapproved

of any pursuit where you couldn't earn a decent living
and always used to say, "Homer died poor."
He was right of course, as I knew then and still think now.
I tried to give it up, to stick to prose
on serious subjects. But frivolous minds like mine attract
frivolous inspirations, some too good
not to fool with. I kept returning to my bad habits,
secretive and ashamed. I couldn't help it.

Here the reader may also experience the supple flexibility of Slavitt's—and W. H. Auden's—eleven-stressed adaptation of the Latin elegiac couplet. It proves in skilled hands to be an adroit handling of a tricky form.

Our best-known poets may or may not be facile and/or frivolous; but, with the possible exceptions of Merrill and Ashberry and Richard Howard, they do not like to confess either quality. Silly? Well, maybe. There is, after all, James Tate, the Steve Martin of American poetry. But pretty much everybody else, even Norman Dubie, at least claims that the enterprise is hard labor and takes talent. The Sweet Singer of Michigan put it best, and once and for all, for our time, though long ago: "Literary is a work very difficult to do." Not even Greg Kuzma or Lyn Lifshin argues that it's as easy as it looks. Of course, Ovid was talking about something else, the difficulty, the serious danger of possessing a very great gift for the craft. Scholar W. R. Johnson's happy description of the qualities of Ovid's work will indicate how little Ovid has in common with the most prominent of our poets: "He has elegance, variety, urbanity; he is capable of an easy radiance, of a style as smooth and iridescent as watered silk." Although glitz and glitter are common enough today, among us all probably only Richard Wilbur has "an easy radiance."

Publius Ovidius Naso (43 B.C.–A.D. 18), born into an equestrian family situated at Sulmo, a hundred miles east of Rome, went to Rome early to go to school. He studied rhetoric, preparing for the law and public service, studied philosophy in Athens, toured the Mediterranean; and then, at twenty he began a highly successful public career as a poet, deeply involved in Roman literary life and circles. He knew pretty much everyone pretty well, except for the great Virgil—

> I saw Virgil once at a party
> but didn't have the nerve to go up to speak
> to the great man.

He married three times, the last time for love and keeps. He owned a mansion and an orchard property in Rome as well as his part of his family's country estate. And so he prospered, was known and honored and influential until A.D. 8, his fifty-first year, when, for reasons then and still now secret and obscure, he was exiled by order of the Emperor Augustus. Sent off to the Empire's eastern frontier to live at Tomi, chief town of Pontus (now Romania), close to the Black Sea. The particular terms of his banishment, or, more correctly, *relegatio*, were somewhat unusual. He did not lose his property and assets, and his books were not banned from the libraries. Nor was he prohibited from publishing new work. Moreover, his exile was not, necessarily, for life. It could end any day, any time, at the pleasure of the emperor and the powers-that-be. Thus if he always had some reason to hope, Ovid likewise had a constant source of anxiety. It seemed to be within his power and art to change things. All he had to do was make his best case. For ten years he tried to do just that, first writing the five books of verse letters, written to unnamed (except for his wife) recipients, that make up the *Tristia;* then later writing the four books of the *Epistulae Ex Ponto,* these addressed to specific people and written now in the reign of Tiberius. Tiberius who found no reason to bring Ovid back from the deep boonies. After ten years of exile and amazing productivity, Ovid died out there in A.D. 18.

Some of the poet's difficulty with the poem, in its parts and as a whole, derives from the simple fact that, despite his best efforts, nothing changes much for him. Getting there, the journey from Rome to nowhere, occupied some of the earlier sections and gave a kind of narrative line and direction to things. But once he was in place, he could only beg and plead, through various seasons, describe the rude and not very exotic milieu, livened by nostalgic memories of Rome, complain about the absence of civilized amenities and the deterioration of the language far from its true source and home. He must whine, of course, but not so much that his complaints might be taken as irremediable. He must make his best case without claiming that the emperor's action was completely unjust. He can only argue that he has certainly learned his lesson and that, at this point, the punishment of exile is a bit too severe. He can only apologize in a rich variety of ways and in various tones of voice. From this unlikely situation and urgently enforced strategy comes one of the great poems of the classical era and certainly the most openly personal and autobiographical poem of the period. He manages to grovel appropriately and most gracefully:

> I beg your indulgence—as any writer hopes
> his reader will indulge him, will ignore the tangles of syntax,
>   the limitations of style, the graceless moments,
> and by a generous leap of the sympathetic heart
>   arrive at the heart of my meaning. Would that I could
> speak directly, throw myself on the ground before you,
>   and let you hear my sobs as much as the words
> strung upon them like beads upon a knotted string.
>   My life is at your disposal. Father, protector,
> I am a harmless beetle that's landed upon your sleeve.
>   You have not crushed me but only flicked me away.
> I lie on my back, helpless, awkward, and wriggle about
>   begging the further favor that you right me.
> It isn't even return to Italy that I ask,
>   but somewhere civilized, where Latin is spoken,
> safe enough for my wife to come to for a visit.
>   I languish here. O Caesar, I offer thanks
> for sparing my life and beg you only to be consistent;
>   grant me as well a place and a way to live it.

The emotions of the exile (though Ovid repeatedly warns both reader and himself against accepting his confused feelings as true), ranging from cheerful hope to leaden depression, are exposed. And at no time is anger far below the surface:

> You have to give me a little leeway, gentle reader:
>   for me it's life or death; you have the choice

of walking away. Nobody's forcing you to read this.
Do you exclaim how awful this is, how sloppy?
I agree. I urge you to put it aside. Drop it,
read something with polish and wit. I would!
I'll tell you the truth: I don't even revise these things
but send them out as they are, like beggar's children,
feeling a twinge maybe, but knowing that they'll do better
because of their imperfections and how they affront
decent people's standards. They ought to look like hayseeds
just blown in from the country on some ill wind.

Tomi was not a good place for a poet—uncomfortable, unciv-
ilized, far from books and good company, food and talk. But it was
also a dangerous place, one where even an old poet had to help
defend what there was from the raids and incursions of honest-to-
God barbarians:

The wild tribes that charge down from the north think it
unmanly to support themselves by working,
preferring to raid and plunder. They assume we're here
like the game in the fields, and they have only to take
whatever they like. Our farmers must wear swords to plow.
The shepherds go out in armor and listen for hoofbeats
as much as for howling wolves. We live from day to day,
from moment to moment, always a little afraid.
Whenever we get complacent, the savages seem to know it
and swoop down like a flock of birds of prey—
and when they do it's every man for himself out here.
Sure, we have some soldiers and all belong
to a kind of ragtag militia, but mixed among our numbers
are a great many Getae who've settled here, willing
to swap some of their wildness for what they consider comfort.
Loyalty isn't part of the deal. They don't
know what it means—or even have a word in their language
to signify such a thing. They are brutes, beasts,
wearing the hides of beasts, are shaggy and smelly and crude . . .

Those barbarians are real—predatory, savage, and of a different
order of humanity. The hatred and contempt of the Romans (and
thus of Ovid) is real enough, too. So is the fear, the very real dan-

ger. We should keep this in mind, for very few of our poets, a mere handful really, of the generation born in and after World War II have any honest familiarity with real dangers, except, perhaps, in the self-induced risks of drugs, booze, AIDS, etc. They are uniformly much too liberal (in their verses, at least) to name a barbarian when they see one. As long as it is somebody else being mugged, they keep a public silence. Slavitt has never been one to accept the ultimate groveling posture—tongue-bitten silence in the face of genuine provocation. *Vital Signs: New and Selected Poems* (1975) is full of poems dealing directly with our complex political and social problems as they impinge upon the life of the poet and the lives of all of us. From those poems, and from others in the four books of his own poems that have followed, we can come to know a liberal, decent, humane, witty Jewish gentleman, one whom experience has taught to be more than a little skeptical and more than somewhat cynical about almost everything under the sun, including himself. About poetry, and literature in general, he has always been demonstrably what we now call "elitist." Which is merely to say that he uniformly demands of others, *all* others, the same kind and level of knowledge of and dedication to the art and the craft that he asks of himself and of the work that he admires. Seven routinely frantic years as an associate editor of *Newsweek* magazine, dealing mainly with books and movies, toughened him and taught him the hard lessons of experience. Close enough to centers of power and authority, for that time, he learned a great deal about the shifty and sometimes subtle differences between reputation and accomplishment. All that time—before, during, and after the seven-year hitch at *Newsweek*—Slavitt was writing and publishing poetry. From *Suits for the Dead* (1961) to *The Walls of Thebes* (1986) there has, to be sure, been the kind of steady growth and change, an honest development of form and content commensurate with the coming to maturity and toward wisdom of an artist of our times. But there are patterns that are at least retroactively evident from his earliest work to the latest: a virtuoso's love of complex verse forms, traditional and homemade, so gracefully mastered as to be not concealed but not self-conscious either, all written in a various language, at both high and low levels, precisely apt or jokingly indecorous, which is close kin to the real speech, written or spoken, which real people use to talk to each other about the important and unimportant things that really matter to them. His work is always openly literary, easily and intelligently allusive to the great literature, including its classical heritage, which has been a significant part of any honorable poet's worldly goods. And, inevitably, the myths and the subjects (people, places, things) of the classical world have always fascinated him.

About translation . . . well, he had been translating bits and pieces from the Latin and, yes, Greek from the first; but the first major translation, as such, was *The Eclogues of Virgil* (1971). (Like this volume, that one was a handsome piece of bookmaking; and likewise both are elegantly illustrated with drawings by Raymond Davidson.) Puzzled, as so many modern poets have been by the pastoral charade, Slavitt set for himself the tasks of answering a tough question—"If you were ever a living, breathing poem, what could you have conceivably been about?" He arrived at a method that allowed the translator to follow closely the line of each Eclogue, giving us the key passages in flawless and interesting English versions, yet simultaneously offering a critical and exegetical commentary, self-reflexive, on the poem by its translator. It was a means that allowed for the kind of anachronism that gives a sense of the simultaneity of past and present:

> Sixth formers read it now, sweat out the grammar
> furrow their smooth foreheads to get it right,
> but cannot know what we know, you and I,
> Tityrus says it all: "Fool that I was,
> I used to think the city they call Rome
> was like our market town, but bigger."

Or take a look at these lines from the ninth Eclogue, "Moeris":

> We have heard it before,
> at the faculty clubs, at the little dinner parties,
> the stories of agents, of editors, of deans,
> and all of the different masks for the same injustice,
> stupid, envious, arrogant, greedy, mean . . .
> And then the talk turns, as it did then.

This superbly successful and original translation, restoring the *Eclogues* to the contemporary reader, was followed by a double volume—*The Eclogues and the Georgics of Virgil* (1972). Here in the *Georgics* he used some of the ways and means he had developed in translating the *Eclogues*, but with some differences. As he put it in his preface: "My poem, then, is actually a reading of Virgil's *Georgics*, which is something a little closer than the ruminations on the *Eclogues*, and yet not quite strictly the poem itself." The *Georgics*, large and tightly structured and very difficult, really, was perhaps as successful as the *Eclogues*, perhaps not; but it was, in Slavitt's version, surely a work of great energy and bravado and (on Slavitt's part) originality. It proved an excellent preparation for the *Tristia*. Along the way from Virgil to Ovid, Slavitt paused long enough to translate elegantly the love elegies of a poet contemporary to both and much admired by Ovid—Aulus Albius Tibullus. *The Elegies to Delia of Albius Tibullus* (1985), besides giving us these poems again freshly, allowed him to polish his own skills with the work of a different order than the language of either Virgil or Ovid.

Meantime his own life and work were changing, deepening and darkening in such a way as to create an even closer sympathy with Ovid, the loser far in time and space from all he loved, dangerously exiled. *The Walls of Thebes* is a sharing, as its jacket asserts, of "the wisdom bred of pain and loss." And this quality is nowhere more explicit than in the poem "Bloody Murder," dealing with the murder of Slavitt's mother, from which these two stanzas will give some sense of the formal feeling following (as Ms. Dickinson noted) close on the heels of great pain. And the kinds of rude and rapid juxtapositions of sacred and profane, deadly serious and sadly frivolous, which Slavitt (like Ovid) has always been master of:

> After the burglar bludgeoned my mother
> to death with a bathroom scale and a large
> bottle of Listerine, the police
> recommended Ronny Reliable's
> Cleaning Service—one of a growing
> number of firms that make it their business
> to clean up after messy murders,
> suicides, and other disasters.

They have the solvents and strong stomachs
for such work. I still wonder
who would choose that kind of employment
or what the men who performed this awful
and intimate task looked like. We only
spoke on the phone; detectives let them
in; and the charge showed up on my next
Mastercard bill. But I know they were there.

Coming to the Ovid as a changed, different person and poet, Slavitt changed his method very slightly, though significantly. In this matter it is best to let the poet speak for himself, from the "Prefatory Note":

> These are witty, angry, passionate, amazing poems. I have tried to be true to that general quality rather than to any particular instrumentality by which Ovid managed his achievement. My poems are the same length as his—so the scale is right. That's the only rule I've observed scrupulously. Otherwise, I've tried to *be* Ovid, which is, I admit, a crazy thing to attempt—but then all translation is always crazy to attempt, probably because that very transformation is what it requires.

The success of this attempt may be indicated by the (rare) blurbs for the book by Karl Shapiro and Richard Wilbur (among others). Shapiro says, plainly enough, that what we have is "the actual voice of Ovid himself, the anguish." Wilbur's praise is more precise: "Tone and personality, so often lost in translation of whatever kind, are captured here; someone clever, passionate and heartbroken comes very near us, and I think it is Ovid."

Ironically, there has been another verse translation of the *Tristia* in our lifetime, a good one, really, in a scholarly sense, by L. R. Lind: *Ovid: Tristia* (1975). But Slavitt is a poet of very considerable gifts and accomplishment—and, if truth could somehow ever be known in this era of hype, false images, and inflated reputations, a major poet, to be counted among the few and best of those writing poetry in our language. That he should have managed to achieve a great translation and restoration of the work of a master from another time is at once appropriate and astonishing. We should be grateful that he has come to this and, thanks to Bellflower Press, it has come to us.

Short Takes
Miscellaneous Reviews

Most newspaper reviews, magazine notices, too, have to be short, too short to say a whole lot of critical things. By definition they have to present a kind of brief abstract of the book, deformed yet somehow accurate. And they also have to offer some kind of judgment, somehow an honest and authentic response to the experience of reading the book. Not least, the review has to be an announcement to fellow readers, a recommendation or, in some cases, a warning.

These are also arranged in alphabetical order of author.

Stephen Becker:
When the War Is Over

I wrote this for the "Lost Words" section, devoted to recommended books from the past, for the *Washington Times.*

The secret at the dark center of the American experience is the Civil War. Not that we lack information. The weight of information, pure and impure, accurate and distorted, is already overwhelming and growing constantly, irrepressibly, like kudzu. Herein lies a superb example of St. Paul's warning that the letter kills and only the spirit giveth life. Problem is and has been that, for all kinds of reasons, we cannot well and fully imagine what happened.

What happened to us is simply revealed in one sentence of Shelby Foote's magnificent three-volume history, *The Civil War.* Near the end Foote writes: "Approximately one out of ten ablebodied Northerners was dead or incapacitated, while for the South it was one out of four, including her noncombatant Negroes." He is speaking of military casualties. What that means is that for the victorious North the war was far worse than it was for any nation in World War I or World War II. For the defeated South it was far worse than any war we know about except maybe for the nineteenth-century

Taiping Rebellion in China. Thus, in terms of the ratio of deaths to population, the Civil War was the most terrible and devastating conflict in modern history. And somehow we have not been able to grasp the truth of it. The generation of witnesses knew it well enough, but did not pass on the truth of it, indeed, in a public sense, lacked the means and inclination to do so. To approach the truth in our time demands an act of imagination. When facts fail us, we turn to fiction. Mostly our fiction, even some celebrated works of art, has failed us also. I can think of three wonderful exceptions, each by a veteran of World War II: Shelby Foote's *Shiloh* (1952), Mary Lee Settle's *Know Nothing* (1960), and Stephen Becker's extraordinary *When the War Is Over* (1969). Settle's novel concerns the loss of national innocence and ends just as the war is beginning. Foote's is a classic combat story, gritty with authenticity and one of the best by any American, an initiation rite performed as the green troops of both sides are well bloodied in a major battle. Becker's story has a different stance. It is set during the final days of the war, the story of veterans of that utterly lost generation—the young who had somehow survived an indescribable hell to become cynical and compassionate, bitter and hopeful, bone-weary and half-mad. At the center of a large cast of characters, both "real" and fictional, is twenty-four-year-old Marius Catto of Illinois, an orphan who has endured to find a home as "a lieutenant of infantry in the Army of the United States." On a casual patrol in fairly peaceful Kentucky countryside Catto is wounded by a teenage "Johnny," Thomas Martin (who was "real"), a kind of guerilla, who is captured and carried along with the outfit when they move to garrison duty in Cincinnati. Catto heals; Martin becomes a well-liked mascot of the unit; and the war winds down elsewhere. Given a pro forma court-martial, Martin is sentenced to death as a kind of legal gimmick to allow for his eventual full pardon. But the panic in Washington, following upon the assassination of Lincoln, turns the whole system inside out. For a brief period all pardons are ignored, all sentences are to be carried out. Thomas Martin "falls through the cracks," as we say, and must die and dies, breaking the hearts of all who knew him, especially Marius Catto, whose life is changed for keeps by this final senseless act of war.

Lean, lithe, and evocative, constructed in a driving sequence of swift, crisp scenes; written in a language that allows a full range of acting and talking, feeling and thinking, the plainly quotidian and the lyrical, an appropriate and splendidly lucid language Becker taught himself to invent by deep immersion in the "real" language of the times; and peopled with both real and fictional characters who are equally and altogether true and memorable—from Jacob, the freed slave, to General Joseph "Fighting Joe" Hooker, all of them given their future in a final epilogue, a Mozartian fugal coda. *When the War Is Over* is a masterpiece of our national literature, an achievement on the order of *Billy Budd*, no less, and one that fulfills the ("real") hope and words of Cincinnati's Judge William Martin Dickson, who in the 1880s wrote briefly about the need to remember the story of Thomas Martin: "If it is to be told, let us have it whole. Let the young not be misled: the dread reality has something else than the pomp and circumstance, however glorious." The dread reality of the dark American secret is all there, made accessible to the contemporary imagination. Stephen Becker is continuing to create first-rate novels of all kinds, most recently *Rendezvous in Haiti* (1987). But *When the War Is Over* is a very special achievement, a timeless work of art and passion, one that must not be allowed to be lost amid all the glare and gilt of today and tomorrow.

A. Scott Berg:
Goldwyn: A Biography

"It's not his life, it's a fairy story," wrote John Dos Passos of the life of Sam Goldwyn in a documentary section of *Mid-century* (1961). Even though Dos Passos had to depend almost entirely on canned "facts" and public relations handouts, together with an extended personal interview, his little seven-page section, "The Promised Land (old style)," manages to say more, more truly and deeply, than A. Scott Berg's massive (580 pages), much-promoted, widely advertised, and extensively reviewed *Goldwyn: A Biography*. But the comparison and contrast is not quite fair. Dos Passos was a major writer. You don't read Berg for the fine writing or for the refinement and depth of his perceptions; you read him for information he has gained and gleaned from years of honorable hard labor and for his undeniable knack at organizing and refining a heap of factual raw materials into some cumulative and chronological patterns. Dos Passos was dead right, though. The life of Schmuel Gelbfisz of Warsaw, Poland, who became Samuel Goldfish in Birmingham, England, and finally, in America, the one and only Samuel Goldwyn, can justly be taken as an old-fashioned fairy tale of magical transformation—sow's ear into silk purse. It would make a pretty good movie, all in all, following the inexorable rise, from anonymous glovemaker to famous filmmaker, of a passionate, rootless, and ruthless (and lucky) survivor who escapes from the grinding, almost hopeless material poverty of one country and century to find great wealth and eminence and some tokens of honor in another nation and century, ending his days at last physically "reduced to a vegetable," as his son says. And although his actual bones rest and rot appropriately in opulent and vulgar Forest Lawn, there is a sad and symbolic sense in which he may be said to rest forever in an intellectual and spiritual potter's field, that haunting place the dictionary describes as "a burial place for strangers and the friendless poor." It could, thus, be a tragic tale, certainly a pathetic one, if Goldwyn had not also been so uniformly and famously funny—this biography has the greatest collection of "Goldwynisms" yet assembled—and, behind all the fun and games, if he were not so consistently and irresistibly wicked in his dealings with all other creatures great and small, friend and foe alike. And, too, if his line of work, almost wholly exploitative and parasitical, show business pure and simple, were not, after all is said and done, asserted and debated, essentially inconsequential.

Something else inhibits the shadows and undertones of pathos—our nostalgia for the rough and ready hard grabbers of an earlier, simpler time. It is so much easier to like Blackbeard the Pirate than Ivan Boesky, Captain Kidd than Donald Trump, Lucretia Borgia than Leona Helmsley. Slick contemporary corporate people, CEO's and even the lesser lords and ladies, are boring (and dangerous to health and welfare) with a capital *B*. Sam Goldwyn lived and died as an independent producer. In the years between *The Squaw Man* (1914) and *Porgy and Bess* (1959) he produced a long list of picture shows, some of them pretty good, and one of them, *The Best Years of Our Lives* (1946), earning him a belated Academy Award. Goldwyn knew and worked (and fought) with practically everybody in the history of Hollywood. (The photographs of them are well chosen, great and good fun.) And allowing for the enforced limits of seeing the world from a single, unheroic point of view, *Goldwyn* is a solid history of the movie business and, as well, of this nation, which supported that business. There is an odd and interesting inversion there; for the movie industry thrived most when the nation's economy was in worst shape and vice versa. It could be said, though it hasn't been, that our national best interests and theirs are often contradictory. It is probably a good idea to compare and contrast Berg's *Goldwyn* with more general recent histories, most pertinently Neal Gabler's excellent *An Empire of Their Own: How the Jews Invented Hollywood*. But *Goldwyn* is solid and scholarly and interesting and easy to read, worthy of all the excellent reviews it has been receiving; although the very best of these (so far), John Gregory Dunne's "Goldwynism," in the *New York Review of Books* (May 18, 1989), has serious reservations and revisions to make.

I, too, would like to make a couple of minor corrective points.

One of these has to do with the claim made by Berg, in his book and in a number of recent published interviews, that he has enjoyed nearly perfect freedom in the making of this book. Anybody who has ever done any biographical work knows that unless the subject has been dead for several centuries, only an unauthorized biography, built upon materials in the public domain and depending in no way on the resources and good will of the subject's estate, can ever be "free." Berg tells us that Samuel Goldwyn, Jr., sought him out to write the biography and that he, Berg, refused the task unless he had complete access to all materials and freedom to call it any way he saw it. Well, maybe. Just *maybe*. But I kind of doubt it. In the absence of a published copy of the actual contract, we are asked to take this unlikely tale on faith. What Berg really tells us in the book is: "He [Goldwyn, Jr.] assured me that he would make himself available to discuss his mother and father and that he would exercise no control over the contents of the biography." It is virtually unheard of for anybody to relinquish all rights of review and revision; and, chip off the old block, Sam Jr. certainly seems an unlikely candidate to render himself highly vulnerable on the basis of some kind of vague authorial honor system. The old man probably never said, "A verbal contract isn't worth the paper it's written on." But you can believe he could have.

Berg offers many of the warty details of Goldwyn's life and career; so that, in a relative sense, *Goldwyn* is far removed from your typical puff job. But Berg remains uniformly kind to the memory of old Sam; and he is especially generous to (and unquestioning of) the life and times of Samuel Goldwyn, Jr. Not that Berg has suppressed anything, or, anyway, anything we can know about; but the context he creates tends to understate the insatiable greed, insufferable arrogance, the brutal indifference to the needs of others, including his own family, the chicanery and manipulation, the lying, stealing, and cheating that seem to have characterized old Goldwyn's ways and means from the beginning to the end.

It is probable that Goldwyn was a somewhat better human being than most of the other old-timey Hollywood tycoons, but whether that should be emblazoned in heraldry remains to be seen. It can be and probably should be mentioned that these colorful, freebooting, clawfingered barbarians who truly created the myth machine, the dream factory of Hollywood, these alien pirates of whom Goldwyn may have been the best man, are not entirely blameless in some serious matters of our social and cultural history. Sure, they fed us a diet of dreams and we paid them very well for the pleasure of it. But are not some of these dreams, whether formed out of ignorance or shrewd design, almost antithetical to the larger (truer?) American dream? Are not some of those dreams false and corrupt? Once upon a time there certainly was much more to the American dream than the ruthless, obsessive, and rapacious pursuit of success, status, riches, comfort, and celebrity. There were also, from our beginnings, the ideals, especially for the privileged and the lucky, of duty, honor, service, and sacrifice. And for all of us there was the dream of liberty, the hope for brotherhood and equality.

By their highly profitable art and by the example of their dedicated, if dissolute lives, the Hollywood dream salesmen helped to change all that for the worse. And our generation has lived to witness a deadly serious confusion of show business and self-government, a world in which the distortions of publicity and contrived perception replace facts as, in Frost's phrase, "the sweetest dream that labor knows." Though, sooner or later all skulls are reduced to smiling, Sam Goldwyn's must be grinning broadly.

One of the most contemptible times of the Hollywood old-timers was the McCarthy era. It was show business, from the beginning, and it was chiefly Hollywood that fueled all the sad nonsense and created and kept the blacklists. There are strong hints in the subtext of Berg's book that blacklisting was an old Hollywood tradition and a useful weapon in Goldwyn's armory. Nowadays it is Hollywood that tells us, repeatedly, that the whole country was tainted and sick with McCarthyism. Maybe so, maybe not. But there can be not the least doubt that Hollywood was infected. According to Berg's book, Sam Goldwyn, true to form and his guardian inner spirit, took and held the moral middle ground in this matter as in everything else that matters.

Well then. A lively, at times a fascinating story, a modern fairy tale where dungy straw is spun into threads of gold. Yet in a real sense Berg's *Goldwyn* fails in exactly the same way that so many Hollywood movies fail, the way Goldwyn, even at his finest, failed, by finally avoiding or anyway slighting the hard truths, by ignoring the really hard questions and hard sayings that are the very blood and guts of this nation, its people, and their aspirations. Blood and guts he could do without, though he once apologized to Thurber for making a story of his too "blood and thirsty."

"It turned out just as he had dreamed," Dos Passos writes. "He'd reached America and he'd made his fortune. It was what they called freedom."

Sallie Bingham:
Passion and Prejudice: A Family Memoir

Passion and Prejudice offers an insider's view of the fall of the house of Bingham, that family that for seventy years ran the highly regarded Louisville *Courier-Journal* and the *Times* and sold them to the Gannett Company in May 1986 for $307 million.

This proves to be an interesting book, sometimes simply fascinating. There seems to be something here for everybody. First there is the behind-the-scenes account of boardroom battles and squabbles as the various Binghams plotted and schemed and finally managed (very profitably to one and all) to bring an end to the family's control of the newspapers. This is an emblematic contemporary story. The papers were among the most liberal in the South, fighting good fights in New Deal days and standing early (and almost alone) for racial integration. The family, compared to some other baronial newspaper clans, had earned a reputation for community involvement ("a commitment to service rather than personal gain"), and though growing hugely rich, for a lifestyle of elegant, yet reasonable rectitude. They were more admired than envied, more honored than feared. They did not know much about the virtues of serious self-sacrifice. But, then, who does? Behind all that, stretching all the way back to early colonial days, there is a Southern saga of several family lines over generations. There is plenty of sex and violence, tainted money and mysterious deaths, famous names and curious connections. It is as lively a miniseries as you are likely to encounter. Then there is a powerful mother-daughter story threaded through the book, a *Mommie Dearest* with class. There is an autobiographical story, the story of the teller of the tale, Sallie Bingham, how she was somehow able to raise her consciousness and to embrace the assumptions of feminism, among other things, and how she established her identity and independence and discovered the inward and spiritual resources, including an undeniable courage and integrity, to break free from the family's power and reticent habits and to write this book. Finally there is a larger pattern in the story, intimated by allusion and evocation, linking the sins and sorrows of family history to Greek myth and tragedy, even to certain Biblical parallels. Some readers may be touched, satisfied as to the validity of these shadowy implications. Others (this reviewer, for instance) may prove a bit too cynical to accept, without an emphatic raising of eyebrows, the claims of these fat cats to a heritage of archetypal, mythopoeic nobility. Either way, though, their idea of themselves is part of the whole story.

And that's what Sallie Bingham—this generation's family poet, playwright, storyteller, novelist, and, briefly, book editor—has sought to do. To tell the whole story. Her success is remarkable; and, in context, even the flaws and failures of the book are instructive.

Something of a problem for readers is that there are other recent accounts dealing with the same general subject. David and Mary Chandler's *The Binghams of Louisville* (1987) and, especially, *House of Dreams* (1988) by Marie Brenner, were widely reviewed and discussed. For a limited few there will be the pleasures of comparison and collation, some new facts, some corrections, a slight difference in emphasis. For instance, the consensus has tended to blame brother Barry, Jr., more than Sallie does. She is sympathetic, though a little condescending.

But her book can stand on its own. Since both confession and autobiography approximate fiction, and since we are not likely to have to test the facts or to meet any of these folks anyway, it may be profitable to approach *Passion and Prejudice* as a kind of a novel, based upon factual truth. Taken as a fiction, the story has a remarkable and complex character at its center. The narrator, Sallie, is an electric bundle of contradictions, of disparate energies and forces. Compassionate and caring, she is also demonstrably uncharitable—in thought, word, and deed—to those she disagrees with and of whom she disapproves. Self-aware, though not burdened with an excessive sense of guilt, she can be savagely judgmental with other people. She is analytical and intellectually adventurous; yet, at the same time, her writing and thinking are often clotted with the clichés of a somewhat dated radical rhetoric. She has some original, not to say very odd, notions about American and world history. But narration is most of all a matter of voice, of finding a voice; and she knows this, arguing that "finally we must take possession of our own voices." We see that take place. We also see where the narrator's heart lies, where the writing shines and glows—in tales of her wildest and woolliest antecedents, in memories of childhood, in reactions to nature, and in her descriptions of beautiful and expensive things.

The exposition is uneven; some things we are told over and over again, others we will never know. There is some confusion of chronology and a lot of thoughtless (unedited) repetition. In a novel, these bad habits would attest to the narrator's sincerity. There is sympathy and sorrow for many among the living and the dead; there is real anger against perceived injustices. There is only a little love, shy and inestimable, revealed in all of these pages. *Passion and Prejudice* is no Greek tragedy, but it is a sad and moving story; and Sallie Bingham, as she must surely know, is part of the sadness of it all.

John Ciardi and Karl Shapiro: Small Presses Come to the Rescue of Two Elder Statesmen of Poetry

Two books by respected poets have recently come to us from new and "small" publishers. John Ciardi's *Selected Poems*, handsomely made, is from the University of Arkansas Press. Karl Shapiro appears, with a beautifully designed book, elegant to eye and touch, bearing the imprint of Stuart Wright, a new trade publisher who has this year published new books by Eleanor Ross Taylor, Barry Hannah, Ellen Wilbur, and Eleanor Clark. An impressive list.

It might seem discouraging to consider poets such as Ciardi and Shapiro having to depend on small and little-known publishers, but it may well be that in this fact, and in their acceptance of this fact, these remarkable elder statesmen of poetry are still pioneering, pointing the way to the future.

The accidental juxtaposition of these books, arriving separately, yet almost simultaneously, suggests some interesting developments in the ongoing story of contemporary American poetry. Poets of the same generation (Shapiro, born in 1913, is three years older than Ciardi), each had already published collections before World War II. Shapiro's *Poems* appeared in 1935; Ciardi's *Homeward to America* came along in 1940. Both poets saw combat and came of age in the war. And they lived to write some of the finest poetry to come out of that time. Veterans, they returned to a long season of literary success, of considerable honor, of impressive and steady productivity, and of exercising a real influence on the American literary scene. Shapiro won the Pulitzer Prize in 1945, the first of many prizes he would win; served as poetry consultant at the Library of Congress; was editor of *Poetry* magazine (1950–1956). Ciardi was for a long time director of the Bread Loaf Writers' Conference (1947–1973) and poetry editor of the *Saturday Review* (1956–1973). Though he has not yet won a Pulitzer, Ciardi received a string of prizes, including the prestigious Prix de Rome, and has acquired a full deck of honorary degrees.

Both poets were teachers: Shapiro at Johns Hopkins, Nebraska, the University of Illinois at Chicago, and the University of California at Davis; Ciardi at Missouri, Harvard, and Rutgers. Both have written and edited many other books, including criticism, anthologies, and textbooks. Shapiro produced a novel, *Edsel*, in 1971. Ciardi has written children's books, limericks with Isaac Asimov, a celebrated translation of Dante's *Divine Comedy*, and lately, in keeping with the theme of his regular program on National Public Radio, two volumes of *A Browser's Dictionary* with the third one on the way.

By the middle of the 1960s each of these poets possessed solid credentials, an earned place of honor firmly based upon enviable accomplishments. Their peers—Jarrell, Lowell, Schwartz, Berryman, Roethke, and so many others—are dead. Only Wilbur and Eberhardt continue in the practice of the craft. Ciardi, always wryly aware of the incongruities of fortune, must have guessed what was coming his way. "Any man who believes he has succeeded," he once wrote, "has settled for a limited engagement."

Both men suffered a serious eclipse of reputation beginning in the late 1960s. The world that gave us television commercials to live with and media images to admire and even to vote for, has also demonstrated it knows how to handle and dispose of unfashionable poets. Where achievement is too deeply rooted, then something can be gained by simply ignoring what cannot be openly denied.

The gradual decline of respectful attention for Shapiro began about the time he gave up the power center of *Poetry*. For Ciardi the decline of attention can be more precisely plotted. In 1973, after seventeen years, he gave up the poetry editorship of the *Saturday Review*. That same year he was removed from the directorship of Bread Loaf.

What happens to an American poet who loses the power of his

public offices? Before 1973, the *New York Times Book Review* had reviewed every book of poems by John Ciardi. Since then he has published eight collections, including this latest. None of them has been reviewed by the *Times*. None has been widely reviewed anywhere. One, *Lives of X*, fortunately reprinted entirely as the final section of *Selected Poems*, received so little notice that Ciardi reports never having seen or heard of any review of it. Composed of powerful, autobiographical, narrative poems, written in a dexterous and flexible blank verse, *Lives of X* may well prove to be a great influence on the work of many young poets who are turning away from the smoggy vapors of homegrown surrealism in favor of a poetry that can include real places and things and people and words that these people might conceivably say to each other.

Here, then, we have two skilled and mature poets whose ratings have been up and down on the literary stockmarket. Neither has been crippled or stricken into silence. Shapiro's book, *Love & War Art & God: The Poems of Karl Shapiro*, is a rigorous revision and rearrangement of all his work so far, together with at least a dozen new poems, all organized thematically. The critical rigor is demonstrated by the fact that *Collected Poems, 1940–1978* was more than twice as long as the present volume. *Collected Poems* was chronological. Here, early and late poems stand side by side and at ease together. Shapiro's poems show a deep sense of form, a fine, yet relaxed technical virtuosity, a love for the living American vernacular and a concern for the people of our times and the things of our world.

Ciardi's poems, also strictly selective and thematically organized, share the same general characteristics, though his voice is distinctly different—tougher, harder-edged, more various in both subject and treatment thereof. Ciardi has elsewhere declared that he now writes "only unimportant poems," by which it is clear that he, like Karl Shapiro, is a mortal enemy of pretension and hype. Both poets prove to be much closer to the hard facts of our lives and times than most of the younger poets. Readers who care about the health and welfare of American poetry will be glad to know that a couple of first-rate new books by a pair of major American poets are here for the asking.

Frank Kermode:
The Uses of Error: Selected Essays

The Uses of Error is a gathering by the distinguished scholar and critic Frank Kermode of essays and reviews from among the critical and scholarly pieces and personal memoirs he has published from 1967 to the very recent past (1990). Divided into six parts, the book contains forty-four pieces of varying length, forty-three of them taken from a variety of heavy-duty, high-visibility places. Seventeen of the essays originally appeared in the *London Review of Books*; ten more were first published in the *New York Review of Books*; others appeared in such contexts as the *Listener*, the *Times Literary Supplement*, the *New York Times Book Review*, the *New Statesman*, the *New Republic*, the *Atlantic Monthly*, and the *Observer*; one (each) were first found in the *Times Higher Education Supplement* and the *Daily Telegraph*. "On Being an Enemy of Humanity," a critical meat-cutting exhibition more in the manner of a Japanese chef than any supermarket butcher, devoted specifically to Dame Helen Gardner ("the doyenne of English academic criticism") and her book *The Defence of the Imagination*, appeared first in 1982 in the trendy literary quarterly *Raritan*. The title essay, the final piece in the book, is a sermon built on the text of Job 2:6–10 and preached by Kermode at King's College Chapel, May 11, 1986. The book is wittily and allusively dedicated ("il miglior marinaio") to John Updike, specifically referred to in the introduction as "the admirable Updike," author of *Picked-Up Pieces* and *Hugging the Shore*. With characteristic authority and irony, Kermode writes: "It might be thought that lesser persons should accept ephemerality as the penalty appropriate to their coastal caution; but it is hard to see why, if they can get away with it, they shouldn't be allowed to enjoy the measure of permanence, and the measure of vanity, proper to their station, especially if they believe, as I admit I do, that some of their best writing has been 'buried' in reviews."

For those like myself, who have turned away from much of the ingenious, over-complicated, and all too often self-aggrandizing nonsense that passes for literary criticism, even literary "scholarship," in our time, *The Uses of Error* will prove to be a remarkable restorative tonic. There was a time, twenty or maybe thirty years ago, when literary criticism was worth a grown-up's time. There was a whole gallery of critics to pick and choose among, one for every mood and occasion. From among very many some remain still in the easily summoned off-the-top-of-the-head pantheon, among them Lionel Trilling, R. P. Blackmur and Allen Tate, Cleanth Brooks and Robert Penn Warren, John Aldridge and Leslie Fiedler, Caroline Gordon, Mary McCarthy, etc. Some, like Fiedler and Aldridge and the estimable Monroe Spears, are still very much in action, voices to be reckoned with. Using these distinctly American examples as a critical context for the British, though transatlantic, Frank Kermode, I mean to claim him not as a throwback to better times (for he's nothing if not precisely up to date), but to assert that the critic and scholar who comes across in these pages is a prime example of the old-fashioned man of letters, splendidly trained by hard labor, precept, and example (as we learn in a personal piece like "My Formation"), able, with grace and authority, to deal with scholarly problems—biblical scholarship; the texts and implications of Shakespeare, Freud, and Beethoven; the Victorians at home and on the printed page; the modern and contemporary movements, especially the British, but apparently with a full awareness of the American literary establishment, at least as it is maintained and preserved in the *New York Review of Books*. For our assertively uncivil times, he is astonishingly open-minded, able to identify many interesting, even worthwhile things in such practices as implacable and implausible as deconstruction ("Paul de Man's Abyss" and "Talking About Doing"), not even above an appreciation of some of the finer points of the arguments of Stanley Fish. There are just enough zingers to keep the text from becoming a sweet love feast; he dutifully notes the "curious provincialism" informing the work of Frederick Crews. Of the work of Jerome McGann he writes: "The manner is not, as in so much of the writing I've been discussing, vulgar, but it is ponderously modish, its intention seemingly rather more to impress than to please." On a somewhat larger scale he gives a deceased, one-time culture hero both his due and what-for in "Sic Transit Marshall McLuhan"; and the aforementioned "On Being an Enemy of Humanity" proves that challenged and given occasion, Kermode can come out swinging at the bell, as dangerously dedicated to destruction as Joe Louis in round one of the second fight with Max Schmelling. Coming late in the book this essay may be intended to serve as a warning sign for any smart-aleck reviewers.

The maker of these essays, made both a character and a narrator by the five essays and the sermon of the book's final section, is somebody worth knowing. Impeccably knowledgeable, himself, able and undaunted, a model of integrity, brilliant and stylish in both his writing and the tactics of persuasion, Kermode creates the kind of criticism, instructive and delightful, that should engage anyone who cares about reading and writing. We have the well-staged drama of a man thinking and feeling as he responds to texts and ideas. At moments the writing is so good and alive you can almost start to believe that literary criticism is the honorable art form it claims to be. You could fill a fair-size commonplace book with elegant examples, pithy and witty, of his sentences. There are superb rhythms, oddly interesting transitions; sudden surprises, moments of fine excess. He is so good at it that one actually enjoys the structural predictability of many of these essays (why *not* cultivate successful and rewarding habits?). And one is untroubled by the sly and requisite stratagems by which he manages to avoid some of the insoluble political controversies of this politicized age of ours. Well? Courage is one thing, self-destruction another. Meantime what a joy it is to encounter a literary critic who can really write and is doing just that.

James McConkey:
To a Distant Island

Author of several novels, a critical study of E. M. Forster, and a couple of highly personal and innovative books that defy easy and familiar categories, James McConkey has become something of a literary cult figure in the last few years. And this remarkable new book arrives with the endorsement of two very different and distinguished writers, each of whom has earned a dedicated following which might well be called a cult—Annie Dillard and May Sarton; these together with a strong blurb from Benjamin DeMott, a maker and shaker, wheeling and dealing big-time critic. For the doubters and scoffers, all those who may start from the premise that anything favored by DeMott can't be *all* good, let me say rest easy. *To a Distant Island* is a fascinating book, deeply engaging both in form and content; and in a number of ways it is an important book, "important" in the sense that it speaks to issues and interests well beyond those so adroitly addressed by the author. It is a work of high style and literary sophistication, an intricate construction that, in specific details and general execution, is dazzling in its virtuosity. Yet, for all that, it is not a "difficult" book. A brief description of *To a Distant Island* unfairly makes it sound more formidable by far than it is. Cornell English Professor McConkey brings literary scholarship and criticism, as well as his acute memory and imaginative creativity, to bear upon Anton Chekhov and a journey he made in 1890 of some 6,500 miles clear across Russia to the Czarist penal colony on the island of Sakhalin. It was a strange and dangerous journey, begun in a state of despair (what the book flap copy calls "a severe depression") and ending, after adventures and misadventures, dangers and extraordinary discomforts, and, finally, the shocking experience of the brutal inhumanity of the prison system, renewed, restored to something like a state of grace. The outward and physical journey is something of a nightmare. The inward and spiritual journey, like most genuine pilgrimages, is a joyous mystery. Which is why we need a guide, someone there in person. McConkey is with us on two levels. First, he appears as he was when he first encountered the letters of Chekhov and the biographical studies that deal with the journey to Sakhalin. At that time, more than a dozen years ago, McConkey was on a sabbatical leave from Cornell, living in Florence with his family, and recovering from the damage which the late 1960s and early 1970s, a time of uproar at Cornell, had done to him. His own despair was real, and so the anguish and triumph of Chekhov spoke to him most deeply. Following Chekhov in his imagination, he also wrote, as if in direct response, a novel called *Journey to Sahalin* (an old-fashioned way of spelling the island's name in English), a story about "a man who, with his family, is caught up in racial animosities that resonate against an ugly and incomprehensible war"; that is, something firmly based on his Cornell experiences. In the novel his protagonist is killed, but McConkey, the author, was thereby freed from "a discredited social identity," a death he now calls "a necessary act if I were to liberate my soul for the purposes of life." This book, then, *To a Distant Island*, brings everything together now in a complex new counterpoint, which here celebrates life, creativity, joy, and the victory of love and charity over cruelty; in short, it is a celebration of human freedom.

The amazing thing is that it works and works so well, without sweat and strain, succeeding gracefully and, in fact, simply. What makes it work, I believe, is that the author, though obviously a man of subtle literary sophistication, is clearly a classical example of the contemporary American academic, the best of the breed. His innocence and sincerity shine through everywhere, banishing obscurity. He is as honest and trustworthy as an Eagle Scout. He demonstrates the considerable strengths (high seriousness, integrity, courage, and compassion) and the undeniable weaknesses (arrogance, moral pedantry, reflexive group-think, gnarled paralysis of the will) of the American academic liberal. Here is a fully dimensional self-dramatization of that type which, in itself, would make the book a valuable document. But it is so much more than that. All things considered, *To A Distant Island* is a triumph of intellect and imagination and of the literary craft.

Caryl Phillips:
Cambridge

Set firmly and with a sustained and vivid sensuous immediacy in the nineteenth century, mostly taking place in the exotic world of the British West Indies, though with some scenes set in London and the English countryside, *Cambridge* tells two stories that are closely related, indeed inextricably joined in time and place. These two stories ought to be one (and are united in the novel), but prove to be more separate than the central characters are able to imagine, because of a multitude of assumptions, prejudices, and fundamental misapprehensions that isolate individuals not so much from one another as from the possibility of any clear and present understanding of each others' motives, actions, or points of view. These personal and social misunderstandings here lead directly and inexorably to tragedy. At the center of the human tragedy is the institution of slavery, by then unlawful in Britain, but still legal and practical in the West Indies.

Among many credible, well-realized characters, black and white, the two major figures are a sensitive and thoughtful English woman of thirty, Emily Cartwright, and a proud and powerful slave called Cambridge, whom Emily dubs Hercules in the privacy of her diary. In a story with layers of irony, it is ironic that Cambridge never knows about Emily's nickname for him. Nor can or does she ever know the names that he has had—"his true Guinea name, Olumide"; his first slave name, Thomas; his Christian name, under which he preached as a missionary in England, David Henderson. She, in fact, knows next to nothing of his personal history and she figures less in his life and thoughts than one might have imagined. Though both of these central characters reveal themselves to be complex, ambiguous, conflicted characters, they also come across (a triumph of Caryl Phillips's craft and art) as fundamentally good and decent people who try to be honest with themselves and who mean to do well, but who fail out of personal limitations and huge social forces beyond their control.

The core of *Cambridge* is in the stories of Emily Cartwright and of Cambridge, as told by themselves in their own words. They speak to us in a written language, she first in the form of a fairly leisurely journal of her voyage out and visit to the Indies and the sugar plantation of which her father is the absentee owner; he, Cambridge, near the end in an urgent recounting of his life and times, and a different version of some of the events in her account, all of it written in the hurried, intense concentration of someone whose undeniable expectation is that very shortly he will be hanged.

Emily's story begins with the voyage out from England to visit her father's deteriorating sugar estate, after which she is expected to return and, by arrangement, marry a middle-aged, well-to-do widower. The voyage is recounted in detail and proves to be marked by extreme discomfort and a number of deaths, including that of Isabella, Emily's companion and best friend. This is a nice touch by Phillips. Creating the almost unimaginable hardship of an ocean voyage as experienced by a privileged and paying passenger, he trains the reader for the worst when, much later, he allows Cambridge to tell of his two hellish voyages in a slave ship.

Emily is a superb witness, one for whom all things in the Indies are legitimately new and whose journal is the appropriate place to record not only fresh first impressions but also her ideas and feelings. Almost an abolitionist at the outset, she never uncritically approves of slavery, but for various reasons she becomes more moderate in her disapproval. Emily recounts her months there and her impressions of the various white men of the estate—Mr. McDonald, the doctor; Mr. Wilson, the former manager; and, above all, the brutal and somewhat enigmatic Mr. Brown (suddenly, later, to be known as Arnold). He is, aptly, a kind of Heathcliff in Emily's imagination. There are also a number of slaves whose lives impinge directly on hers, especially Stella, her maid and companion, and Christiania, who is believed to be a witch, an obeah (in American terms, a conjure woman), but who proves to be, in Cambridge's account, a mad woman and his wife. Before all is said and done, Emily is sorely tried, loses her illegitimate baby by miscarriage, and is last seen in a state of suicidal despair. Her lover, Arnold Brown, has been murdered, and Cambridge is hanged for it. No one, not Emily or Brown or even Cambridge, knows the whole truth of things. Only the reader is so privileged.

Emily's section is by necessity longer than his. For each of them Phillips has created a plausible nineteenth-century writing style, slightly elevated and abstract, old-fashioned in its rhythms, literary echoes, and, sometimes, allusions, and slightly, subtly different from each other. "Pardon the liberty I take in unburdening myself with these hasty lines," Cambridge begins, "but thanks be to God for granting me powers of self-expression in the English language." No question, he has powers and so does Emily. Yet it is typically paradoxical in this swiftly moving and adroitly told novel that these characters are shown to be at once gifted writers and, at the same time, prisoners of the language and rhetoric of their age. This paradox allows for two kinds of irony in both their stories—those ironies which they, themselves, recognize and highlight, and those which the modern reader sees but for which the characters lack both words and awareness. Both are fully dimensional, credible characters whose perceptions of the world have authenticity and validity.

Their two voices dominate *Cambridge* but, in fact, there are four distinct voices. First and last there is the third-person narrator's voice, found in the brief, poetic prologue and epilogue. Likewise there is a third part of the central narrative, a very brief (three and a half pages) version of the climactic events of the story, told in a journalistic, semiofficial style. This section is important; for with its misapprehensions and misjudgments of both events and characters that we already know, it casts the shadow of doubt over the possibility of any "objective" account of the events and, more generally, questions the validity of any purely "factual" history. The truth lies within the whole of it—in the committed imagination of the novel we read and experience.

Phillips is fascinated by the ways and means of storytelling, and he is especially concerned with the creation of memorable characters. There is action aplenty—sex, violence, beatings, madness, murder—in *Cambridge*, as, separately and equally, the English woman and the displaced African find their sad endings. Events and ideas matter in this fictional world, but not as much as the humanity, with depths and nuances, of the characters. Phillips's artistry and integrity overwhelm all stereotypes.

Born in St. Kitts, raised in Britain, educated in Oxford and widely traveled, Caryl Phillips has proved himself among the best and most productive writers of his generation with plays and documentaries, three previous works of fiction, and his brilliant, tough-minded, prize-winning nonfiction—*The European Tribe*. Now with *Cambridge* he takes a firm giant step toward joining the company of our literary giants.

Darden Asbury Pyron:
Southern Daughter: The Life of Margaret Mitchell

Amid all the hype and hoopla attending the publication of *Scarlett: The Sequel to Margaret Mitchell's Gone With the Wind*, it is appropriate and propitious that we should also be given the chance for another serious look at the original and its creator, this time in the form of a first-rate biography of Margaret Mitchell. The legend is widely, if vaguely familiar: how a New York editor, Harold Latham, visiting Atlanta for publicity purposes and to look for new manuscripts, happened across a local newspaperwoman,

Margaret Mitchell, who at the end of his brief visit impetuously pressed upon him a huge mass of typescript, a novel she had been shyly and secretly working on for years; how Latham read it and loved it and accepted it at once, and pretty soon it became our all-time best-selling novel (also winner of the Pulitzer Prize), and next, thanks to the persistence and genius of David O. Selznick, was transformed into an incredibly successful movie, making Peggy Mitchell rich and honored and world famous and probably as happy as could be until the evening when she was hit while crossing the street in Atlanta by a taxi driven by a drunk.

Some of the above is more or less true. All of it is nonsense.

In what proves to be an exemplary model of what a literary biography can be and should be, Darden Pyron has carefully examined and analyzed the pertinent secondary sources, including a couple of earlier biographies, and explored and evaluated the available primary materials (letters, journals, manuscripts, documents of all kinds) for himself, adding a significant number of personal interviews, to bring forth not only the story of Margaret Mitchell and her book as completely as can be, but also a larger story, an accurate accounting of the changing South and of America in her time and ours. Because Pyron is an established historian, able to evoke the precise climates of opinion as well as the ambiance, both detailed and general, of this nation's story, the narrative of Margaret Mitchell is played out not in a vacuum but in and against the living forces of a palpable world. Deceptively leisurely (for soon enough even apparently idle facts are fully pertinent to *Gone With the Wind* and its creation), this re-creation is as much fun as it is good history. We learn the story of her large network of family on both sides and their place in the history of Georgia and Atlanta, with special emphasis, of course, on the Civil War and its aftermath. It is for us, the readers, to judge the likeness and the validity of the myth of her fiction when compared and contrasted to the "true" history; and we are given enough solid information and hard evidence to make sound judgments. Margaret Mitchell comes across as a true child of her ancestors and as very much a creature of her times and particular generation, the first twentieth-century generation of the South.

If the outward and visible world is accurately presented, even more so the inward and psychological reality of Margaret Mitchell is first discovered and then revealed. Mitchell was a complex and conflicted being, at once generous to a fault and miserly, gentle and charming yet steely and stubborn, highly intelligent and sensitive yet also often thoughtless and tactless. A severe hypochondriac, she nevertheless suffered real pains and many ailments even as she gave much of her time and energy to nursing her dying father and her sickly husband. Without being either sentimental or defensive, Pyron manages to present Mitchell as a deeply sympathetic and gifted woman whose extraordinary accomplishment was achieved in the face of overwhelming personal and social odds. By the time we come to the writing and publication of the novel, we can see clearly how Mitchell managed to focus herself in all her separate parts and her inner and outer problems in all their shapes to inform with great intensity the characters and events of her novel. It is in large part this intensity which defines the very essence of the story of *Gone With the Wind* and lifts it to the level of myth. The mystery of the making of the novel remains, but both its art and its effect upon readers become believable. It is also possible to understand how, at the end of things, Mitchell had nothing left to put into fiction, nothing more to say.

One of the chief faults of literary biographies is the felt necessity to defend a given artist and to argue against all negative criticism in favor of the importance of the work in question. Pyron avoids that trap. He assumes the worthy significance of Margaret Mitchell and her work and makes his case only by that basic assumption and by some brilliant analysis of her literary art wherever it appeared—in feature articles, in early stories, published and unpublished, and in the multitude of letters, early and late, in which she created fictions about herself and imaginary self-images.

Pyron's own writing is accessible if not easy, often more complex than transparent, as it has to be to dispel firm stereotypes about Mitchell and the book and to deal with the elusive and shadowy images of Mitchell's psychology. The writing seldom calls attention to itself and never seems to divert attention away from the subject. Pyron is, himself, charming, witty in appropriate places; and when, as guide and narrator, from time to time he interrupts to add a personal note, in both the text and in the excellent footnotes, it serves a useful purpose, usually as an explanation of southern history, custom, or habit. Richly detailed, the story is astonishingly uncluttered with trivia and only sometimes burdened with the weight of repetition and redundancy. Its structure, essentially chronological and set out in five large parts (twenty-one chapters) plus prologue and epilogue, works to keep the story moving forward, creating maximum possible suspense for a story where climax and ending are fixed and known.

Southern Daughter is a fascinating book, one that will change and modify many simplistic notions we may have allowed ourselves to believe about Mitchell and her book. It is a unique story of a greatly gifted woman, blessed and cursed almost beyond endurance. And as Pyron tells it, it is the full story of the book, how it came to be and what happened to it, and of the movie, which turned the book inside out, denying the truth of it in favor of another kind of myth. *Southern Daughter* is not flawless. (What is?) But its faults are few and puny balanced against its undeniable achievement.

Philip Roth:
The Facts: A Novelist's Autobiography

We are now in midseason of the postmodern autobiography game; and so it is no wonder that Philip Roth—who has always been well aware of (if often indifferent to) the cut and jib of literary fashion and who has, anyway, ever since *Goodbye Columbus* (1959), mostly been writing, as this new book clearly shows and tells, close enough to the facts of his life to confuse many people, friends and strangers alike—should feel the need to come forward and offer a personal, factual accounting of himself; one which, within reasonable limits of rectitude, tells us a good deal about the truths of his real life as related to, and yet distinct from, the truths of his personal fictions. It is a process already consciously underway, at least since 1975 when *Reading Myself and Others*, a gathering of various interviews of Roth and essays by him, which was described by his publisher as "chapters in the autobiography of a writer," appeared. And the Zuckerman series, featuring the fictive yet Roth-like writer Nathan Zuckerman, has been around since the late 1970s, and most recently in the complex metafiction *The Coun-terlife* (1987). The Zuckerman of that novel furnishes the epigraph for this one. Roth opens his autobiography with a letter from Roth to Nathan Zuckerman from which we learn (if we don't mind reading somebody else's mail) that this text was composed rather quickly, beginning *after* the spring of 1987 when "what was to have been minor surgery turned into a prolonged physical ordeal that led to an extreme depression that carried me right to the edge of emotional and mental dissolution." The letter is, then, at once an explanation and an apology and a request for critical reaction and guidance from Zuckerman. The book to follow will be, for Roth, a general meditation on the subject of "where I had started out from and how it had all begun." Essentially chronological, though with the full freedom in time and space of a deftly exe-cuted first-person narration, the story begins with his childhood in Newark in the 1930s and goes forward to the auspicious begin-ning of his professional career with *Goodbye Columbus,* up to and including the astonishing breakthrough he came to with *Portnoy's Complaint* (1969), "a book," he tells us, "imprinted with a style and a subject that were, at last, distinctively my own." The truth is, he goes well beyond the time of *Portnoy's Complaint* whenever it is relevant, as, for example, in his treatment of *My Life as a Man* (1974), which, it seems, proved to be a supplementary "break-through" for Roth in which he was able, through the fictional Lucy Nelson, to deal with the real, if fantastical and troubled character of his wife Josephine Jensen. But essentially the story of *The Facts* is complete with the rousing success and scandal of *Portnoy.*

Following the letter to Zuckerman we have a prologue, chiefly devoted to honoring his living father and the memory of his mother. Next comes the core of the text, in five sequential chapters: "Safe at Home," treating his childhood and adolescence in Newark in the 1930s and 1940s; "Joe College," recapitulating school days at Bucknell during the early 1950s, with Roth moving and shaking among "the unrebellious sons and daughters of statusquo Amer-ica at the dawn of the Eisenhower era," where, helped by some memorable good teachers, he acted, edited, wrote, stirred up a couple of controversies, and managed to get laid; "Girl of My Dreams," concerned with his time first as a grad student, later as an instructor at the University of Chicago, where he found himself "fortified, intact, and hungry for literary distinction," and where he met and was unlucky enough to be hooked by his wife, the divorced mother of two and a few years older than he, a woman he took to be an ambassador from "the menacing realms of benighted American life that so far I had only read of in the novels of Sherwood Anderson and Theodore Dreiser," also as "the legendary old-country shiksa-witch, whose bestial inheritance had doomed her to become the destroyer of every gentle human virtue esteemed by the defenseless Jew," and whose accidental death some years later would cause him to whistle, cheerfully if unconsciously, in the taxi taking him to the funeral home; "All in the Family," dealing with the troubles he had with some Jews over the presumed self-hatred and antisemitism of some stories in *Goodbye Columbus*; and finally "Now Vee May Perhaps to Begin," picturing Roth in the 1960s, having an affair with an attractive gentile, becoming mildly involved in the turmoil of the times, getting free from the haunting of his wife, having a close encounter with death, himself, from a ruptured appendix, and managing to pull himself and a lot of things together in *Portnoy*. The final chapter of *The Facts* is a letter from Zuckerman to Roth, urging him not to publish this book, pointing out some flaws and problems, and changing everything slightly (again), turning the facts into fiction.

Those who follow Roth will learn some new and different things about him and the intricate relationship of his "real life" to his art. Because it is (except for a number of affairs with interesting women) a fairly calm and unadventurous life, its greatest strength is Roth's assertive honesty, supplemented by sharp wit and edgy irony. That very honesty may hurt him with readers who are not familiar with and sympathetic to his other work. For the character who emerges in these pages has self-centered habits of arrogance and is often ungenerous and overly judgmental. He is subtle and precise in his fine-tuned discussion of the story of Jews in contemporary America. He is less interesting and exact in his comments on mainstream American society, and his political and social judgments of the times he has lived through often seem more like television punditry than earned wisdom. But, all in all, *The Facts* is an honorable and worthy book, certainly an interesting and valuable one to anyone who has been actively engaged in the appreciation of the shadow and substance of the art of Philip Roth.

James Seay:
The Light As They Found It: Poems

One basic rule of thumb, a tentative guide to serious and interested readers of contemporary poetry, is that any book endorsed by poet Stanley Plumly can't be all good. I am happy to report that this book, handsomely and expansively and (maybe more pertinent) accurately endorsed on its jacket by Plumly, seems to stand as a notable exception to that rule. Besides there are also other earned endorsements by other writers worth listening to—Reynolds Price and Henry Taylor among them. The nineteen poems, structured and arranged in four separate, untitled sections, represent Seay's first full-scale book of poems (not counting a couple of limited editions) in fifteen years. Readers who enjoyed his earlier books, *Let Not Your Hart* and *Water Tables*, and who have been wondering, waiting for the next one, this one, will find themselves amply rewarded by the new work presented here. Poetry, finally, is not a product like any other; nor is it a matter of schedules and calendars, clocks and hourglasses, blurbs and reviews. It comes and goes like a ghost in a dream, and the best poems, however much in and for a time, haunt us timelessly, ever after. There are deeply haunting poems in Seay's new book, appropriately so when his fundamental subject, offered in a variety of lengths and forms and mostly ghosted and drummed in by a steady, graceful, iambic beat, is so often the persistence of memory and its accumulated patina of irony and pity. As in his earlier work, though here with more depth and maturity, Seay tells stories, large and small, works in narrative lines threaded with a design of lyrical moments that are more than merely decorative. His tone and voice are Southern, mostly spoken and vernacular, always readily accessible, aiming for clarity, resonance, and evocation. People (public and private), places (familiar and exotic), and hard-edged, accurately summoned and rendered things all join together to give these poems the grace of art beyond pure craft. Seay is a mature poet, now at the peak of the powers his earlier works promised. He writes with more openness, directly about himself—"Years later I was processing a compensation claim / for an insurance company I was working for." And, paradoxically, he asserts more sophistication about the ways of the world:

> such parades in life, for instance as lunch
> with the woman in Georgetown
> whose every emblem was Camelot
> right down to sterling frame for the Presidential scrawl
> on a scrap of teletype
> thanking her for the intro to Ian Fleming and 007.
> —"Tiffany & Co."

There is a renewed confidence in himself and his art, evidenced by, among other things, the dedication of individual poems to old friends including Roy Blount, Jr., William Harmon, Elizabeth Spencer, James Dickey, and Louis D. Rubin, Jr.

Isaac Bashevis Singer:
Scum

"Just when you think you've vanquished the demons, they stick out their tongues," thinks Max (born Mordkhe in Roszkow, Poland) Barabander, the long-suffering antihero and more or less eponymous central character of *Scum*. Set in Warsaw in 1906, the novel swiftly and gracefully tells the story of Max's return, after twenty years, to his Polish homeland from Argentina, where he has made a large fortune in real estate and various and sundry shady enterprises. Max's only child, Arturo, has just died, and his wife, Rochelle, a former prostitute, now a lady, has sunk into a deep depression. Max is not feeling so good, himself, as he journeys alone, ostensibly to have a reunion with kinfolk in his old hometown. Max is restless, at times almost suicidal, inwardly suffering *verzweiflunc* (a "Germanic-Yiddish word for despair"), horny as a jack rabbit, and yet, and worst of all from Max's point of view, afflicted by impotence. At least at the outset. Arriving in Warsaw—which Singer wonderfully and efficiently reinvents, depending on evocative details, on rich bouquets of scents and odors,

and on the recitation of neighborhoods and street names, the Warsaw where Max first began his rise as a petty criminal and jail-
bird—Max soon has his hands and life full of complicated women:
Esther, a baker's wife; Tsirele, a rabbi's rebellious, socialist daughter; Basha, a hot-blooded housemaid; Madame Theresa Shkolni-
kov, a mysterious medium; and, most of all, Reyzl Kork, faithless
girlfriend of the gangster Shmuel Smetena. Handsome, youthful
in appearance, strong and rich, Max is a born con man, "enchanted with his own words," gifted with a glib and almost independent mouth. Max usually starts talking fast and just wings it,
never knowing exactly what he may say next. He has sudden,
gusty impulses and all too often acts on them. He manages to talk
his way into and often out of a whole lot of trouble, inadvertently
creating for himself a string of genuinely comic situations that can
only be broken, as they in fact are, by some real trouble, by violence and personal tragedy at the tag end. It is this comedy, while
it lasts—which is almost to the end of things—together with the
demonstrable, undeniable charm of Max, which combine to keep
the reader fully engaged in and finally deeply touched by his fate.
It is an utterly unsentimental destiny that is dramatically satisfac-
tory because it is so deftly plotted, as exact as a balanced equation,
by a master storyteller.

True to the ways and means that Singer has carefully developed
and refined over many years and more than forty books, *Scum*
joins together gritty, realistic details with a world of dreams and
magic, the stuff of fable and folktale. As an artist, Singer is a master of swift and sure exposition; his dialogue is electric and shining even in translation; his characters, even in minor and cameo
roles, are individually unforgettable—see the brief appearance
of "Blind Mayer, King of Krochmalna Street, rabbi of the under-
world." Like other Singer fictions, *Scum* is at heart a parable. And,
like the best parables of the Judeo-Christian tradition, the truth,
the meaningful core of it, is a clash (Jacob and the angel) between
opposite forces. Blind Mayer says: "Nowdays a man is worth less
than a fly. He lives, and in a moment he's gone." Earlier the Rabbi
tells Max: "The Talmud says that a person doesn't sin unless a
spirit of folly enters him. Well, there are choices and everything
can be overcome if there is the will to do so." It is the magic of

Singer's art, in *Scum* as so often, that hope and despair go hand in hand.

Gay Talese:
Unto the Sons

Gay Talese's eighth book, his most ambitious and finest so far, begins and ends in Ocean City, New Jersey, where Gay was born in 1932 and where he grew up with his mother and sister and his father, Joseph, a tailor originally from the ancient and "precariously situated" southern Italian village of Maida, in the mountains of a region described in an awkwardly translated but accurate guidebook as "uncontrollable territory," inhabited by "strange rustics with peculiar customs and leading backward lives." The primary time, the present time of telling, also firmly, vividly established at the outset and returned to at the end, is the 1940s, the years of World War II, a deeply troubling time for Joseph who, although an American citizen and a proudly loyal one, too, had a crowd of close kinfolk—his own mother, brothers and sisters, a wealth of cousins—still in the old country and dangerously vulnerable, Maida being, as it had been from the earliest known times, in the path of invading forces. Talese describes his father, at that time, as "an emotional double agent."

Both place and time are efficiently presented, summoned directly and sensuously out of the memory of Gay Talese, who begins this story as a first-person narrator, creating himself as a voice, an entirely trustworthy witness, a reliable *source*. But very soon he vanishes gracefully into the telling of the tale, a tale (tales within tales, in fact) of others. He does not reappear until the final scenes and then only in the third person, "he" not "I"; for the young Gay Talese is now a remembered character, himself, fixed in a time and place forever, though likewise free of time and space in the minds and memories of readers and the writer. The story begins, then, as a personal account and ends as a communal one, a shared experience.

This is a wonderful structure for the story and for one of the basic things it is all about—the simultaneity of the past in family history, which lives in the long shadows of memory, gossip, rumor, fireside tales, myths, and legends, and which somehow adds up to something more than the sum of all our family and tribal stories, becoming what we call history. The book and the world it contains are appropriately dedicated to Talese's two daughters. It is passed on to them and, not incidentally, to us.

Essentially, but not by any means exclusively, the story line of *Unto the Sons*, loosely chronological, follows the lives of Domenico Talese, Joseph's grandfather and the ruler of the family farm and fortunes; all his children, including Gaetano, Joseph's father, for whom Gay is named, who lived by a familiar and adventurous pattern of his times, coming and going from America, earning his living there, and keeping his wife and family at home in Maida. Another major character, standing out significantly amid a gallery of memorable minor ones, is Antonio Cristiani, a tailor also and Joseph's older first cousin, who ventured not to America but to Paris, where he lived to enjoy considerable success and became a prominent and respected man. In his "Author's Note," Gay Talese particularly acknowledges his direct influence on the making of this book both because of his "retentive memory I tapped often and at length prior to his death in 1986, when he was in his nineties" and for his diary, "which preserves much of the history of his native village and of our family as it was related to him by his maternal grandfather, Domenico Talese." And finally, of course, there is the full story of Joseph Talese, who came to America to stay, arriving in New York on December 23, 1920, to make a new life.

These central stories are abundantly surrounded by a wealth of other stories, moving freely, as free as the play of memory, in time, stories within stories, asides and digressions within digressions. But there is nothing idle or wasted by the master storyteller. With virtuosity verging on a magician's sleight of hand, he lets the tale seemingly tell itself; yet, in the end, everything large and small smoothly, unobtrusively relates to everything else. Sooner or later everything pays off handsomely. For example, on page 151, Don Achille, village schoolmaster, makes a pedagogical remark to his pupils—"So cruel were the Spanish authorities that even our word 'spagnarsi,' meaning 'to be afraid,' refers to the Spaniards. When we are afraid we say, '*Io mi spagno.*' When we say, 'Do not be afraid,' it is *'Non ti* spagnare'." Much later, 474 pages later, the next use of those words will break your heart. This is subtle plotting. Even the last lines of the book are carefully plotted on page 123.

It requires time and space to allow the reader to profit from the steady accumulation of experience until the people and the places of the book seem real. So it is a long book. But, with the arguable exception of the history and background, detailed and interesting in itself, of Dr. Richard V. Mattison, Gaetano's eccentric American employer, everything seems necessary; and perhaps Mattison's story really has to be there, too, if only to compare and contrast with the Italian stories and to show and tell a little of America's history as well. One concludes that our own story would be poorer and blander without the rich gifts of the southern Italian immigrants.

At one point old Domenico Talese asserts that the family name comes from a Greek word, *telein,* meaning "to initiate to mysteries." Certainly that has been the task and the triumph of Domenico's great-grandson, the American writer. Full of life, the family stories are mostly a matter of courtships and marriages, births and deaths, joys (much is marvelously funny; look for the story about three Gypsies, disguised as nuns, who tried to run a scam on Domenico) and heavy sorrows, and all the subtle, shifting nuances of caste and class. "Southern Italy was a fountainhead of dark fantasies, turmoil and hope," Talese writes. And he depicts a world riddled with old superstitions and rich with the inheritance of traditional customs—for example, the blessing of the livestock, beginning always with the sheep, by the bishop on the second Sunday in March. Maida and the region are haunted by history. The Greeks came there and built cities no later than 750 B.C. Cicero had a villa nearby, and Spartacus raised rebellion there. Followed by ravaging, punishing Romans. Sometimes "real" historical figures came to Maida: Alaric, the barbarian king; the Emperor Frederick II, who paraded his retinue, "a traveling circus," right through town. Sometimes there was direct contact between the family members and public figures in Maida and elsewhere: Joachim Murat, Napoleon's brother-in-law; Giuseppe Garibaldi; King Victor Emmanuel II; Benito Mussolini, among others. And under the sad gaze of Maida's patron saint, Saint Francis of Paola, our brutal history has left its huge, impersonal marks—Joseph's older brother, Sebastian, shell-shocked in the horror of Caporetto in World War II; Domenico, the youngest brother, fighting in Spain in the 1930s; others in North Africa and on the Russian front in World War II. There is some first-rate expository narrative history, deftly introduced without breaking the spell and freshly seen from a different angle and point of view.

Unto the Sons is a triumph and fully deserves the good things that are already happening to it and the author. Writing about his father's trade inadvertently describes his own and hints at the secret of this book: "A tailor's eye must follow a seam precisely, but his pattern of thought is free to veer off in different directions, to delve into his life, to ponder his past, to lament lost opportunities, create dramas, imagine slights, brood, exaggerate . . ."

John Updike:
Rabbit at Rest

When a writer lives with and writes about a character in four books and for more than thirty years, as John Updike has done with Harry ("Rabbit") Angstrom—central character of *Rabbit at Rest* and of the quartet that began with *Rabbit, Run* in 1960—author and character get to know each other, strengths and weaknesses, good habits and bad, like an old married couple. Like old feet easy and comfortable in an old pair of shoes. Updike and Angstrom always shared some particular things—a Pennsylvania home and a feeling for it, a fine-tuned and alert sense of perception, a heightened sensitivity to persons, places, and things that easily transcended the differences between their vocabulary and education and experience. Some of these differences: Angstrom was an outstanding high-school athlete, a basketball star, some of whose feats have been remembered for a generation. One reads, here and there, that Updike shoots a little golf (so does Angstrom, as it happens) and both in print and by the twitching grapevine one is told that Updike is a country fair golfer. But nobody that I know of has ever yet singled out and identified John Updike as a jock. Nevertheless it needs to be said that some of the best writing in *Rabbit at Rest*—lively, energetic writing, concerns Angstrom shooting golf and playing basketball (in memory and in the present), and Updike writes with equal authority and authenticity about both. If Angstrom's feats are well remembered, Updike has earned and enjoyed another kind of fame during the same years. Updike went to Harvard and Oxford. The less fortunate Angstrom missed out on college, but served two years in the army. Updike was spared his generation's military experience, gaining at least a couple of crucial career years thereby. And, inevitably, he makes less of the army in Angstrom's fictional life than he ought to. It is highly unlikely that it meant as little to Angstrom, in fact and in memory, as it seems to. But this is a very slight weakness and is more than compensated for by the power and capacity of Updike's imagination first to create, then to enter into, every aspect of Harry's life and, indeed, equally the lives of all the others, men and women, young and old, who play parts in this story.

I can report that something happens to us when we start growing old and the body begins, in bits and pieces, to fail. Somehow those of us who are survivors and veterans are able to get around the shapes and configurations of different circumstances and distinct experiences and finally see each other as fellows, a judge and jury of peers. This has now happened to Updike and Angstrom. If, once upon a time, Updike was more than a little bit smirky and condescending with Angstrom and his ilk, that's pretty much over and done with by now. There is compassion and understanding here. True, Angstrom does his share of dumb, sometimes ridiculous, occasionally even wicked and unforgivable things, adding his full share to the world's weight of woe; still, his faults and foibles, even his sins, are those of an old friend, someone whom we wish well even as we wish that he did better by himself and others.

A plump book of more than five hundred pages, its jacket lined with the traditional purple and black of penance, *Rabbit at Rest* gets going, outwardly in time, in the aftermath of the explosion of the Pan Am 747 over Scotland and ends with the aftermath of Hurricane Hugo. Parallel to this, first in Florida, then in fictional Brewer, Pennsylvania, and environs, then back in West Florida, Angstrom suffers a heart attack, endures angioplasty, enjoys a kind of slow suicide of forbidden consumption, especially junk food, and ends the story, after another more devastating heart attack, in intensive care and at death's door. (If Updike wants to save him for a quintet, the last available possibility is a heart transplant.) The physicality of the story, the sense of Angstrom's body, its hungers and aches and pains, is simply superbly realized. The outline of his inward and spiritual development, beginning in the pure, cold-sweat funk of fear and trembling, and ending with acceptance and a kind of peace, is likewise overwhelming. The world beyond memory and his fingertips comes to Angstrom, as it does to most of us, by "the news," most often delivered by means of TV. Updike is precise in time and wonderfully accurate in his recapitulation of public events and their impact on Angstrom. These are important; for all four books were conceived of as a kind of time-capsule chronicle of the times. This is especially interesting in that Updike comes as close to living a sheltered life, a life in a cave, as any major writer of our times. The world wherein so many of his generation have been forced to live, to sink or swim, comes to his mainly as "the news." Which is to say he and Angstrom may (maybe not) make too much of it all. He does these pieces, not set pieces, but living tableaux, very well indeed, and he adroitly manages to overcome the great danger of sounding like a checklist.

Use of current events as the impact on Angstrom puts Updike at risk, in this peculiar literary day and age, of being uniformly judged as "politically correct" or not by reviewers to whom politics matter more than art or truth (life). Widely reviewed, *Rabbit at Rest* has passed the test. As critic Jay Parini, writing in a slick magazine appropriately called *Fame*, argues, in defense of Updike's work in spite of earlier lapses from grace ("his weirdly blinkered essay about the Vietnam War"), "Updike like so many writers, is smarter in his fiction than in 'real' life." Continuing, Parini welcomes Updike back to the fold: "As Rabbit Angstrom, in late middle age, is forced to deal with, for instance, his son's gay friend, Lyle, who has AIDS; with his son's addiction to drugs; with the general filthy mess that America, through greed and benign neglect, has become; one senses his growing political (and, of course, spiritual) awareness of things." I am happy to be able to report that Updike is a lot better writer than Parini and others credit him with being, and that Updike's elegiac portrait of America, seen and experienced by Angstrom, is a lot more solid and subtle than Parini's view of it. He and Angstrom both are too intelligent and decent to equate virtue with intelligence and the spiritual with the "politically correct."

This is a fine, rich, powerfully imagined novel, abundant in its details, ample in its rewards.

Kurt Vonnegut:
Hocus Pocus

Once upon a time, I, too, was a Vonnegut groupie. In that world, which every day seems a little better than this one, we waited, eager and conspiratorial, for the man who had written the short stories (somewhat later collected in *Canary in a Cat House*, 1961, and *Player Piano*, 1952) to bring out his next one. We few. We happy few.

Then what?

There was a little wait before that marvelous and wacko novel, *The Sirens of Titan* (1959) appeared, offering the wild and woolly and deterministic adventures of one Malachi Constant and his wife Beatrice Rumsfoord and their little boy, Chrono. And best of all, introducing us to what was to become Vonnegut's outer-space Yoknapatawpha—the planet Tralfamador, "where the flying saucers came from." Next we were blessed with *Mother Night* (1962) and its impeccable moral—"We are what we pretend to be, so we must be careful about what we pretend to be"; *Cat's Cradle* (1963), featuring the inimitable Dr. Felix Hoenikker and his three odd children; *God Bless You, Mr. Rosewater* (1965), which introduced us to one of Vonnegut's most enduring characters—sci-fi writer Kilgore Trout. (Moral: "Goddamn it, you've got to be kind.") So far he had endured the services of four casual publishers, very few reviews, next to no money from his writing; and we, his devoted readers, still knew most of each other by name. We knew next to nothing then about Vonnegut's private life, with its full share, and then some, of trouble and woe and even tragedy; but we loved his bleak, black, essentially sophomoric and sentimental humor, and we rejoiced in the crazy quilt of mordant fun and games that was a novel created by him.

Then what?

Then some strange things happened, beginning with a piece by critic Robert Scholes—" 'Mithridates, He Died Old': Black Humor and Kurt Vonnegut, Jr."—in the *Hollins Critic* (1966) and leading, swiftly enough, to a new publisher, a new novel, *Slaughterhouse Five* (1969), at ease, first on the best-seller list, then as a popular movie in 1972; and so to riches, fame, and almost overnight, as these things go, to a bulging, six-foot shelf of books and articles all about Vonnegut, his texts and subtexts, signs and symbols, sneaky similes and sly metaphors. He looks likely to be the last American literary "discovery" of this century, a star of magnitude, soon a public figure, yet one more highly regarded and well-rewarded sage in residence.

Then what?

Then it seemed to us, his old and longtime fans, that he started acting and writing like one, too, sounding more and more like some kind of weird cross between former senator Eugene McCarthy and that ancient and indefatigable flower child—the Maharishi. Maybe a hybrid of Woody Allen and Annie Dillard. And so as the new books came along, nine by my count, we shrugged and yawned and went our separate ways. I remember laughing out loud when I looked among the diet books and cookbooks in our local bookstore and found *Breakfast of Champions* (1973) there.

Then what?

Then please come home, old fans. Gather around, you new ones. The magic is back, the Force is with him. With *Hocus Pocus* and a new, improved publisher, Putnam's, Kurt Vonnegut seems to have rediscovered himself. *Hocus Pocus* is the autobiographical manuscript of one Eugene Debs Hartke (the book is dedicated to his namesake, Eugene Victor Debs, 1855–1926), West Pointer, Vietnam veteran ("If I were a fighter plane instead of a human being, there would be little pictures of people painted all over me"); former college professor at Tarkington College, a school mainly for the dyslexic and learning disabled, where there is a Pahlavi Pavilion, a Samoza Hall, a Vonnegut Memorial Fountain, and a remarkably imaginative computer called *Griot*; a teacher at Athena, a prison run, like much else in America, by the Japanese Army of Occupation in Business Suits; and now, himself, a prisoner awaiting trial for his part in the largest prison breakout in American history. Although the story ranges freely in time, covering all of Hartke's life and a good deal of our history, it is set in the amazing literary year of 2001. (Hartke saw the movie in Vietnam). Now he finds himself "in late middle age, cut loose in a thoroughly looted, bankrupt nation whose assets had been sold off to foreigners, a nation swamped by unchecked plagues and superstition and illiteracy and hypnotic TV, with virtually no health services for the poor." Sound familiar? In this new/old world, I. G. Farben owns Du Pont, Italians own Anheuser-Busch, President Mobutu of Zaire has bought an ice cream company in San Diego, the Sultan of Brunei has the First National Bank of Rochester, N.Y., the Shah of Bratpuhr controls meatpacking in Dubuque, and the *Encyclopaedia Britannica* is "owned by a mysterious Egyptian arms dealer living in Switzerland." For spiritual consolation Hartke has his memories, of course, good and bad, a wealth of events and an album of major and minor and always memorable characters, including, too briefly, a mortician named Norman Updike. And he has some useful books—"the Atheist's Bible," Bartlett's *Familiar Quotations*, as well as the old magazine *Black Garterbelt*, which has a story to it, "The Protocols of the Elders of Tralfamadore," probably by Kilgore Trout, which argues that "the whole point of life on Earth was to make germs shape up so that they would be ready to ship out when the time came," and that human beings, in the cosmic scheme of things, are only "germ hotels." Shades of *The Sirens of Titan!*

The form of any Vonnegut novel always has some new wrinkles. According to "K. V.," who merely edited this book, Hartke is writing it down "in pencil on everything from brown wrapping paper to the backs of business cards." Adding: "The unconventional lines separating passages within chapters indicate where one scrap heap ended and the next began. The shorter the passage, the shorter the scrap." Some scraps are a phrase or one word only; others go on for pages. There are other idiosyncrasies of text, including the author's flat refusal to use "foul language," leading to many a strained euphemism, all of them adding to Vonnegut's familiar and inimitably goofy charm.

Then what?

Form and content, *Hocus Pocus* is a classic Vonnegut novel, weird but good, more fun to read than to review. Are we ready for it in this late sad day and age? I conclude yes, yes indeed; for we are older and so is he, more relaxed and tolerant, if not one bit kinder and gentler, and as funny as anybody in the funny business. You owe to yourself at least to see for yourself.

Then what?

The moral. Read Vonnegut's lips: "Just because we can read and write and do a little math, that doesn't mean we deserve to conquer the Universe."

Jonathan Yardley:
Our Kind of People: The Story of an American Family

People who read the quirky, sometimes cantankerous reviews and columns of Jonathan Yardley, rooting for him or hooting and jeering but always engaged, are in for something of a surprise when they encounter *Our Kind of People*. A kinder, gentler Yardley is at work, displaying a gracious plenty of warmth and wit, no little wisdom and loving kindness, in this accounting of his own family, presented as exemplary "of those Americans whose histories went back to the beginning of the country, who had through the lives of their own ancestors intimate knowledge of the traditions and convictions out of which the nation had been shaped."

Narrated by Yardley, though elegantly enhanced by wonderful letters, memoranda, inventories, and, at crucial moments, apt quotations from The Book of Common Prayer, the story is partly autobiographical, but chiefly concerned with Yardley's late parents, Bill and Helen, and their quietly interesting, often admirable lives. It is a chronicle of their sturdy fifty-year marriage. Their joint past, going back to seventeenth-century settlers (including the splendidly named Temperance Flowerdew) and, indeed, beyond that to include even one witness to the instrument of Magna Carta, and the particular families united in their marriage—Yardleys, Gregorys, Ingersolls, Edwards (the author is, maybe appropriately, named for his ancestor Jonathan Edwards), and Woolseys—shaped them even as that long past formed the first hopes and finest aspirations of this nation. The story is enriched rather than burdened by the past. The fully dimensional central characters are shadowed by history. Bill was an educator, later also a clergyman, who became a much-admired rector of Chatham Hall in Virginia. Helen, a member of the "Pioneer" Class of '36 at Bennington, was unflagging in her traditional role as wife and mother, raising four children, yet likewise managing to accomplish various kinds of work to supplement their income and to use her intelligence and training. Bill and Helen come across as good and decent people who lived by old values (duty, service, sacrifice, labor, courage, honor) and enjoyed WASP pastimes (sailing, woodcrafts, reading, ritual, bathroom jokes, and the perfect martini) in a new age that took both the values and pastimes lightly.

J. P. Marquand is Yardley's model, but the truth is this story has more depth than Marquand's fiction. And it has real authority and authenticity. Yardley's sense of the South may be a bit hazy, but he is right on the money in his evocations of Newport and Tuxedo Park, of Baltimore and Philadelphia (though Chestnut Hill is *not* part of the Main Line), of Woodberry Forest and Groton. His portrait of our first ruling class is accurate and honest. His view of America, then and now, is both lively and challenging. But Yardley's true literary triumph is to have introduced us to some decent and honorable people who are as alive and worthy of interest as anybody you are likely to meet, in or out of a book, for a good time to come.

Acknowledgments

Below is copyright and publication information for the pieces in this collection in the order of their appearance. All are reprinted by permission.

Essays and Reviews

"Courting the Virgin Queen" ("Traces of the Elizabethans"), Copyright © 1991 by The New York Times Company; "Child among Ancestors," from *Traditions and Innovations: Essays on British Literature of the Middle Ages and Renaissance,* edited by David G. Allen and Robert A. White. University of Delaware Press, 1990. This essay was first presented as a paper at the Fifth Citadel Conference on Literature at Charleston, S.C., March 1985; "The Star System," Copyright © 1987 by *Michigan Quarterly Review;* "Once More unto the Breach, Dear Friends," Copyright © 1988 by the *Review of Contemporary Fiction;* "Tyranny by Sloth," Copyright © 1988 by *Chronicles;* "Literary Biography in Our Time," the *Sewanee Review* 92 (summer 1984); "My Silk Purse and Yours," Copyright © 1968 by the *Hollins Critic;* "B. S. Johnson: The Poetry," Copyright © 1985 by Gale Research, Inc.; "A Few Things About Fred Chappell," the *Mississippi Quarterly* 37 (winter 1983–1984); "On Mary Johnston's *The Long Roll,*" from *Classics of Civil War Fiction,* edited by David Madden and Peggy Bach. University Press of Mississippi, 1991; "Foote's *The Civil War,*" the *Mississippi Quarterly* 28 (winter 1974–1975); Reviews of *The Tongues of Angels* and *The Foreseeable Future* by Reynolds Price, *The Year of Silence* by Madison Smartt Bell, and *Love Life* by Bobbie Ann Mason appeared in the August 1990, August 1991, January 1988, and June 1989 issues of the *World & I,* a publication of The Washington Times Corporation, Copyright © 1990, 1991, 1988, 1989; "John Barth's *Giles Goat-Boy,*" from *Masterplots 1967 Annual,* 126–30, Salem Press, Inc. Copyright © 1968 by Frank N. Magill; "*The Tidewater Tales,*" Copyright © 1987 by the *Washington Times;* Reviews of *Cooper* by Hilary Masters and *Wartime* by Paul Fussell appeared in the September 1987 and November 1989 issues of the *World & I,* a publication of The Washington Times Corporation, Copyright © 1987, 1989.

Short Takes: Short Stories

Review of *Living After Midnight* by Lee K. Abbott, Copyright © 1991 by The New York Times Company; Review of *What Was Mine* by Ann Beattie, Copyright © 1991 by *The Atlanta Journal & Constitution;* Review

Short Takes: Miscellaneous Reviews

Index

316 • Index

Vidal, Gore, 33, 229; *Empire*, 229
Vietnam, 186–94, 198, 222, 300, 301
Vietnam War, 48, 58, 101, 131, 207, 250,
    253, 298
Viking, 67
Village Voice, 20, 41
Virgil, v, 143, 205, 258, 262, 263
Virginia, 131, 141, 154, 155, 161, 163,
    164, 167, 168, 303
Vliet, R. G.: *Scorpio Rising*, 21
Vogel, Serenus, 127
Volpone, 204
Vonnegut, Kurt, 33, 134, 248, 299–302;
    Breakfast of Champions, 300; *Canary in
    a Cat House*, 229; *Cat's Cradle*, 299;
    God Bless You, Mr. Rosewater, 299;
    Hocus Pocus, 299–302; *Mother Night*,
    299; *Player Piano*, 299; *The Sirens of
    Titan*, 299; *Slaughterhouse Five*, 248,
    300

Warren, Earl, 116
Warren, Robert Penn, 18, 103, 104, 121,
    128, 129, 157, 278; *Flood*, 129
Washington Post, 20, 21, 33, 38, 50
Washington Times, 41, 265; "Lost Words,"
    265
WASP, 56, 57, 87, 107–42, 303
WASP humor, 107–42
Waugh, Evelyn, 247
Weeks, Edward: "The Peripatetic Re-
    viewer," 123
Welty, Eudora, 103
West, Ray B., 156
West(ern), 49, 50, 55, 188
Weyand, Arline, 188, 189
Weyand, Fred, 188, 189
White, E. B., 246
Whitehead, James, 130
Whitman, Walt, 83, 123, 152, 164
Whittier, John Greenleaf, 124
Wiggins, Marianne, 160–62; *Bet They'll
    Miss Us When We're Gone: Stories*,
    160–62; *John Dollar*, 161
Wilbur, Ellen, 274

Wilbur, Richard, 25, 120, 252, 257, 264,
    275; *The Writer's Voice*, 120
Wilde, Oscar, 209
Wilder, Thornton, 246
Williams, William Carlos, 18, 31, 83, 121
Wilson, Edmund, 115, 119; *Patriotic
    Gore*, 115
Wilson, James Southall, 164
Wolfe, Tom, 33, 125, 131–32, 134–42,
    211, 212; "The Big League Complex,"
    137; *The Bonfire of the Vanities*, 139,
    140, 142, 211; *The Kandy-Kolored Tan-
    gerine-Flake Streamline Baby*, 134;
    *Mauve Gloves and Madmen, Clutter
    and Vine*, 131; *The Painted Word*, 134,
    135–38; *The Pump House Gang*, 137;
    *Radical Chic and Mau-Mauing the Flak
    Catchers*, 132, 135; *The Right Stuff*,
    139, 142; "O Rotten Gotham-Sliding
    Down into the Behavioral Sink,"
    137; "Tom Wolfe's New Book of Eti-
    quette," 137; "The Truest Sport:
    Jousting with Sam and Charlie," 131
Wolfe, Thomas, 29, 63, 199
Wool, Robert, 186
Woolf, Leonard, 11
Woolf, Virginia, 11, 18, 196
Working, 221
World & I, 195
World War I, 113, 164, 234, 243, 252
World War II, 4, 27, 34, 48, 94, 113, 117,
    159, 171, 193, 198, 200, 242–54, 261,
    265, 266, 274, 293, 296
Wouk, Herman, 248
Wright, Charles, 122

Yardley, Jonathan, 33, 302–3; *Our Kind
    of People: The Story of an American
    Family*, 302–3
Yeats, William Butler, 18
Young, Marlyn B., 192; *The Vietnam
    Wars, 1945–1990*, 192

*Zen and the Art of Motorcycle Mainte-
    nance*, 220–21
Zola, Emile, 142